Storm Over Chile

STORM OVER CHILE

CHILE

The Junta Under Siege

Samuel Chavkin

Foreword by Hortensia de Allende

Lawrence Hill Books

Library of Congress Cataloging-in-Publication Data

Chavkin, Samuel.
  Storm over Chile : the Junta under siege / Samuel Chavkin.
      p.   cm.
  Rev. ed. of: The murder of Chile. 1st ed. c1982.
  Includes index.
  ISBN 1-55652-067-0 : $12.95
    1. Chile—History—Coup d'état, 1973.   2. Chile—Politics and
government—1973- 3. Human Rights—Chile—History—20th Century.
  I. Chavkin, Samuel. Murder of Chile. II. Title.
  F3100.C428   1989
  983.06'5—dc20   89-15510
                                                             CIP

Lawrence Hill Books is an imprint of
Chicago Review Press, Incorporated
814 North Franklin Street
Chicago, Illinois   60610

CONTENTS

ACKNOWLEDGMENTS

THERE ARE at least eighty people I want to thank for making this book possible. Most of the men and women interviewed are now living in exile in Italy, Mexico, Spain, France, and the United States. Some of these people have returned to Chile to join the resistance. Recalling their suffering, and the brutality their relatives and friends underwent at the hands of the Junta, took courage; indeed, it was a searing experience. Nevertheless, they took part in this project in the belief that the epic story of Allende and the Popular Unity government, as well as that of the Fascist orgy of sadism that followed, should be told again and again. This book is a collection of personal accounts by the victims and resisters of the putsch, which pieced together gives perspective to the drama of the Chilean tragedy. Though many of the survivors of this group have been hurt psychologically and maimed physically after years of terror in concentration camps, they remain astonishingly optimistic, confident that the Chilean Junta will not continue to rule for long.

A number of individuals are identified by their full names; others, fearing reprisals to relatives still in Chile, are referred to either by initials or by assumed names. To cite but a few: Calambre, the former shantydown dweller in Santiago; the law student Clara; Nora; K.L.; Señora Hortensia Bussi de Allende; Sweden's Ambassador Harald Edelstam; Professor Enrique Kirberg; Joan Jara, widow of famed folk singer Victor Jara; former Foreign Minister Clodomiro Almeyda; Isabel Letelier; Lucho; Fernando Alegría; Dr. Danilo Bartulin; and Dr. Oscar Sotô. I am grateful to all of them for their willingness to share their remembrances with me.

I am particularly appreciative for the help from Jaime Barrios, Director, Chile Democratico in New York, who gave generously of his time and energy in locating the individuals to be interviewed. I am equally obligated to former Senator Hugo Miranda, Director, Casa de Chile in Mexico, who put me in touch with exiles in Mexico City.

I am greatly indebted to Jerry Gross, my editor, for his warm cooperation and incisive suggestions; and to Michael Cantalupo, assistant editor, for his alacrity and readiness to extend a helping hand. Early readings of some of the chapters and comments from my friend Mary Heathcote have been most constructive. Special thanks go to Frances Goldin, my literary agent, for her enthusiastic encouragement and belief in the significance of the project; and to Carol Barnette for her patience and accuracy in transcribing my translations of the dozens of taped interviews from the Spanish language.

SAMUEL CHAVKIN

FOREWORD

DESPITE THE DAILY outpouring of news about political and social developments around the globe, the events in Chile since September 11, 1973—that ill-fated day when the Junta seized power—continue to hold the attention of the world press. But apart from its news value, Chile has also become a matter of conscience for millions of people concerned with justice.

Thus, when the Chilean people repudiated the fifteen-year dictatorship of General Augusto Pinochet in the plebiscite of October 5, 1988, the news of this happening resounded around the world. And the Chileans did it by ballot.

This was a hard blow to the dictatorship and a historic move forward for the cause of democracy and human rights in Latin America. The Chilean people have achieved this victory through unity and organization. After fifteen years of oppression and humiliation, the moment had arrived to overcome the divisive ideologies of the past and to reopen the road towards Chile's common good. In the preparation for the plebiscite Chileans carried out their tasks with responsibility and avoidance of provocation.

The triumph of the "no" vote (the rejection of Pinochet's bid to continue in office for another eight years) was made possible thanks to the unity of the Chilean people. It was also a demonstration of their commitment to a peaceful transition to democracy in Chile. Pinochet is becoming more and more isolated. But even though politically spurned, he refuses to cede power or to make the necessary changes in his restrictive Constitution of 1980.

So once again the case of Chile is big world news. It is indeed astonishing the extent to which interest in Chile is kept alive, considering the number of years that have elapsed since the Junta coup interrupted the tradition of Chile's long-lasting democracy. Evidence of this phenomenon is the new, updated edition of Samuel Chavkin's book *Storm Over Chile: The Junta Under Siege*. This work provides the reader with a picture of what has

9

transpired in Chile via the personal experiences of Chileans from the day of the coup through the plebiscite. It also points to what the future holds for the country, as discussed by a wide variety of Chileans, whether eminent economists, politicians or shanty-town dwellers—the *pobladores*.

Storm Over Chile is an honest, lucid example of conscientious journalism. I know this because I myself am among the people Chavkin interviewed when gathering the information about what had taken place on September 11, 1973, and the tragic days that followed. His report begins with the battle of "La Moneda," where Salvador Allende fell, and then sweeps across a variety of other momentous events. Among these: the incarceration of the principal government leaders at the Dawson Island concentration camp; the deaths of Pablo Neruda and Victor Jara; the courageous stand of several foreign diplomats—the Swedish Ambassador Harald Edelstam and the Mexican Ambassador Gonzalo Martínez Corbalá—on behalf of many of the savagely persecuted Chileans.

When gathering the material for the book, Chavkin interviewed dozens of protagonists and Junta victims who have undergone this most barbaric experience ever recorded in the history of Chile. This is not a work of fiction. Everything in it is based on concrete sources of information, explicitly cited in the course of the text. And yet, in the presentation of his dramatic segment of Chile's experience, the author succeeds in making the book come alive and as intriguing as one would expect of a novel.

I must also comment on the integrity of the author in not concealing or minimizing the complicity of the United States government, through the CIA and other agencies, in the events that led to the paralysis of the democratic processes initiated by the government of Salvador Allende. For the moment, these democratic developments aimed at bringing about major social improvements in Chilean life have been arrested, but I want to affirm that this drive for change will resume once the military dictatorship comes to a close.

With the passage of time and as a consequence of the Junta's many crimes: torture, abuses, persecutions, exile and overall immorality, opposition to the military government has been mounting steadily. In addition, because of the economic ruination of the country—the enormity of the foreign debt, the massive unemployment, the hunger and misery of the poor—Pinochet and his palace cohorts find themselves in a situation they cannot maintain other than by force of arms.

But now with our victory in the plebiscite and the upcoming presidential and congressional elections the road may finally open to bring democracy back to Chile. This is a national responsibility and should not depend on one single party. To that end we must all work jointly for the creation of a government for the next four years that will be truly representative of the people, a government with one objective and with a democratic, pluralistic parliament. And when this happens, I hope there will be many journalists in Chile of the moral and intellectual caliber of Samuel Chavkin to tell the story.

HORTENSIA BUSSI DE ALLENDE

Hortensia de Allende lives in exile in Mexico City. Just prior to the plebiscite, Mrs. Allende returned to Chile for the first time since the coup. She was greeted by a cheering crowd of 350,000 Chileans at the Santiago airport. It was a tribute both to the memory of President Allende and to Hortensia de Allende for her unflagging commitment to pleading the cause of Chile throughout the world these past fifteen years.

This reception was in dramatic contrast to the one she received from the U.S. State Department when applying to enter the United States for a series of lectures several years ago. She was denied a visa, although she had been invited by a Protestant church group, a Roman Catholic archdiocese, Stanford University, the Human Rights Commission of the San Francisco Bar Association, and the Mayor of San Francisco.

In this connection *The Washington Post* observed editorially, "This is incredible. Mrs. Augusto Pinochet, wife of the General who led the coup against the government of Chile in 1973 and who has run a tight and nasty military dictatorship since, is received for tea in the Reagan White House. Mrs. Salvador Allende, widow of the elected president who was deposed and killed in that coup, is now refused a visa to enter the United States to give a speech."

Finally, late in 1985, after much pressure from various quarters, the State Department allowed Mrs. Allende to enter the United States for a short visit.

INTRODUCTION

A TIDAL WAVE of anger, discontent, and demands that the military Junta, headed by dictator-president Augusto Pinochet, return democracy to Chile is sweeping across this South American nation. Despite the violence by the police and the militia to subdue anti-Junta protesters with bullets, clubbings, and water-cannons, Chileans from all walks of life and of different political persuasions are making it clear that Pinochet must step down.

This was made emphatically obvious in the plebiscite of October 5, 1988, when 55 percent of Chile's electorate voted to rebuff Pinochet's attempt to stay on as dictator for another eight years.

For more than 15 years the Junta whipped Chileans into compliance through terror and repression reminiscent of the Nazi period in Europe. From the day it seized power on September 11, 1973, and murdered in the process the democratically elected President, Salvador Allende Gossens, the Junta has been ruling Chile with concentration camps and executions. Hundreds of thousands of suspected opponents of the regime have been jailed and tortured, and an estimated 30,000 have perished. (In 1973, Chile's population stood at ten million. In equivalent population terms, the United States would have suffered the murder of more than 700,000 people.)

Year after year the United Nations Special Rapporteur who monitors human rights violations in Chile presents detailed documentation of the Junta's reign of terror. And the world body, with substantial majorities, denounces the Chilean regime for the "cruel, inhuman and degrading treatment" of its people. (Under the Reagan Administration the United States has voted against these condemnations.)

Junta apologists look approvingly on Pinochet's barbaric, iron-fisted policies. They have been singing hymns of praise to what they regard as the "miraculous" ability by Pinochet to restore order following the coup disorders. However, many observers feel that it is the anti-Junta opposition that has achieved the miraculous. Despite the brutal constraints put upon it, with most trade union and pro-Allende political leaders either killed or scattered in exile abroad, some of the political parties that made up Allende's Popular Unity coalition managed to survive.

It is in the context of the growing resistance that the meaning of Allende's election to the presidency in 1970 can be understood. It is also within this frame of reference that one can perceive the reasons why the Junta is unable to govern Chile except through terror, and why its paranoia is likely to grow as time goes by.

Allende's election was not just a happening. Nor was it, needless to say, simply a testimonial to his personal, indefatigable persistence to get to the country's top office. (It was his fourth try for the presidency over a period of eighteen years.) Essentially it was a reflection of a sustained, growing conviction by labor and elements of the lower-middle-class that Chile's chronic poverty and its economic stagnation could not be resolved unless the country moved toward a basic economic and political reorganization along socialist lines.

The growth of this political consciousness is demonstrated by the fact that when Salvador Allende ran for the presidency the first time, he polled only about 50,000 votes. By 1970, however, he garnered well over a million votes, roughly one third of the total ballots cast. It is this deeply ingrained political commitment nurtured through decades that incites the Junta's armed forces to behave like an army of occupation toward their own countrymen.

The intransigence of Chile's labor and that of the overall Left which the Junta finds so difficult to subdue has been forged through the many years of struggle to attain better living standards and to extend democratic rights. In part, Allende had a hand in shaping these developments since the middle thirties, soon after his graduation from medical school. Though born into an upper-middle-class family in Valparaiso—his father was a lawyer—Allende veered toward a Leftist political outlook. While still at the university he became a Socialist party activist, and soon afterward was elected as a Socialist deputy to the lower house of Congress. In the late thirties, when Pedro Aguirre Cerda became President of the left-of-center Popular Front government, he appointed Allende Minister of Public Health. In this job Allende traveled extensively to check on the health conditions of the country and in the process he became more convinced of the need for an overhaul of the entire Chilean system of government. He was appalled at the conditions of the urban slum dwellers, the barren existence of the half-starved coal and copper miners, and the misery of the peasants in the remote Chilean hinterland.

From the standpoint of the Chilean Left, the country's predicament resulted from the fact that its high revenue-producing raw materials, principally copper, were owned by foreign multinational corporations. And its food scarcities resulted from the stagnation of its agriculture because of the inefficient management by a semi-feudal oligarchy which lorded over most of the land. For nearly thirty years, first as a deputy and then as a senator, and also as a "perennial" presidential candidate, Allende hammered away at shaping legislation aimed at freeing Chile from foreign domination and at bringing about agrarian reform. Not surprisingly, these were also the main features of the program of the Popular Unity government when it came to power in 1970.

However revolutionary these goals were, Allende believed that they could be accomplished through Chile's established democratic process, in keeping with its constitution. Though this program ran afoul in Congress because the Rightists held the majority in both House and Senate, Allende was convinced that eventually the representation in Congress would take on a Leftist character and thus his Socialist-tilting government would get the support of a congressional majority. Indeed, in the first two-and-a-half years of Allende's term the Left did gain more seats in Congress as more of the people rallied in support of the Popular Unity programs. The irony is that precisely because of this pro-Allende trend in the succeeding congressional elections, the Rightist forces decided on a military coup to thwart the possibility of Socialist reforms being approved democratically.

The coup was in the making for a considerable period of time, and it was not strictly a Chilean domestic affair; it had long strings attached to Washington. President Nixon was not only abetting it but was pressuring his Chilean surrogates to bring it about as quickly as possible, particularly after the Allende government nationalized the Anaconda and Kennecott copper mines, and International Telephone and Telegraph (ITT). As was later disclosed in the United States Senate Select Committee hearings, the Nixon Administration was heavily involved in subverting

Allende's regime through the CIA and other channels. Interestingly enough, despite the plethora of testimony in this connection, the Committee concluded that there was not enough proof to link Washington directly with the overthrow of the Popular Unity government, thus exonerating the United States from responsibility.*

However beleaguered Allende had been by the hostile forces about him, whether inside or outside the country, some of his critics feel that the outcome of the Popular Unity government experiment might have been different had Allende moved more decisively when dealing with the Chilean military establishment. Allende was convinced that the armed forces would remain neutral and even loyal to his government because it came to power legally. His belief was bolstered by the pledges of support from the chiefs of staff of the armed forces first, from General René Schneider, who was assassinated precisely because of his loyalty, and then from his successor, General Carlos Prats. But above all, Allende feared that tangling with the military might have triggered a putsch at the very beginning of his administration.

Whatever the shortcomings of his leadership, adherents of all the parties that made up Allende's coalition government continue to pay homage to his valiant stand at the La Moneda presidential palace. With his sacrifice, his supporters contend, Allende told the Chilean people and the world at large that his constitutional government had been violated, and that under no circumstances should the Junta be viewed as anything other than an illegal and an immoral band of conspirators ruling Chile by terror and murder.

Samuel Chavkin

*Former Massachusetts Congressman, Michael J. Harrington, ridiculed this view. Though the CIA did not lead the Chilean putschist forces directly "up the steps of the Presidential palace" to wrest the government from Allende, this in itself, he maintained, was not significant. "Whether that was the controlling or even the decisive factor is not the point," he declared in an article in *The New York Times*, January 2, 1976. "We played fast and loose with the democratic traditions of one of the world's most sophisticated nations. And when the United States penetrates a society as thoroughly and continuously as we did Chile's . . . it is factually wrong and morally wrong to assert that we have no responsibility for the consequences of our actions."

1

The Battle of La Moneda

SALVADOR ALLENDE GOSSENS looked out the window of his private office in La Moneda, the presidential palace, and watched troops and tanks advancing toward the nation's seat of government. They marched with rifles at the ready, and lumbering Sherman tanks took battle positions around the palace. For a few moments, the President looked down with disbelief, as though mesmerized, but he quickly regained his composure. He turned to the ministers and advisors who stood around his desk and said: "I'm going to talk to the people once more. I shall tell them that I will fight to the death to uphold the constitution and Chile's legal government. I will not submit to the traitorous military Junta. I will not resign. I will not agree to the overthrow of this legitimate government."

He picked up the microphone on his desk which was connected to Radio Magallanes, the one station still in government hands. "These are my last words, certain that the sacrifice will not be in vain," he said. "I am sure that there will be at least a moral sanction that will punish the felony, the cowardice and treason.

"Workers of my homeland, I have faith in Chile and its future. Other men will overcome this dark and bitter moment when treason seems to reign. You must never forget that sooner rather than later the grand avenues will be open where free men will march on to build a better society. Long live Chile! Long live the People! Long live the Workers!"

He was as accurate in predicting his own death as he was firm in his resolve to meet it bravely. For on that crisp day— September 11, 1973—he led five hours of battle in which he and a handful of his loyal supporters held off repeated assaults by tanks, shellfire, and continuous sorties by Hunter-Hawker dive bombers. At 2:20 P.M. Allende and many of La Moneda's

17

defenders were gunned down. The huge flames sparked by the bombing attacks enveloped the palace, transforming it into a funeral pyre, not only for Allende but for Chile itself. The Junta had triumphed in one of the handful of Latin American nations that prided itself on a truly democratic tradition and an abiding respect for a constitutional government.

Overnight a torrent of blood separated Chile from the rest of the world. Acting on patterns borrowed from Nazi Germany, the Junta set up concentration camps into which thousands upon thousands of Chileans were herded. Allende supporters tortured or put to death included: workers, some of Chile's most prominent writers, professors, physicians, housewives, students, and artists—even the beloved folk singer, Victor Jara.

The death of Allende and of his Popular Unity government produced reverberations far beyond the borders of Chile or of South America, or, for that matter, of the Western Hemisphere. The word Chile, usually vaguely known to most of the world as the name of some remote country in the grip of the Andes in South America, sprang out of obscurity and became a cause: a symbol of Fascist terror; a victim of the greed of multinational corporations.

Army takeovers of Latin American governments are not novel phenomena. They are generally banana-republic transitions, in which one group within the power establishment seizes power with military assistance from the one in office; there is little or no participation on either side by the disfranchised, poverty-stricken inhabitants. (There are exceptions, of course: The Cuban experience; the recent Nicaraguan revolution; and the current upheavals throughout Central America.) The scenario is usually the same. The triumphant Junta offers the outgoing president and his family a plane to take them into exile, in exchange for his willingness to abdicate. And he customarily accepts, goes off to Miami or to Spain (with a fortune amassed while in office), fades out of politics, and becomes a footnote to history.

Such was not the case with Allende. When the military Junta telephoned him at La Moneda at about 8:00 A.M. on the day of the putsch, telling him that a plane was ready to transport him and his family, and even some of his closest collaborators out of

Chile on the condition that he resign, Allende shouted back: "As traitorous generals, you are incapable of knowing what honorable men are like." And he slammed down the receiver. This is probably the first time in Latin American history that a head of state refused to knuckle under to victorious military usurpers, if only to save his own skin. Instead, he chose to fight against overwhelming odds.

The coup in Santiago was preceded by rumors throughout the night about mysterious troop movements in the direction of the Chilean capital from military bases in the Andes. At about midnight Allende received a report from his palace night staff about these activities at the presidential residence on Tomás Moro Street. These reports came from night laborers on highways leading to Santiago. Considering the growing tension in Chile several months prior to the coup, such reports were taken seriously and yet with a grain of salt, since people were jittery and tended to exaggerate ordinary events. So Allende called Orlando Letelier, the Defense Minister, and asked him to check out the report with General Herman Brady, the recently installed commandant of the Santiago region.

Brady told Letelier he had absolutely no information concerning this report and assured him that everything appeared normal and peaceful. There was nothing to fear, he said. Letelier got back to Allende with Brady's message but promised to be on the alert for further developments for the rest of the night. Both he and the palace staff continued to probe other military officials since the rumors would not abate.

These officials denied having any information that would shed light on these reports. Only one general volunteered the idea that such troop transports might have something to do with the Independence Day parade scheduled for the following week, September 19th. "These soldiers," he said, "might be en route to Santiago to rehearse for the military parade."

At 6:30 in the morning of the day of the putsch Allende was awakened by a phone call from the palace and was told that the navy was in rebellion and had occupied Valparaiso, Chile's main port and second largest city. All communications with it were cut. He immediately called Letelier and told him to order

General Augusto Pinochet, chief of staff of the armed forces, to arrange for maximum security for the presidential palace and for Santiago as a whole. But Letelier had already tried to reach Pinochet and could not locate him; nor could he reach Pinochet's next in command. Moreover, he was astonished, he said, to find Admiral Carvajal answering the phone when he called his own office at the Defense Ministry. What was the admiral doing there, and at that hour in the morning?

In the next forty-five minutes Allende was on the phone with government officials and leaders of the various political groups that formed his Popular Unity party. He still was uncertain how widespread the uprising was. But he summoned his personal bodyguards at Tomás Moro who quickly loaded three vehicles with bazookas, automatic rifles, and machine guns. This group of twenty-seven young men, devoted to Allende and highly trained sharpshooters, were known as the G.A.P.—Grupo de Amigos Personales.

At 7:15 A.M. he entered his car, his head covered with a helmet and in his hand a light machine gun, a gift from Fidel Castro, who had visited Chile some months earlier. Going at breakneck speed, with the three-car convoy immediately behind him, Allende arrived at the presidential palace at 7:30. At first glance everything seemed normal. There was the usual detachment of *carabineros* and their tanks standing guard. But minutes later various ministers, close friends, and trusted advisors began rushing into the building. Among them were Carlos Briones, Minister of the Interior; Clodomiro Almeyda, Foreign Affairs Chief; José Tohá, former Defense Minister, and his brother Jaime Tohá, Agriculture Minister; Daniel Vergara, Undersecretary of the Interior; Jaime Barrios, an eminent economist and close friend of the President, with his wife, Nancy; Frida Modak, the President's press secretary, and Miriam Contreras, his personal secretary. Soon after there also arrived Allende's two daughters: Beatriz, a close political aide to the President, married to a Cuban diplomat and mother of a three-year-old daughter; and Isabel, who was married to a Chilean scientist. But Letelier was not among those present. While this group was conferring with Allende or with each other in the President's office, Augusto Olivares, the journalist, then director of Chile's national television network, was glued to the telephone, desperately trying to get news of the latest developments.

As yet there was nothing definite about the army's role in connection with the navy uprising. Santiago appeared tranquil. And those who had driven to La Moneda had experienced no problems getting there. Allende phoned his wife to reassure her that while things were difficult, all was not lost. "The situation is serious," he told her, "but do not despair. Though the navy mutinied, I am confident there are enough loyal army units to deal with the situation."

About ten minutes later Allende made his first radio address, telling the Chilean people about the Valparaiso rebellion. He urged his listeners to remain calm. So far as Santiago was concerned everything looked peaceful. However, he appealed to all members of trade unions to be on the alert and to take all necessary means to defend their factories and plants should the need arise. He pleaded with them to avoid provocations and stand ready for further instructions.

At 8:15 Allende made a second radio broadcast, very much along the same lines. But even as he spoke, the hoped-for dependability of the military quickly began to evaporate. Growing concern about Letelier's absence was reinforced with the arrival of Colonel Valenzuela, the Undersecretary of War. Valenzuela was certain that something must have happened to Letelier. He himself had just come from the Ministry of Defense, where soldiers had barred his way to his own office. And as Allende finished his second speech there was a phone call from the air force headquarters.

Scarcely did he place the receiver to his ear when his face clouded with profound disbelief. He muttered, "The traitors, the traitors . . . they don't even have enough guts to tell me this directly . . ." The voice on the other end of the wire was that of Roberto Sanchez, the President's air force aide-de-camp. He was telling Allende that a junta composed of the three branches of

the military had demanded that the President resign and that the
air force was making a plane available to fly him to exile to any
country of his choice.

"Tell them I am the President," Allende shouted into the
phone, "and it is here at La Moneda that I am going to remain."

It quickly became clear why Letelier had not found General
Gustavo Leigh when he tried to trace the reports of troop
movements, and why it was impossible to reach General Augusto
Pinochet, whom Allende had named supreme commander of the
Chilean armed forces the month before. Allende could not have
been entirely surprised at the turn of events, considering the
thickening conspiratorial atmosphere of the previous several
months, but it must have been a particularly heavy blow to
discover Pinochet's deceit and betrayal. This was the man who
reached the pinnacle of his career because of Allende. Posturing
as a friend of the Popular Unity government, he had cultivated
close personal relations with the people he eventually put to
death. Only two months before the putsch he had personally
helped put down an incipient mutiny by an army tank battalion.
Chileans who suffered torture at the hands of the Junta recall
how slyly Pinochet wormed himself into their homes and even
their hearts.

At 8:30, within minutes after Allende's indignant rejection of
the exile offer, the Junta repeated its ultimatum in a nationwide
broadcast. "The President should immediately relinquish his
authority to the armed forces and the *carabineros* of Chile. All
press, radio and TV channels, formerly in the service of the
Popular Unity parties must immediately suspend their operations
or face punishment by air and ground forces."

In the next half hour, Allende's three aides-de-camp—from
the navy, the army, and the air force—suddenly appeared at the
door of his office urging that he see them at once. They all
attempted to persuade him to resign. The Junta was really in
earnest about taking La Moneda by force, they said. But Allende
remained adamant; moreover, he said, there was no longer any
point in talking to anybody in uniform, since even his own aides
were taking orders from the Junta. Trust had run out, he told
them. He had been especially fond of Commander Sanchez,

who was close to the Allende family and had accompanied the President and his wife on many official missions abroad. He gave Sanchez a warm handshake as he bade him farewell and told the three men to leave the palace.

Waiting to see Allende next was General José Maria Sepúlveda, commanding officer of the *carabineros*, and known to have been loyal to Allende. Downcast and angry, he told the President that he had been relieved of his command and that the Junta had ordered him and the *carabinero* security guard to remove their gear, tanks and all, and withdraw from the palace.

Dr. Danilo Bartulin, one of several physicians on the staff of the palace medical corps, who remained with Allende to the end, describes the President as solemn but composed, very much in command of the situation. As the *carabineros* began to abandon the palace, Allende told his ministers and friends that regardless of the outcome at La Moneda, Chile's war against fascism would have to continue. He discussed strategy for the future with calm and determination. His chief concern centered on the means to salvage the progressive legislation his regime was able to bring about for Chile's disfranchised sections of the population. For this reason as well as for their own safety, he urged certain political leaders, in particular, to leave the palace at once, while there was still time. A number of those around him shook his hand and left through side doors.

Allende then made his historic last address to the Chilean people. Dr. Bartulin recalls that the President spoke in a firm voice and without reference to notes. There was a decisiveness in tone and a somber serenity at the same time. Immediately after his address he went about the business of setting up the last-ditch defenses of the palace.

His helmet back on and machine gun in hand, the nation's commander-in-chief sized up his total "army" of forty men. A somewhat portly figure dressed in maroon trousers, a pullover sweater, and a gray tweed jacket, he moved about quickly, directing his men to the various battle stations. Allende showed no panic, even though the ringing telephones brought increasingly bad tidings.

There was no longer any doubt about Valparaiso. It was now

fully in control of the Junta forces, who overnight had executed
hundreds of marines and sailors who refused to go along with the
mutiny. Similar reports were coming in from the port city of
Antofagasta, from Valdivia, and from other key cities. Even at
this juncture, after nearly three years of precarious tightrope
maneuvers to keep the Rightist sections of the army from
mutiny, and constantly defusing situations which were ready to
explode into a civil war, Allende still had some hope that cooler
heads among some of the generals and admirals would prevail
and halt the onrush to disaster.

La Moneda was a busy place. Under the portraits of Chile's
former presidents and generals, who looked down with a sense of
confidence at having added to Chile's proud history, Allende's
staff rushed about preparing for battle. Some were destroying
documents and rosters of names of Allende supporters whose
lives would be in jeopardy if these papers fell in the Junta's
hands. Others made a quick inventory of the weaponry and
ammunition in the small palace arsenal. Dr. Bartulin, Dr. Oscar
Soto, a cardiologist, and others of the medical staff, were
preparing the infirmary for emergency treatment of the battle
casualties that were bound to come.

At about 9:40 A.M., soon after his farewell address, Allende
called a meeting of all those still in La Moneda, except the men
already at their battle stations at windows and doors. Allende was
serious but unruffled. He seemed almost relieved that his mind
was made up; that there were no options; that the only honorable
alternative was to show Chile and the world that anti-Fascists
would not surrender without a fight.

The meeting took place in Sala Toesca, the largest conference
hall at La Moneda. A huge chandelier lit up the unadorned,
pale-yellow walls of this ceremonial chamber, usually reserved
for high-level official functions. Allende sat down behind a huge
table on the platform, at the head of the hall. Frida Modak
remembers that the President outlined the nature of the insurrection, reported on the latest developments, and spoke of his
decision to fight it out at La Moneda. But, he explained, this was
to be a political action, and should not be viewed in terms of
personal martyrdom. Dispassionately he went on to declare that

the battle of La Moneda was only the beginning. "That is how we write the first page of history," he said. "The next page will be written by the Chilean people and by all Latin Americans." And once again he called on those in the palace who had no experience with firearms to get out, and help develop the resistance against the Junta on the outside. Also, he added, those who did not agree with his decision to make a stand in La Moneda should leave, and should do so without guilt, without remorse. "The struggle against fascism need not result in useless deaths; there will be plenty to do outside the palace."

He then turned to yet another immediate problem, the presence of nine women at the palace. In addition to his daughters, there were his private secretary; Nancy Barrios, the wife of the economist who decided to remain with the President; two newspaper reporters; Frida Modak; and two clerical assistants.

Allende insisted that all of them get out of the palace as soon as possible. The women, however, protested vociferously, demanding to stay and fight alongside the men. Beatriz was especially obstinate. (Devoted to her father, she shared many of his philosophical views. She was keenly sensitive to the plight of Chile's poverty-stricken workers. Like her father, she was a doctor. And like him she was convinced that Chile's political and economic structure must be changed if meaningful health improvements were to be made.)*

For several minutes the exchange between Allende and the women was contentious and heated. After yet another tilt with Beatriz, Allende said his mind was made up—the women had to go. With this final statement, Frida Modak says, "he rose and strode out of the room in the direction of his private office. There were no special words for his daughters or for anyone else. A short, steely silence followed. There was scarcely any time for us to react. Events were moving quickly and preparations for the

---

* A few days following the coup Beatriz left Chile with her husband. For the next few years she traveled in Europe and other parts of the world campaigning against the Junta and raising funds for the resisters. Though tireless in her activities, she became progressively depressed with the plight of Chile and especially with the murder of her father by the Junta. She took her own life in 1978.

*The Junta used tanks, troops, and aircraft
in its assault on La Moneda. (Wide World Photos)*

defense of the palace took on a grim reality. As if to underscore
the gravity of the moment, shots were heard from the direction of
the main square in front of the palace."

In a matter of seconds the attacking forces opened fire, Dr.
Bartulin recalls. "And we in the palace returned the fire. The
battle was joined. The noise of rifles and machine guns was
deafening. Most of the shooting was aimed at the section of the
palace which housed the President's private office. But out of
that very office a bazooka was seen protruding from the window
out of which a shot scored a direct hit at a tank as it neared the
building.

"Momentarily it was heartening because our counterattack
appeared to stop the Junta soldiers. Two of their tanks had been
destroyed and many of their men were in retreat. The commanding officer of the Junta forces was enraged; he warned us by radio
that unless we surrendered the air force would blow us to

smithereens. He told us that we had until 11 o'clock to make up
our minds; that bombardment would begin exactly at that hour."

With the palace surrounded, Allende could do nothing to get
the women out until he could arrange a temporary truce. Still
protesting, they were sent into a small storage room in the
interior of the building, presumably a safer haven. In the shuffle,
the President's private secretary managed to separate herself from
the group and hide, determined to see it through.

"Word got back to Allende of our resistance," Frida Modak
said. "During a brief lull in the battle, the President rushed down
to our shelter and began imploring us to leave. 'You are so
young,' he said. 'And you have so much to contribute in the fight
against the Junta.' He addressed us individually, in turn,
pointing up our value in the struggles ahead. He then pleaded
directly with Beatriz and Isabel. To Beatriz he said, 'Think of
your child at home, and think of your unborn child. [She was
eight months pregnant.] You owe it to them to stay alive.' And to
Isabel: 'Your mother will need all the help you can give her.'
And then his voice took on an urgent, hard timbre, as though
saying 'Enough is enough,' and he ordered us to leave the
palace. Some of us argued that a truce would not be honored.
Beatriz insisted that there were no guarantees of safety once the
women were outside La Moneda; there was only a Junta general's
promise. And suppose the general reneged on his word and
decided to hold them hostage, thereby forcing Allende to
surrender to protect his daughters and others? Increasingly
impatient, Allende snapped that if that happened, then 'the
entire world would indeed be jolted by the horror that will have
descended upon Chile!'"

To make sure his order would be carried out Allende accompanied the women to the side door on Morandé Street. He
hugged his daughters and the others. Nancy Barrios held her
husband in a brief embrace, but there was no time for talk. She
pressed a note into his hand: *"Te amo siempre."* (I love you,
always.)

At the door Allende picked up a telephone which was still
connected to the palace intercom and to the administrative
guardpost across the street, now occupied by the Junta general.

He said: "There is a group of women who are going to leave La Moneda. And even though you are a traitor, General, I would expect that you will at least have the decency to give these young women safe conduct and provide them with a jeep to get them out of the area of combat." There was dead silence for about two minutes and then the general replied that he would agree to Allende's plan.

Frida Modak continues:

"I shall never forget that last time I saw Allende, his head covered by a helmet, his hand holding the machine gun. There were no further last-moment embraces or farewells. We suddenly found ourselves out on the street, with the door shut behind us. But there was no jeep at the door, nor any soldiers in view. Nor was there any shooting. Cautious and bewildered, we crossed the street toward the palace guardpost. But again no one was inside or near the buildings. What had happened was that the military had already been pulled back to a safe enough distance to be out of range of the air attacks that were to follow soon after. There were only two drunkards standing in the middle of the street, totally oblivious to the world about them. As the bomber aircraft began their initial reconnaissance sweeps, buzzing La Moneda at a rooftop level, the two men would stagger about on rubbery legs, throw their arms about in all directions as though directing traffic, and mindlessly keep lurching on.

"We, for our part, must have looked as though we were adrift, without compass or direction. We walked a bit farther but saw no jeep nor any human being except the two intoxicated men wandering off in their own world. There was an eerie silence as we neared the vacant broad avenues and the plaza in front of the palace. As we huddled together for a moment, trying to consider what to do next, Beatriz said that she was going back to the palace and tell Allende that we would probably be better off inside La Moneda than outside, should the bombing raids commence. And before anyone else could offer an opinion, Beatriz just took off. She crossed the street and ran back toward the Morandé Street door.

"Beatriz knocked frantically but only the small lookout window was opened. Dr. Bartulin was at the door. Beatriz told him there was no jeep and that we were in an exposed position. She begged him to let us back in. But Bartulin handed her his car keys, told her where his car was parked and said he was sorry but the president's order was not to let us reenter the palace. Beatriz rejoined our group. A quick inspection of the parking area at the palace showed that the cars had been demolished during the morning battle. We had to escape on foot and it was now 11:15, a quarter of an hour past the promised bombing of the palace.

"As we turned the corner we were greeted by a deafening roar of bullets from what seemed like all directions. This was an infantry-softening attack on La Moneda, but to us it appeared as though we were the targets, with unseen enemies taking aim. We dashed across the street to a two-story building, but the doors were locked and there was no response to our frantic ringing of the bell. We then made our way to the building housing *La Prensa*, a newspaper belonging to the Christian Democratic Party, some of whose leadership conspired with the Junta to bring down the Allende government. As we were about to enter the building, two of our group, very young women whom we didn't know and who may have been with the custodial staff of one of the ministries connected with the palace, suddenly broke away, turned the corner and disappeared from view.

"So here we were, six women entering the *La Prensa* building, totally empty except for the doorman. He eyed us with a kind of disbelief. We certainly looked bedraggled. Our hair was wind-blown, our clothes a mess, and one of us decidedly pregnant—all suddenly emerging from a deserted street with bullets ricocheting around us.

"We told him we were employees at one of the ministries, that we had come to work totally unaware of the developments that were in the making. He didn't recognize any of us, and he didn't ask questions. He led us to the open stairwell saying that it was probably the safest place from whatever stray bullets might reach the building. Meanwhile his transistor radio continued to crackle with an endless series of Junta proclamations, and with warnings of the imminent bombardment of La Moneda.

"No sooner had we sat down than the bombardment began.

Our faces were drawn, eyes staring ahead. We were numbed with pain, and the radio kept jabbering away as rocket after rocket slammed down on La Moneda with thunderous explosions. From time to time our host would utter such philosophical comments as, 'Why don't those people in La Moneda give up? They probably aren't even there. They probably found a hiding place outside. And in the meantime—beautiful La Moneda will be destroyed.'

"We looked at each other without saying a word. Beatriz was sitting next to me. But she and the rest remained fully in control of their emotions. Suddenly the door swung open and a young *La Prensa* reporter dashed in. 'It's a terrible, terrible thing,' he exclaimed to no one in particular. He looked at us and quickly sized up the situation; he knew exactly who we were. But he said nothing and walked away in the direction of his office.

"We remained at *La Prensa* for about half an hour, within a short walking distance from La Moneda, where bombs came crashing down to pulverize a historic edifice and everyone in it; where some of us had a father, a husband, or a close friend. Were they still alive? Were they killed by bullets, or were they being burned to death by incendiary bombs?

"Suddenly the bombing stopped. And the radio announced that there would be a half-hour bombing reprieve to see whether Allende and his men would surrender. We left our shelter hoping to get out of the palace area as quickly as possible. We couldn't see La Moneda itself because of the enormous plumes of billowing smoke darkening the entire area. We walked for about two blocks when once again bullets began whistling about us. Apparently it was still another attempt to wear down the Moneda defenders and allow the infantry to take over. The cacophony was overpowering. There was the staccato rattle of machine guns, rifle fire, and occasional cannon salvos. We turned the corner and there, on Ahumada Street, was a hotel only one block away. For some reason two more of our group, the two women journalists, suddenly left and ran off in the opposite direction. We were now only four: Beatriz, Isabel, Nancy, and I.

"We walked into the lobby, which was jammed with joyous

merrymakers, men and women, all obviously upper class, judging by their dress, all celebrating the Junta seizure of power. It was a spree. Since the lobby looked out on a street which led directly to La Moneda, these people had a front-seat view of the bombing attacks on the palace. No one recognized us as we shuffled quickly to a corridor-like extension, slightly away from the lobby. Weary, tense, forlorn, we settled down for a moment in the comfortable leather chairs. But only for a moment. We noticed the telephone booths and some of us quickly made for them. I was able to call my mother and tell her I was safe. Isabel got no answer from her mother who, we thought, was still at Tomás Moro. Amazingly, some of the phones in La Moneda were still functioning. Nancy was able to get through to her husband, who told her that despite the bombardment some of the people were still alive. But then there was a buzzing sound and the line was cut off.

"For a brief moment our morale was somewhat restored. While the horror of the final outcome of La Moneda was oppressively clear to all of us, the very fact that Allende and others had managed to survive gave us a momentary euphoria. But all this was dashed as the hotel lobby radio began reporting that Tomás Moro was also under bomber attack. Isabel crumpled in her chair, her eyes flooded with tears. Beatriz ran to console her, whispering that their mother might have gotten away before the bombing began.

"All this was unfolding against the background of joy and a spirit of fiesta in the adjacent lobby, as champagne bottles popped and the revelers shouted themselves hoarse congratulating themselves that the Allende era was about over. 'Hooray, the show is over,' someone bellowed. 'Down with the Marxists. Let's drink to our generals . . . to our glorious Junta.' And as the bombing resumed, there were more cheers and more hoorays. 'What a pounding,' someone screamed with relish. 'They'll be broiled chickens . . . look at those flames . . . it's a regular bonfire . . .'

"Each exclamation was like a dagger in our hearts. It was unbearable, suffocating. We had to get out. While we were in a huddle deliberating where to go next, a man who seemed like the hotel manager approached us and said, 'It is not that I want you out of here. But as you can see for yourself this is not a very safe place for you. And since the 3 P.M. curfew is almost upon us it would be better if you leave as soon as possible.' We weren't sure whether he knew who we were, but obviously we didn't belong.

"So we filed out of the hotel lobby, turning our faces away from the direction of La Moneda, where enormous flames were shooting skywards, with sections of the horizon covered by a wall of black smoke which could be seen from every part of Santiago.

"Nancy lived close by but it would have been suicidal to go to her apartment since the Junta people were probably already there, ransacking her belongings. One of our group remembered

Fire and smoke enveloped La Moneda, the presidential palace,
following a bomber attack. President Allende and a handful of guardsmen
put up a last-ditch stand in defense of the Popular Unity government
for nearly five hours. (Wide World Photos)

a dentist friend whose office was in the vicinity. We thought we could rest there, make our phone calls, and sort out our alternatives as to the next move. But when we reached his office we found it was closed. This was the dentist's day off, the porter told us. I remembered a seamstress I had known who lived in the same area. We made our way there, but the door was locked. We trudged about in the lonely, deserted streets. There was only occasional traffic when troop carriers or cars covered with Fascist slogans or with names of such Rightist organizations as Patria y Libertad (Fatherland and Freedom) streaked by, as though driven by madmen.

"Suddenly a car driven by a man, with a woman beside him, and two children in the back seat, came along and slowed down. 'We are going toward Parque Forestal. If you need a lift, hop in.' We climbed in and somehow were able to make it in the back seat with the children sitting on our laps. When the car reached Plaza Italia, at the beginning of a residential area, we spotted a military patrol stationed in the middle of the street, checking each car as it came along. There was a tank and several black army vans. None of us uttered a word at the sight of the patrol. I was especially concerned about our good samaritans, the driver and his wife, who might easily wind up in tragedy for having helped us, not knowing our identities. If the soldiers should recognize us it would be most difficult to explain that our meeting with this couple was entirely uncalculated.

"The soldiers were quite young, and apparently from the provinces. As we filed out of the car, one of them said to Beatriz in a worried tone, 'Señora, are you all right?' 'Not quite,' she responded, 'I am afraid I may be having my baby right away.' Actually Beatriz was indeed experiencing occasional contractions brought on by the tension. Whereupon the soldier told his buddy to hurry with the examination of our bags and then turned to our driver and said, 'You better get going, and get her to a doctor fast.'

"As the car began rolling away we noticed that the young wife of our driver was very nervous. From time to time she would look back, stare at me as though trying to place me. This was not altogether surprising. For a period of two years I was seen frequently on television conducting press conferences, or otherwise involved in news programs having to do with Allende and the government. Fortunately we soon came to a street where a friend of Nancy's lived with her mother. We thanked our driver profusely and quickly walked away in the direction of the new shelter. We entered the house precisely at 3 P.M., the hour the curfew went into effect. We remained there for thirty-six hours."

When Allende finally took leave of the women, he quickly returned to his office to check on further developments. There was little to cheer him. However, taking advantage of the lull in the fighting, Allende made a final inspection of his tiny army. He paid meticulous attention to measures designed to fortify the positions of those left to defend La Moneda. In addition to ammunition the palace arsenal also had a supply of gas masks, which were distributed to everybody.

Of course La Moneda was a fortress in itself. Built in the eighteenth century, it was a massive gray edifice in downtown Santiago. Despite its thick, three-foot walls it had a pleasant as well as an enduring character. In its center there was an open, cheerful ambiance. Wide, glass-covered corridors led to the various conference halls and adjacent ministries, filled with plants and semi-tropical flowers. During the Allende years there was little formality in the halls of La Moneda. Its corridors resounded with the sound of hundreds of peasant and worker delegations whose counsel was sought by ministry officials on trade union problems, health safety measures in the mines and industrial plants, and plans to nationalize major foreign and domestic multinational enterprises. It shed its former official, crusty bureaucratic trappings. As one American observer put it, it was something like an indoor Boston Common in the early days of the American Revolution, allowing all political groups to sound off.

Unless attacked from the air, La Moneda would be a difficult bastion to breech. And Allende and his supporters made doubly sure that this was how it was going to be. The Junta generals would have to rip La Moneda apart stone by stone, and thereby reveal themselves as the destroyers of one of Chile's proudest national monuments. For Allende and his last defenders, La Moneda became their Madrid of the Spanish Civil War, during which the Republicans vowed that the city would not be surrendered to the Franco legions, and *No Pasaran* (They shall not pass) became the rallying cry of early anti-Nazis the world over.

While doing his inspection, constantly interrupted by phone calls and questions from his anxious aides, Allende suddenly turned to Dr. Bartulin and said, "I sure am hungry. I certainly could devour a sandwich." And miraculously enough, somebody produced a slice of bread which he began munching immediately. Dr. Bartulin ran down to the palace restaurant to see if something more substantial was on hand. Much to his surprise he discovered that the refrigerator contained several chickens ready for broiling, obviously prepared by the kitchen staff the day before. He was almost gleeful at this find. And as he lit the stove and placed the chickens inside, the first bomb slammed into La Moneda, within close range of the kitchen. In seconds shattered glass, twisted metal, crumbling walls, powdered plaster, and the raw chickens became all one unrecognizable mess. Dr. Bartulin, gasping for air as he wrestled with his gas mask, was among the first to be wounded: a cut hand and a mild concussion.

Then came the second bomber attack, and yet another. All told, about twenty-five sorties within forty minutes. Olivares, the Chilean journalist, was mortally wounded. The others were dazed, coughing, and choking from the noxious gas of the exploding rockets. Apparently the gas masks were not effective. Parts of the roof caved in. Splintered furniture, pieces of sculpture were scattered in all directions. But most ominous was the wall of fire and smoke advancing from the left side of the palace, known as the Red Room. This is the area in which a dozen defenders must have been killed outright from several direct rocket hits. There was no way of reaching these men since a roaring blaze was now enveloping the entire area, threatening the office of Allende and the remaining defenders.

In a desperate effort to contain the fire, Allende ordered all faucets opened in the lavatories and in what remained of those in the kitchen. As one survivor described it, "We were about to be burned to a crisp and drowned at the same time." There was a brief pause following the bombardment. Allende once again reviewed his beleaguered forces. He himself had been in the thick of it. His fingers and hands bore gunpowder smudges from having fired his machine gun.

Suddenly, to everyone's amazement, the intercom phone began ringing. The call came from the Junta general directing the assault. He offered a temporary cease-fire and asked Allende to send two emissaries to discuss a proposal to halt the hostilities. Allende was strongly opposed to such negotiations since he was certain that the Junta would again demand his resignation, something he vowed not to do. Moreover, he warned that the Junta offer might turn out to be a trick, and those undertaking the mission would never get back.

There were those in the group who felt that there was nothing to lose, since it was obvious that their position was hopeless, but all agreed that there would be no compromise on the issue of Allende's surrendering the presidency. Allende assigned a negotiating committee of three: Fernando Flores, chief of the presidential staff, Daniel Vergara, and Osvaldo Puccio, the president's executive secretary and confidant. Puccio's nineteen-year-old son, also named Osvaldo, became the fourth member when he insisted on accompanying his father.

Minutes went by and more minutes went by. But no word reached the Allende people about the negotiations. And then it became clear that Allende's prediction was correct—the four emissaries were not heard from again.

The Junta's truce came to an explosive end as the assaulting ground troops began attacking La Moneda from all sides with recoilless rifles, cannons, and heavy machine guns. At 1:30 P.M., the first contingent broke through one of the doors and suddenly some of the defenders on the ground floor of La Moneda found themselves surrounded. Allende and about a dozen men were on the second floor, with some of the group continuing to shoot at the invaders.

Those taken prisoner on the ground floor were kicked, battered with rifle butts, and shoved out into the street. They were ordered to drop to the ground with their arms outstretched as soldiers frisked them for weapons and kicked them again. One of the commanding officers walked over to Dr. Soto and demanded that he identify himself. When he did so, the officer told him to go to Allende's office and tell him to give up or face immediate execution. Soto ran up the partly destroyed marble staircase shouting to warn Allende that he was coming with a message. He saw Allende sitting at a desk, the machine gun still in his hands and a group of about fifteen people standing guard around him.

Allende listened to what Soto said and then ordered everyone to go down to give themselves up to the Junta officers below. "There is no point in useless deaths. I order you to go," he told the men around him. Most of them obeyed. And so with their hands up in surrender, Dr. Soto and ten others began their walk down, single file. They were stood up against the wall, cursed and kicked by the soldiers who searched them for guns. In the meantime, a platoon of heavily armed soldiers rushed into the building and up the stairs. There was a brief exchange of gunfire. And then a perspiring, somewhat bedraggled but smiling officer rushed down to announce to other officers and soldiers at the door that Allende was dead.

Allende was killed with five of his personal bodyguards, young men between the ages of eighteen and twenty-five, who would

Surrendered prisoners were kicked, hit with rifle butts, and then forced to lie on the pavement face down while trigger-happy Junta soldiers stood watch. (Wide World Photos)

not leave their President. The battle of La Moneda was over at 2:20 P.M. on September 11, 1973.

Of the dozen or so survivors who were taken prisoner, ten of them were tortured and executed within the next twelve hours. Among them were the economist Jaime Barrios; the nationally known psychiatrist, Dr. Jorge Klein; Dr. Enrique Paris, the director of education and science research; and the sociologist, Claudio Gimeno.

The Junta thought that by killing Allende and some 30,000 of his supporters it would blot out his memory and his social reform programs in one fell swoop. It appears, however, that quite the reverse has happened. Allende has emerged as Chile's greatest martyr. In giving up his life to uphold a constitutional principle he converted himself into a symbol of national honor, a sort of reference point for those continuing to fight against the Junta. Regardless of party origins or previous political labels, Chile's exiles scattered across the globe, whether in Mexico, South America, Italy, France, or Sweden, are united in their resolve to bring down Pinochet and the Junta and return democracy and liberty to their country. The same is true for those inside Chile who are willing to take extraordinary risks in organizing the resistance, notwithstanding the daily menace of torture and the firing squad.

2

The Coup and the CIA Involvement

> *President Nixon informed CIA Director Richard Helms that an Allende regime in Chile would not be acceptable to the United States. The CIA was instructed by President Nixon to play a direct role in organizing a military coup d'etat in Chile to prevent Allende's accession to the presidency.*
> "COVERT ACTION IN CHILE"—*Staff Report of United States Senate Select Committee to Study Governmental Operations with Respect to Intelligence Activities. Washington, D.C., 1975*

THOUGH THERE ARE no eyewitness accounts as to what transpired on the morning of the coup at the United States embassy in Chile, it is safe to surmise that there was a good deal of backslapping and self-congratulating among the small group of top-ranking CIA and State Department officials as they raised their whiskey glasses to toast a job well done. After all, as the Senate Select Committee later disclosed, it took years of conspiratorial preparation and many millions of dollars. But what a payoff! The sound of every exploding bomb, the stutter of machine guns, the whine of bullets—all were telling evidence that everything was going satisfactorily. And if they had looked out of the windows they could have seen the Allende regime not only tottering but literally wiped out by rocket and fire. Huge clouds of smoke were billowing out of La Moneda, the presidential palace where Allende made his last stand. Squads of soldiers poured out of personnel carriers, scurrying in all directions, exchanging rifle fire with half-hidden snipers. The shantytown pockets of resistance were now smoldering heaps of ashes; the flattened tin cans and strips of wood, the building

39

materials for the hovels that were homes of thousands of families in and around the nation's capital, were charred rubble.

But immediately after the overthrow of the Allende regime, Washington rejected charges that it had had a hand in the coup, and it disclaimed having had advance knowledge of its imminence.

America's "covert" activists had first stopped Allende from becoming President in 1964. It was a lot easier then; there was less fuss and things were kept in lower profile, although it did cost some three million dollars to finance the anti-Allende electoral campaigns of the opposition parties.

This time it was much more complicated and very expensive for the American taxpayers, well over eight million dollars. As the Senate Select Committee,* headed by then-Senator Frank Church of Idaho, subsequently discovered, from 1969 to the day of the coup in September 1973, the CIA handed out its largess freely to just about anybody who could be useful in bringing down the Allende government. These "covert" activities, the Senate Committee disclosed, "covered a broad spectrum, from simple propaganda manipulation of the press to large-scale support for Chilean political parties, from public opinion polls to direct attempts to foment a military coup."

If translated in "unminced words," a former Chilean diplomat said, "this meant that this CIA undertaking, first known as Track I and then as Track II, included everything from cloak-and-dagger operations, involving the murder of generals and civilians, to strangulation of Chilean economy and subversion of its legally elected government."

Chileans admit grudgingly that much of this performance was enacted via a subtly handled script in which only the tragic consequences were allowed to surface. The faces of the main actors and directors in Washington remained secret. Allende and his government were jousting in a lethal chess game with an

---

* In addition to Frank Church, the Select Committee included these senators: John G. Tower, Philip A. Hart, Walter F. Mondale, Walter D. Huddleston, Robert Morgan, Gary Hart, Howard H. Baker, Jr., Barry Goldwater, Charles McC. Mathias, Jr., and Richard Schweiker.

*President Allende addressing the United Nations, December 4, 1972.
He charged that Washington and the multinational corporations
were plotting to overthrow his government. (United Nations)*

adversary who remained out of sight but who had the advantage of striking out while the Chilean President and his people had their backs turned.

As Allende put it, in his speech to the United Nations, December 4, 1972, "We find ourselves faced with forces which operate in the shadows, without a flag, with powerful weapons, posted in the various places of influence. . . . From the very day of our electoral triumph on the fourth of September 1970, we have felt the effects of a large-scale external pressure against us which tried to prevent the inauguration of a government freely elected by the people, and has attempted to bring it down ever since, an action that has tried to cut us off from the world, to strangle our economy and paralyze trade in our principal export, copper, and to deprive us of access to sources of international financing. . . .

"We are the victims of virtually imperceptible activities, usually disguised with words and statements that extol the sovereignty and dignity of my country. We know in our own hearts, however, the distance that separates these words from the specific activities that we have to face."

The Chileans knew that the hostile acts were directed from Washington and played out by Chile's Rightist surrogates, but they seldom had black-and-white documentation to prove their case. However, on March 21 and 22, 1971, Jack Anderson, a Washington columnist, published an exposé citing documents that the International Telephone and Telegraph Corporation (ITT), a multinational giant, was involved in a plot to torpedo Allende's election the year before. Moreover, Anderson revealed that the CIA was directly involved with ITT to precipitate economic chaos in Chile leading to a military coup to stop Allende from getting to the presidency. Among other things Anderson charged that ITT had been ready to contribute "up to seven figures" to the White House to make sure that the plot would be carried out effectively.

But it was only after the fact, after Allende had been assassinated, after some 30,000 Chileans had been tortured to death or shot by firing squads, after upwards of 100,000 others were languishing in prisons and concentration camps, that official documentation of this conspiracy came to light before the Senate Select Committee in 1975.

There were a number of reasons, the Committee learned, why Washington was preoccupied with the Allende development in Chile. Only a decade before, a Socialist Cuba had come into being; it was something new and threatening to the status quo of Latin America. Soon afterward, at the other end of the hemisphere, the possibility of a Socialist Chile hove into view. With Chile's proximity to such unstable governments as those of Bolivia, Peru, Argentina, and Brazil, the old Dulles domino theory was perceived to have a realistic potential. As seen from the Pentagon and the State Department, the United States' hemispheric preserve was coming apart.

In addition to political considerations, there were powerful economic interests at stake. American corporations, such as ITT and the two copper multinationals, Anaconda and Kennecott, were imperiled by the mounting, broad-based demand in Chile that they be expropriated. Because Anaconda and Kennecott controlled 80 percent of Chile's copper production, which in 1970 accounted for four-fifths of Chile's foreign exchange, these corporations held the lifelines to Chile's economy.

Considering these fast-breaking developments and the far-reaching hemispheric implications should these companies be nationalized, Washington found it compelling to derail an Allende victory, regardless of the legitimacy with which it would come to power. And as far as the American people were concerned their views on the desirability of U.S. intervention in Chile were neither sought nor expected to play a role. Thus, in fact, the Nixon administration, in subverting the Popular Unity government, had also chipped away at the American constitution by going to war, covert war though it was, without the consent of the Congress.

Not even the Congressional Oversight Committees were fully informed on the extent of the CIA's activities. The Senate Select Committee disclosed in 1975 that "of the thirty-three covert action projects undertaken in Chile . . . during the period of 1963–1974, Congress was briefed in some fashion on eight. Presumably, the twenty-five others were undertaken *without Congressional consultation* (author's italics)." One of these concerned an attempt "to foment a military coup in 1970." Withal, the Senate Select Committee commented, "the CIA did not volunteer detailed information; Congress most often did not seek it."

Both the Republican administration under Nixon and that of Democrats under John F. Kennedy and Lyndon Johnson looked with anxiety at the growing unrest in the Southern Cone (Chile, Peru, Bolivia, Paraguay, Argentina, Brazil, and Uruguay), where "widespread malnutrition, illiteracy, hopeless housing conditions and hunger . . ." the Senate Select Committee said, "were seen as communism's allies." This anxiety was the reason Kennedy launched the Alliance for Progress program which provided millions of dollars to start up national development projects to ease the acute economic crises of these areas and, it was hoped, stave off Castro's influence.

That anxiety was also the reason why the United States began

training Latin American army and police forces in "counterinsurgency techniques" to combat urban and rural protesters and
guerrillas intent on bringing about speedier social and economic
change. As the Senate Select Committee pointed out, "The
vicious circle plaguing the logic of the Alliance for Progress soon
became apparent. In order to eliminate the short-term danger of
Communist subversion, it was often necessary to support Latin
American armed forces, yet frequently it was those same armed
forces who were helping to freeze the status quo which the
Alliance sought to alter."

Because of Chile's traditional widespread labor support for
Socialist, Communist, and other leftist parties, and because of its
overall political sophistication—save for a few interruptions,
Chile had, after all, been a democracy for a hundred years.
Washington tried to wean it away from Castroism by making it a
showplace for the Alliance for Progress program. Between 1962
and 1969 the United States extended over a billion dollars in
loans to support a variety of projects. However, little of it filtered
through to the needy sectors of the population. The "have-not"
Chileans were not mollified. And Allende, a former Minister of
Public Health, and for years a Socialist senator in parliament,
decided to run for the presidency for a third time in 1964, on a
broad leftist program. The program then, just as it did six years
later, called for a more equitable distribution of Chile's wealth.
This was to be accomplished by trimming the large estates of the
landed gentry and giving the land to peasant collectives and
cooperatives, and by expropriating domestic monopoly industries, as well as foreign holdings in copper, iron mills, and
communications. The expropriation, however, was not confiscation; it was to be done with compensation to the owners
along internationally recognized legal guidelines.

In the 1964 presidential race between Allende and Eduardo
Frei, the candidate of the middle-of-the-road Christian Democratic party, the latter received three million dollars from the
CIA, enough to defray half of the costs of the campaign. Frei
won, but his promises concerning social and economic reforms
remained generally unfulfilled.

Six years later Chileans had another chance to cast their votes for a candidate they felt would represent their interests. This time, in 1970, there were three presidential candidates: Jorge Alessandri, of the Conservative Party, Radomiro Tomic, of the Christian Democrats, and Allende. Allende ran as a candidate of the Popular Unity Party, a coalition of the Socialists, the Communists, the centrist Radical Party, and several small leftist parties.

Initially, United States involvement in the 1970 elections was modest compared to 1964. Differing views on tactics in Washington, especially between the State Department and the CIA, limited U.S. participation for a while. For one thing, some officials felt that the United States should keep as low a profile as possible in whatever machinations were to be undertaken. There was also confidence that either the Conservative candidate or the Christian Democrat would withdraw at the last moment and the two parties would join to stop Allende.

American corporations such as ITT, however, were considerably more apprehensive. Two months before the election ITT representatives met with the Chief of the Western Hemisphere Division of the CIA to confer on how best to finance the anti-Allende candidates. According to the Select Committee, the CIA officials counseled ITT on the best Chilean intermediary to make the transaction possible. Thereupon ITT and other American companies kicked in $700,000 with a good deal of money going to Alessandri and to the fascistic National Party. And the United States, for its part, finally decided to do its bit and on the command of the 40 Committee * chipped in some $400,000 for what it called "spoiling" activities. These were aimed at disrupting the growing strength of Allende's Popular Unity Party while shoring up the opposition parties. It was also to sow dissent within the Popular Unity Party itself.

In detailing this undertaking, the Senate Select Committee

---

* The 40 Committee was a sub-Cabinet-level body of the Executive Branch whose mandate was to review proposed major covert actions. The Committee has existed in similar form since the 1950s under a variety of names. Since 1969 it included among other officials, the Undersecretary of State for Political Affairs, the Deputy Secretary of Defense, the Chairman of the Joint Chiefs of Staff, and the Director of Central Intelligence. Heading the Committee at the time of the Allende election was Nixon's National Security Advisor, Henry Kissinger.

said the CIA helped prepare a series of propaganda materials to accomplish these goals. An anti-Allende newsletter was mailed to 2,000 Chilean journalists, members of the academic community, and opinion makers warning of the catastrophes to come following an Allende victory. The CIA financed the hiring of sign-painting teams that covered some 2,000 walls with the slogan *su paredón* (your wall), evoking the image of firing squads for Allende opponents should Allende get into office. This scare campaign was orchestrated with the help of many newspapers and periodicals, all in the pay of the CIA. But most important was the wide utilization of *El Mercurio*, the *New York Times* of Chile. CIA-dictated editorials and slickly edited special features and "straight" news articles, all assailing Allende and his supporters, were served up regularly in this most prestigious newspaper with a daily circulation of 350,000. The paper also operated a chain of provincial editions.

"Access to *El Mercurio* had a multiplier effect," the Senate Select Committee pointed out, "since its editorials were read throughout the country on various national radio networks. Moreover, *El Mercurio* was one of the most influential Latin American newspapers, particularly in business circles abroad. A project which placed anti-Communist press and radio items was reported in 1970 to reach an audience of well over five million listeners."

In the course of a six-week interim period, the Senate report went on to say that "726 articles, broadcasts, editorials and similar items" resulted " . . . directly from Agency [CIA] activity." Incidentally, *El Mercurio*'s cooperation was not without fringe benefits to the owners of the paper. They received one-and-a-half million dollars to present "objective" news as edited by CIA operatives.

But after all was said and done, Allende won the presidency. True, he squeezed by with only 36.3 percent in a plurality vote, but he triumphed; almost, that is. Because he did not obtain 51 percent of the vote, the Chilean constitution called for Congress to choose one of the two candidates who received the largest number of votes at the polls. The election took place on

September 4, 1970; Congress was to vote on October 24th; and the inauguration was scheduled for November 4th.

This sixty-day interval was seized upon by Washington for a final attempt to stop Allende at all costs, regardless of the consequences. There was still time to sway public opinion and have the Congress turn against Allende. Every effort was to be made to frustrate Allende's coming to power. This was a direct order from Richard Nixon, the President of the United States.

In testifying to the Senate Select Committee, Helms recalled his impression that the "President came down very hard, that he wanted something done, and he didn't care how and that he was prepared to make the money available . . . if there were one chance in ten of getting rid of Allende, we should try it; . . . and aid programs should be cut; [Chile's] economy should be squeezed until it 'screamed.' . . . This was a pretty all-inclusive order. . . ." Helms added that the President shouted and cursed and said that he would authorize ten million dollars to pay for whatever was needed to stop a Socialist government from coming to power.* Nixon's Secretary of State, Henry Kissinger, is reported to have said, "I don't see why we should have to stand by and let a country go Communist due to the irresponsibility of its own people."

In keeping with the President's directive, the CIA moved quickly. According to the Senate Select Committee, "as part of its attempt to induce the Chilean military to intervene before the October 24th congressional vote, the United States had threat-

---

* Nixon's emotional, high-pitched involvement with the Allende phenomenon was recalled by former Ambassador Edward Korry in a television documentary program on the national network of the Public Broadcasting Service in 1980. Korry said that shortly before he was replaced as Ambassador to Chile in 1970, he flew to Washington to report to Nixon. Korry said: "As I came through the door the President greeted me and then shut the door. And while we were still standing at the door (together with Henry Kissinger), Nixon started saying, 'That son-of-a-bitch, that son-of-a-bitch,' as he smacked his fist. I must have looked sort of surprised, thinking, 'Who me?' And he said, 'Ah, not you, Mr. Ambassador, you always tell it like it is. It's that son-of-a-bitch Allende.' And he launched into a ten-minute monologue describing how he was going to smash Allende. . . ."

ened to cut off military aid if the military refused to act." That inducement, the Committee added, "was accompanied by a promise of support in the aftermath of a coup." *

Within a week following the elections *El Mercurio* unfolded a hysterical campaign warning its readers that Allende's presidency would doom the country to economic collapse. With headlines screaming that the solvency of the nation's banks was in doubt, depositors rushed to queue in endless lines to withdraw their savings. The Chilean *escudo* tumbled precipitously in relation to foreign currencies.

In addition to the subsidies to *El Mercurio* and much of the other media, the CIA distributed yet another three million dollars to those willing to abort an Allende administration. Among the recipients of such financial favors was the Christian Democratic Party, led by outgoing President Frei, the Rightist National Party, and the out-and-out Fascist organization, Patria y Libertad. The CIA didn't appear to be squeamish about handing out laundered dollars to Patria y Libertad despite the fact that this organization took to the streets with Hitler salutes, dressed its members in Nazi-like uniforms, and waved banners decorated with swastika-resembling insignias. The initial grant to Patria y Libertad was $35,000.

Alongside the insidious press campaigns, the CIA-directed Rightists whipped up a radio blitz scare. Typical were these one-minute spots. A woman's voice came on with a scream: "The Communists will kill my son! The Communists will kill my son!" This was followed by a somber male voice: "This will happen if Chile goes Communist. This message was brought to you by 'Women's Power,' an organization devoted to protecting the well-being of women." Another example: "The streets are unsafe," a panicky voice would interrupt a soap opera produc-

---

* Because of its unique role, the Chilean army was something of a power unto itself. Chile's heads of government would tread softly where it concerned defense appropriations for the purchase of weaponry, presumably to safeguard the country from some of its neighbors. Thus the paradox: Though Washington was cutting back its economic ties with the Allende government drastically, it still continued to extend bountiful credits to Chile's armed forces, so as to maintain its influential hold upon it. For his part Allende would not intervene in this U.S.-Chilean army liaison for fear that it would harden the army's resentment against him.

tion. "Street fights may erupt at any minute. Don't let your children play in the streets. Run to fetch your children from school."

In the continuing psychological warfare to involve the mothers against Allende, wall posters carried a photograph of a schoolboy, against the background of a picture of the same lad dressed as a guerrilla fighter with a gun in his hand under the headline YOUR CHILD . . . OR YOUR ENEMY? And the subhead drove the message home. It read: "In Socialist countries, children are forced to spy on their parents."

The CIA's "spoiling operations" was not confined to Chile. They even reached out to "disinform" the American public. Especially noteworthy because of the magazine's importance, was the coverage of Allende in a *Time* cover story. According to CIA documents the *"Time* correspondent in Chile apparently had accepted Allende's protestations of moderation and constitutionality at face value." But, "briefings requested by *Time* and provided by the CIA in Washington resulted in a change in the basic thrust of the *Time* story on Allende's September 4th victory and in the timing of that story."

The Chilean media campaign was aimed not only at the economic and political aspects of Chilean life. More and more this battle offensive was also designed to condition the Chileans to associate Allende and the Popular Unity Party with a breakdown of social mores, with schisms within the family, and with perils to personal security. In many ways it was conducted cunningly. In the reportage of an ordinary crime, whether a burglary or a murder, the newspapers would carry a front-page headline concerning this incident and alongside it run a large photograph of Allende or some other important personage associated with the Popular Unity Party. The photograph had nothing to do with the crime story, but the effect for the cursory reader was that somehow Allende was connected with the felony. As slum dwellers, led by Allende activists, began to participate more fully in their respective community affairs—and this included the organization of self-defense groups for the protection against assaults from right-wing hooligans—the anti-Allende press charged that the shantytowns were becoming armed camps. And since the shantytowns were relegated to the periphery of Santiago, there were such headlines as SAN-TIAGO ENCIRCLED, as though the shantytowns were the launching pads for the seizure of the nation's capital. These stories were accompanied by maps pinpointing the alleged concentration areas from which the so-called invasion would get underway.

In the attempt to solidify the opposition against Allende in Congress as it was about to vote for either Allende or Alessandri, the two front runners in the popular vote, rumors were spread that the military would not tolerate Allende's taking the presidency, that a coup would be sprung. Actually, the leadership of the armed forces, such as Commander-in-Chief René Schneider and General Carlos Prats were committed constitutionalists. For them, their pledge to uphold the constitution and defend the country meant that the military had no business becoming involved in politics or interfering with legitimately elected governments. In other words, the armed forces were to be neutralist, not taking sides though some of the other generals as well as junior officers were already knee-deep in anti-Allende conspiracies.

Despite Schneider's public statements, the rumors of a coup d'état would not go away. The atmosphere throughout Chile crackled with apprehension. There was good reason to be alarmed, especially if the facts had been known. For toward the end of September, Richard Helms, Director of the CIA, went into a huddle with other operatives and an ITT executive to consider stop-Allende measures should the Chilean Congress approve Allende's election.

When commenting on this plot and on the subsequent murder of Schneider by Chilean military conspirators in his 1972 speech at the United Nations, President Allende obviously made reference to the United States without naming it. He said, ". . . terrorist activities took place in my country which were planned outside our frontiers in collusion with internal Fascist groups. Those activities culminated in the assassination of the Commander-in-Chief of the Army, General René Schneider

Chereau, who was a just man, a great soldier, and a symbol of the constitutional attitude of Chile's armed forces."

Despite the attacks on the Popular Unity Party, Allende himself began to prepare to take office with the fullest confidence that the Congress would support him in the October vote. As Gonzalo Martner explained to me, "It was a confidence born out of forty years of proximity to Chilean reality, to vast sectors of the population who had suffered continuous privation and who now were not likely to stand aside and see their moment of triumph slip by." Martner, an economist, a former Minister of National Planning in Allende's cabinet, said, "The reality which Allende had come to know through the years, first as a public health doctor and then as a political spokesman for Chile's impoverished, was spelled out for him in many ways: through the hunger that plagued hundreds of thousands of people, whose two meals a day consisted of a few slices of bread, a cup of coffee, or just hot water; through the thousands of children with mental retardation because of malnutrition; through the profound loneliness of tiny villages whose men went off to eke out a miserable wage in the nitrate mines in the far north, and who eventually were swallowed up by time and distance, never to return to their families. It was a reality in which Mapuche Indian peasants were expected to do a day's work for less than a dollar."

Convinced that he had the support of Chile's masses, and the likely Congressional vote in his favor, Martner says, Allende went to work with his principal economic experts to prepare for the implementation of the Popular Unity program "that was to give Chile's disfranchised a break to a better life, their first taste of a New Deal.

"Allende, two economic experts, and myself," Martner recalls, "left the nation's capitol for a secluded inn in a mountain retreat for the first such meeting on September 19th, when the armed forces traditionally marked Chile's independence observance with a parade." Because of the growing tensions, Allende and his aides felt it prudent to work outside Santiago. "Some of us were very concerned that the military activity that day might tempt the Rightists in the armed forces to pull a coup, including an assault on Allende. We four were in one car, and five of Allende's bodyguards—young, very dedicated activists—were in the car behind us. We negotiated the one-hour trip with considerable anxiety. We changed cars four times on secluded side roads to avoid the possibility of falling into a trap or an assassination attempt."

At the inn, Martner says, Allende and his counselors went to work straight away. "Allende was in full command of the discussion. There's no question, however, that he was somewhat nervous, something which could be noticed on his very sensitive and mobile face. From time to time he'd turn on the TV to scan the military parade in Santiago—to make sure that everything was normal. Though Allende was virtually sitting on top of a volcano which was about to erupt," Martner adds, "he controlled his emotions and pressed on with the most detailed examination of the program at hand."

On October 22, 1970, two days before Congress was to vote on Allende's confirmation, Martner says, "We were again with the President putting the final touches to the economic program which the Popular Unity Party was to unfold. While we were reviewing some of the text, Allende was called to the phone. He was told that an assassination attempt had been made on General René Schneider, and that the general appeared to be near death. The assault took place when Schneider was driven to his office. Three cars blocked his path. The general drew his pistol, shots rang out, and Schneider fell back mortally wounded. He died three days later."

On hearing the news, Martner recalls, "Allende said, 'Well, here comes the putsch.' He was sure that Schneider's murder would be blamed on the leftists and used to arouse the country and the Congress against him, a move that would lead to nullification of the election and bring about a takeover by the armed forces."

His hunch was well-founded. He hadn't suspected, however, the close connection between this plot and Washington. The Senate Select Committee disclosed there had been two previous attempts on the general's life, only a few days prior to his death, in which the CIA provided tear-gas grenades and three sub-

machine guns to the conspirators. However, in the testimony
before the Committee the CIA seems to have obfuscated the
matter so that its role and responsibility for the assassination
remain up in the air.

The Select Committee report puts it this way:

"It quickly became apparent to both White House and CIA
officials that a military coup was the only way to prevent
Allende's accession to power. To achieve that end, the CIA
established contact with several groups of military plotters and
eventually passed three weapons and tear gas to one group. The
weapons were subsequently returned, apparently unused. The
CIA knew that the plans of all groups of plotters began with the
abduction of the constitutionalist Chief of Staff of the Chilean
Army, General René Schneider. The Committee has received
conflicting testimony about the extent of CIA/White House
communication and of White House officials' awareness of
specific coup plans, *but there is no doubt that the U.S.
government sought a military coup in Chile* (author's italics)."

"Allende was visibly shaken," Martner says. "He made several
phone calls and talked to the outgoing President Frei, who was
still at the helm of state, urging him to order an immediate
investigation. He then returned to our group and asked that we
speed up a bit so that he could hurry to the hospital to be with
Schneider. We tried to dissuade Allende from taking this trip
because of the obvious dangers. But he insisted on going and on
taking personal charge in mounting a counteroffensive to blunt
the Rightist accusations we were sure would come." Martner
added parenthetically, "In the six weeks before Congress confirmed Allende as President, Chile experienced a steady rise in
sabotage and terrorism with threats made to many individuals
directly associated with Allende or the Popular Unity Party. We
were increasingly menaced with the possibility of 'liquidation.' I
myself received dozens of warnings that I was on the hit list of
those to be murdered.

"Notwithstanding our entreaties for caution, Allende was
determined to be at Schneider's side so the public would
understand that neither he nor the parties of the Left had had
anything to do with the assassination attempt. As usual Allende

was very decisive once he made up his mind. This was typical of him. Although he was careful to consult on policy matters with his cabinet as well as the leaders of the parties that made up the Popular Unity coalition, he would not equivocate in carrying out a decision, whether that of a group or one depending on his own judgment. He abstained from negotiating with his political confréres on matters of detail, but he certainly took an active part in giving his views on basic substantive questions. In the Schneider matter, uppermost in his mind was the shrill Rightist press campaign charging that the Left would try to insure its electoral victory by 'decapitating' the leaders of the armed forces." The newspapers and television had tried to propagandize the public into believing that Allende was out to get to the presidency at all costs, including the murder of top officials, but the campaign was a flop. The Schneider assassination boomeranged, and most Chileans tended to link the atrocity with the Rightists.

"Allende lost no time in persuading the nation that 'the sinister reactionaries' were behind Schneider's murder. He also hammered away at the armed forces, telling them that the plot was not only against Schneider but was aimed as well against others of the high command who were fulfilling their patriotic duty to uphold the constitution. The public was so outraged at the assassination that many of the wavering Christian Democrats went against their leader, Frei, an implacable personal foe of Allende, and decided to go along with the Popular Unity coalition. And so two days later the Chilean Congress voted 133 to 35 in favor of Allende over Alessandri.

"Allende's inaugural, November 4th, represented not only a personal victory—this was his fourth election try for the presidency—but also a victory for Chile's labor and the poverty-stricken citizenry, who had long craved for a fundamental change in the nation's order of priorities, in other words, a New Deal."

Allende supporters poured into the streets to celebrate the event. The festivities continued into the early hours of the morning. As L.R., an attorney and former official of the agrarian reform program, describes the celebration: "There was a feeling that for the first time in Chilean history it was the people and not the politicians, or the very rich, who were going to have a say regarding the destiny of the country. In the midst of this revelry I was especially struck by the poignant look in the eyes of some of the older trade union and peasant leaders, some already in their seventies, who couldn't quite believe that a program embodying so many of their long-sought objectives had come into being within their lifetimes. These were people who took part in the nitrate and copper strikes all the way back to the twenties, who for years thereafter continued to agitate for little victories: a bit more pay, better health protection on the job, and old age pensions. They were always extending the vision to their followers—one day, sometime in the future, there would be a kind of millennium for working people. And now it was here, beyond their wildest expectations."

At that very moment of triumph the war against Allende directed from Washington got under way in earnest. The signals of disapproval and enmity from the United States now became unmistakable. For instance, Allende received congratulatory cables from every head of state except Richard Nixon, the President of the United States. This snub broke long-standing traditions in international protocol. Was it just heat lightning growing out of a personal pique or an augury of a calamity to come? Allende wasn't sure, but at that moment he felt he had a good chance to ride out the storm. (Nixon did send Charles Meyer, Assistant Secretary for Inter-American Affairs, to represent the United States at the inauguration.)

Scarcely installed in La Moneda palace, the Allende regime began making good on its previously publicized program: to enable the impoverished sections of the Chilean nation to begin eating better, to provide them with greater employment opportunities and to solidify the Chilean economy. "Almost at once the government began expanding Chile's productive capacity in industry and in the agricultural area," Martner says. "It was to be done according to a carefully projected program in which only the very large agricultural estates would be expropriated. The same principle was to be applied to Chile's monopoly industrial enterprises—ninety-one in all—and to the foreign multinationals which controlled most of Chile's resources—copper, nitrates, steel, and telecommunications.

"Within days Allende, trying to implement the overall economic program, ran into opposition from Chile's Congress and the judiciary. In Congress the Popular Unity Party had less than 40 percent of the seats and only about 26 percent in the Senate. As for the judiciary, it was hidebound conservative: Rightists could look to the judges to halt rather than to advance whatever social reforms were proposed. Despite these obstacles, nationwide support for Allende soared during the first year of his administration." As Martner explained, "The new government began to generate near-miraculous results in the improvement of people's living standards. Inflation went down by 22 percent, and unemployment was reduced from 8.3 percent to 3.8 percent. Industrial production increased by 14 percent. There were also benefits for medium-sized manufacturers and producers of consumer goods through liberal credits from government banks. Because many more people now had jobs and because their salaries rose to catch up with the cost of living, people were spending freely. They were confident of their job security and wanted to live it up in the present. Minimum wages rose significantly. The Allende government went on to improve housing conditions and extend public utility services in the shantytowns by investing capital reserves it had inherited from the previous regime on construction and public works.

"Because of greater employment and better wages, workers' demands for consumer goods grew quickly. Some manufacturers expanded their production capacity to meet these demands. However, many of the larger industrialists, eager to cash in on this new development at a much higher rate of profit, actually cut back on production and concentrated instead on encouraging black marketeering and hoarding so they could boost prices sky high."

In the countryside the agrarian reform program was also making headway. As L.R., the legal counselor, points out, agricultural productivity in 1971 began to rise rather than decline as the critics had insisted it would. "As a matter of fact," he added, "it almost would have been impossible to reduce productivity to a lower level than had existed before the Allende regime came to power. The new regime inherited an agricultural economy that was stagnant, muddling along without purpose or program. We've always had to import such basic dairy products as milk and butter; the same holds true for wheat and meat. Through the ages the problems of Chilean agriculture were very similar to those existing in other Latin American countries. More than 60 percent of the land was in the hands of the oligarchy, a handful of families. Their properties extended into many thousands of acres and usually operated on a very marginal basis. Even though 30 percent of the country's population—farm workers, Mapuche Indian peasants—was involved with agriculture, these people had little to say on how the land should be tilled or what products should be cultivated. Almost traditionally the oligarchs do not live on their estates; they go off to revel in the nightclubs of Paris, Madrid, or Rome, and more recently in New York; they are, indeed, absentee landlords. The administration of the estates is handed over to managers who are not especially interested in extending the productivity of these lands.

"Whenever consumer demands rose in the cities for certain farm products, the tendency was simply to raise the price of these products, not to enlarge the output by intensifying cultivation. This underplowing of the land continued to yield a favorable profit for the owners and their managers, but it scarcely benefited the livelihood of the farm workers. In effect, therefore, 30 percent of Chileans—the farm population—were excluded from the country's market economy; they had not the means to purchase the products manufactured by the nation's industries in the cities.

"It was only with the expropriation of some of the major estates and their conversion to farm collectives that production output was increased. The farm workers were now in effect the owners of the land and had every incentive to enlarge agricultural output since their income would be directly related to it."

Simultaneously the Allende regime hurried to renegotiate with Anaconda, Kennecott, and ITT for the expropriation of their holdings. "The move to nationalize foreign investment in Chile was by no means an original Allende idea," Martner points out.

"The hope to liberate the nation from the foreign economic domination is something that was shared by both the Left and the Center for many years. It was a matter of national pride. Chileans from different walks of life knew that most of the profits derived from the country's basic resources, particularly copper, were pumped out of the country to the companies' home offices in the United States with barely a pittance left over for the Chilean economy. When touching on this matter in his address before the United Nations, Allende said that in little more than forty years Anaconda's and Kennecott's exploitation of Chile's copper mines yielded a profit of four billion dollars; their initial investment was only thirty million dollars.

Again, Martner, the former Planning Minister, points up the specifics: "Anaconda's returns in Chile between 1955 and 1970 averaged 21.5 percent on its book value. In other countries Anaconda's profits were only 3.6 percent per annum. In the case of Kennecott, the profit margin over the same period was even more dramatic. It zoomed to 106 percent in 1967, 113 percent in 1968, and over 205 percent in 1969. Kennecott's average profits in other countries in those years amounted to less than 10 percent per annum.

"Even the governments that preceded the Allende regime clamored for a greater share in these earnings. They felt that if at least the productivity of these mines could be expanded there would be greater revenues with larger increments trickling down to Chile's treasury. But Anaconda and Kennecott had little incentive for the reinvestment of some of their gains to enlarge the scope of their operations. When they finally did agree to modernize their technology so as to extract greater copper yields, they had the Chilean government assume the entire responsibility of getting international loans to pay for the cost of this undertaking. This move meant that Chile was stuck with an external debt of $727 million in the copper area alone.

"The Allende government's position was that Anaconda and Kennecott should be compensated, but at the rate of 12 percent per annum from the year 1955. The profits in excess of 12 percent should be deducted from the compensation agreement. The government's expropriation proposal received widespread support. In Congress no one dared challenge it."

Both the Senate and the lower house unanimously approved the constitutional amendment permitting the nationalization of the copper industry. As *The New York Times* editorialized in July 1971: "Every one of the 158 senators and deputies present—from revolutionary Socialists and Communists on the left, to the Nationalists on the right—had voted for the amendment."

Washington's reaction was to intensify its covert activities to undo the Popular Unity regime. In quick succession the United States lashed out to strangle Chile's economy, to create panic among the people and to disrupt normal life. First, Nixon's order that Chile's economy "should be squeezed until it screams" was applied fully.

In October, executives of six American corporations with holdings in Chile met with Secretary of State William Rogers for "an open discussion" of their predicament. Rogers opened the meeting by stating that "the Nixon administration was a 'business administration' in favor of business and its mission was to protect business," and voiced concern that Chile's actions would have a domino effect throughout Latin America in the absence of strong U.S. retaliatory action. He also raised the issue of an embargo on spare parts and materials being shipped to Chile.

As the Senate Select Committee put it, "The bare figures tell the story of how the United States proceeded to choke off the financial-economic viability of Chile. Export-Import Bank credits, which had totaled $234 million in 1967 dropped to zero in 1971. Loans from the multilateral Inter-American Development Bank (IDB), in which the United States held what amounted to a veto, had totaled $46 million in 1970; they fell to $2 million in 1972. . . . The availability of short-term United States commercial credits dropped from around $300 million during the Frei years to around $30 million in 1972." At the same time, because of its predominant position in international financial institutions, the United States prevailed in its efforts to dry up the flow of credit to Chile from other countries. Further, it exerted its pressure on foreign credit nations not to renegotiate Chile's foreign debts.

Despite the threatening roadblocks that were thrown in the way of the new government and the never-ending augury of doom for the Popular Unity program, the Allende regime continued to broaden its base of support. Certainly during the first year it became ever more evident that the economy was bouncing back and the New Deal was working. Even those in the lower-middle class, generally found in the ranks of the Christian Democratic Party, were ready to draw closer to the Popular Unity people.

The litmus tests of success were the mayoralty elections throughout Chile, only five months after Allende's inauguration. The country was stunned by the results. In March 1971, more than 50 percent of the electorate voted for pro-Allende candidates; the Popular Unity vote across the country rose by 14 percent over what it had been in the presidential election of September 1970.

These electoral gains were a green light for the Allende forces to move with their programs full steam ahead. For Washington and the Chilean Right, as Martner put it, these developments spelled disaster: "Allende's opponents were greatly concerned that if the Popular Unity coalition were to grow at a pace reflected by the elections, it would ultimately inveigle the Christian Democrats to join them into a kind of united front. This would make it possible for the Leftist-liberals to capture the majority in the Congress, enabling them to change the constitution in such a way as to install a socialist economy in Chile democratically. And this Washington would not tolerate."

Thus Allende's halcyon days resulting from the March elections were to be numbered. Within a year the U.S. financial and economic blockade began to take its toll. Because of Chile's traditional dependence on American-made transport as well as on technology used in its copper mining, Washington's order to halt the delivery of spare parts dealt the country a paralyzing blow.

By 1972, the Senate Select Committee reported, ". . . almost one third of the diesel trucks at Chuquicamata Copper Mine, 30 percent of the privately owned city buses, 21 percent of all taxis, and 33 percent of state-owned buses in Chile could not operate because of the lack of spare parts or tires. In overall terms, the value of United States machinery and transport equipment exported to Chile by U.S. firms declined from $152.6 million in 1970 to $110 million in 1971." These developments were entirely in keeping with the prediction made by former American Ambassador Edward Korry who vowed that "not a nut or bolt would be allowed to reach Chile under Allende."

Simultaneously with this economic squeeze the CIA stepped up and widened its psychological warfare against Allende. The plan now was to keep the nation in a state of continuous agitation, to sow dismay and defeatism. Rumors, half-truths, and outright falsehoods were deliberately planted in the press, on television, in the workplace, in cafes, and wherever people got together, Martner says. "The anti-Allende war took on an inflammatory character," he adds. "Sabotage became widespread. Huge textile mills suddenly went up in flames. Industrial plants were bombed. In the copper mines complex machinery would suddenly break down.

"But most important was the attempt to create a scarcity of foodstuffs and essential consumer goods. There are eyewitness accounts of outright destruction of these products; baby foods, nipples for baby bottles, medical supplies dumped into rivers. Right-wing dairy and vegetable producers cut back on shipments of milk, fruit, and greens to city markets. And many of the truck farmers who were cooperating with the government were often intimidated by hoodlum assaults.

"When deliveries did reach supermarkets or neighborhood stores, saboteurs would rush to the phones and alert rich friends and family groups to buy up supplies as quickly as possible, warning them that these items would disappear from the markets for good." As Martner describes it, "It didn't matter whether it was toothpaste, toilet paper, matches, or condensed milk. These people would descend on these stores like ants. They'd empty the shelves immediately, buying up hundreds of cans of milk at a time. The same thing happened with coffee, milk, cosmetics, or clothes.

"Many merchants would deliberately stash away some of the merchandise for black-market operations. The dwindling supply of goods led to widespread grumbling and disquiet. And as the queues became longer and longer many of the discontented housewives were led to feel that it was all because of Allende and the Popular Unity government.

"To denigrate Allende and the other government leaders, the propaganda campaign drew upon a vicious satiric arsenal. This included cartoons and jokes which characterized Allende and his associates as filthy, vulgar, violent opportunists. The overall attempt of the CIA and the Rightists was to create an image of Allende as a fuzzy-headed, incompetent administrator who was plunging the country into chaos."

This avalanche of ridicule and hatred was being launched against Allende and his government with warlike strategy through the media, 80 percent of which was controlled by the Right. The counterattack of the Allende people via the media it controlled was "pathetic," according to Martner. The government had only two television channels and was supported by only two large newspapers, *El Clarín* and *La Nación*. The smaller papers which were published under the sponsorship of the various parties that made up the Popular Unity coalition were poorly produced, usually by non-professionals. In many instances local or national leaders of the Popular Unity Party wrote the lead pieces and often they sounded more like propaganda than political analysis. Moreover, they reflected the ideological viewpoint of the specific party in the coalition rather than its overall policy. In contrast, the Rightists' newspapers were skillfully edited, their stories written with deceptive, seeming objectivity.

Martner says that the anti-government media campaign preoccupied Allende at that time. On many occasions, he says, Allende got on the phone with various editors stressing the need for them to focus on given national issues and thus coordinate a strategy to repel the Rightist attacks.

Martner recalls "the extraordinary stamina and alacrity that Allende possessed in those critical days." As the CIA blueprint for his government's destruction came into sharper focus, the President seemed to be everywhere organizing countermoves. "For a man nearing his mid-sixties, in an on-and-off bout with a chronic heart condition, Allende appeared bouncy and spry, as though ready to take on all challengers. He met with his cabinet or expert committees on a daily basis, sometimes several times a day. At the same time, he was also in touch with the leaders of the coalition parties.

"On a number of occasions Allende carried on government business outside the nation's capital. In keeping with his pre-election pledge that he would stay close to the citizenry, Allende traveled to different parts of the country where he conferred with county officials, representatives of trade unions and peasant organizations concerning their regional problems. He made himself available to individuals of whatever party, listened to their complaints or suggestions and dealt with them in a serious but informal fashion. Throughout the day, of course, he'd be in touch with his office in Santiago. And if he found it necessary to prolong his talks with regional officials, he'd summon some of his ministers to fly down from Santiago and help carry on the business of the national government.

"His cabinet meetings in Santiago were usually held at his office at La Moneda palace. It was a rather small room, with a high ceiling in the colonial style of architecture used throughout La Moneda. We usually sat around a big mahogany table on chairs that were hard-backed and not particularly comfortable. There was only one wall decoration, the Chilean Independence Charter from Spain.* There were no pictures. Red curtains covered a large window that opened out to a patio. In this somewhat severe atmosphere Allende would sit at the head of the table with several telephones beside him. He began the meetings with a short résumé of the day's most important developments and then proceeded to more specific points on the agenda. He asked various ministers to give their reports, to which he listened very attentively and took notes. (I might add that the discussions were of a high intellectual quality. I was educated at universities in Chile and in the United States, and I've taken part in many world conferences. But rarely have I witnessed anything like the

---

*On September 11, 1973, the day of the coup, Allende removed this historic document (issued in 1811 and inscribed on parchment) and gave it to Miriam Contreras, his secretary, with the hope that she would leave with the other women before the battle got underway, and save the historic scroll from destruction. But his secretary remained in the palace throughout the bombing. She survived, and on her way out of the palace she turned to one of the officers, showed him the charter, and said, "Please safeguard it." The lieutenant examined it for a moment, laughed and said it was all a lot of nonsense and ripped the scroll to shreds. Thus, Chile's great historic document, which was respected by all previous governments for 163 years, disappeared forever.

consistent intellectual level at which the Chile cabinet meetings were conducted.)

"Although a number of the ministers were Allende's close friends, the meetings were conducted on a formal basis, each addressing the other as 'Comrade Minister' or 'Comrade President.' From time to time the discussions were punctuated by flashes of humor, but often they took on a somber character. We had to cope with too many mounting adversities.

"It was quite astounding," Martner recalls, "how well Allende was able to remember details of whatever subject was under discussion, and then to refer to it in future conferences. There were times, of course, when Allende strongly expressed a differing view from those of the majority, whether at cabinet meetings or in discussions with leaders of the various parties of the coalition, but he always remained calm and careful not to become acrimonious in a personal way. There was only one occasion that I recall Allende losing his composure. This was shortly after his taking office. While at a cabinet meeting he got word that a Santiago policeman shot and killed a peasant, something that was quite frequent in previous administrations.

"Allende flew into a rage, and got on the phone with the Director General of the *carabineros*. He shouted, 'One of your men has just slain a poor laborer. Don't you know,' he demanded, 'that there has been a change in the government? Don't your men know that the time is over when you shoot down poor people and peasants at will?' He ordered an investigation be conducted immediately, with the accused officer brought to trial.

"Despite a life-long preoccupation with the poverty of peasants and the cities' downtrodden, he enjoyed humor and savored good company, good food, and good wine. Allende had a passion for life. Basically of an optimistic nature, he walked with a vigorous stride, remindful of a man at least twenty years his junior.

"Somewhat stoutish, with a full face interrupted by a well-groomed mustache, he'd be at his desk until two in the afternoon. Usually at that hour, he'd have lunch either with members of his cabinet or political leaders and then take a half-hour nap. After this respite he would resume his work well into the evening and then take supper, usually with government officials or foreign diplomats."

Paradoxically, the successes of the first year of the Popular Unity government spawned disunity within the Popular Unity coalition itself. Martner recalls that "the wrangling centered on two considerations: whether the Christian Democrats, basically middle class, should be drawn into the government as allies; and the speed with which Chile's economy should go socialist. The Communist Party, the centrist Radical Party, as well as Allende, who was a member of the Socialist Party, argued that the presence of the Christian Democrats within the coalition was imperative in order to overcome the growing resistance of the Right. Even if certain program compromises were to be made, they felt, it was still worthwhile if only to thwart the threatened coup from reactionary forces.

"Allende encountered the greatest opposition to this approach from an important sector in his own Socialist Party, the group led by Carlos Altamirano, the party's Secretary-General. Altamirano contended that those in the Christian Democratic Party who wanted to come along in support of the new regime should do so, but not in a way that might dilute and slow down the basic program. On the contrary, confident that the March 1971 vote had underscored the readiness of labor and the impoverished sectors of the nation to move at a faster pace toward nationalization of industry and agriculture, the Altamirano forces put forward the slogan, *Avansar Sin Transar* [Let's Advance Without Yielding]. The Altamirano group, in effect, rejected the need to develop any dialogue with the Christian Democrats. The Communists and Allende, for their part, argued that these talks should continue. Notwithstanding the objections of the Altamirano people, Allende on his own initiative tried to resume talks with certain representatives of the Christian Democrats on several occasions, but these never took hold and eventually fell apart."

Martner continued, "The Altamirano position found a responsive echo especially among the younger members of the Socialist Party. Altamirano also appeared to bolster the approach of MIR

(Movimiento Izquierdista Revolucionario). MIR was not a participant in the Popular Unity coalition and had a limited membership. But it enjoyed a popularity among the youth as it pressed for more militant actions and for a speedier expropriation program than proposed by the Allende government. This agitation occasionally prompted employees and peasants to seize small businesses and farms in the name of nationalization. Often these 'nationalized' enterprises employed fewer than a dozen people. By no means did they fall into the category of the large-scale monopoly industries and agricultural estates that were targeted for expropriation within the Popular Unity economic reform program.

"These unauthorized takeovers were relatively few, and in many cases the government made quick restitution to the owners whose property had been confiscated, but they were welcome grist for the anti-Allende propaganda mills. Scarcely a day passed that these developments were not taken advantage of to stir anger and fear among the small-time entrepreneurs such as grocery and butcher shop owners, neighborhood pharmacists, and small truck farm operators. Many of these people may have wavered in their support for Allende at the outset or assumed a neutral, wait-and-see attitude regarding the initially announced program.

"But as the din of press, radio, and TV barrage regarding the unauthorized seizures intensified, a considerable number of the apolitical waverers felt that they had been 'taken'—been deceived—and they then began turning against Allende. Some eventually drifted toward the most reactionary groups, those determined to bring down the Popular Unity government.

"With scarcities of food and consumer goods ever more acute, with black marketeers cornering what there was, and with an inflation soaring again—more than wiping out the initial salary increases—the situation became desperate when truck owners went on strike. The long stretches of Chilean territory, which run down the Pacific coast of South America for some 2,500 miles, depend on motor transport rather than on railroads or ships. Angered by the breakdown of their equipment, unable to secure the needed spare parts because of the Washington blockade (and also many right-wing prejudices anyway), the truck owners went into collusion with the CIA to deliver a body blow to Chile's economy. The extra-special inducement for the truck owners not to move their vehicles was, simply, money. Just how much money was made available has never been disclosed, but in some cases the cash flow must have been substantial since even some trucking company employees were known to have received as much as $50 for every day they did not show up to work."

The Senate Select Committee, in referring to these truckers, observes: "It is clear that anti-government strikers were actively supported by several of the private sector [political] groups which received CIA funds." Since it wanted to maintain a very low profile, the CIA was vexed to learn that "contrary to the Agency's [CIA's] ground rules," some of its disbursements went directly to the strikers rather than by an indirect route. The committee added, "The CIA rebuked the group but nevertheless *passed it additional money next month* [author's italics]."

"The truckers' strike was launched in October 1972 by the Confederation of Truck Owners," Martner states. Interestingly enough, press reports abroad, and especially in the United States, usually glossed over the fact that this strike was principally a truck-owners stoppage rather than that of employees, thus giving the impression that a section of labor had defected and no longer supported the Allende government. The truckers were soon joined by the Confederation of Retail Storekeepers and various professional organizations.

"The strike went on for twenty-six days. During this critical period Allende suffered a heart attack, which was kept secret lest word of his illness spark a move to have him retire from the presidency. For ten days Allende remained bedded down in his private office in the presidential palace under the care of his cardiologist, Dr. Soto. Despite severe chest pains and a high fever Allende insisted on being involved in the day-to-day proceedings concerning the strike. Since he was unavailable for interviews, the press was told that the President was too busy drafting a solution to the strike. Soon after the strike came to an end, Allende snapped back to normal. It was a near-miraculous recovery. Only two months later he was in New York making his denunciatory speech of the United States before the United Nations.

"The truck owners' strike not only disrupted the nation's economy for many months, but it also polarized the Chilean society as never before. Doctors, lawyers, teachers, and engineers in their respective professional organizations were split down the middle, each faction regarding the other as an enemy. Even some doctors joined the strikes to sabotage the government by refusing to provide essential services in clinics and hospitals. Other physicians worked round the clock, sometimes twenty hours at a stretch, to insure the continuity of emergency care. Even family dinners became scenes of controversy. Political discussions, so typical of family gatherings, usually took place with traditional Chilean civility, regardless of the different points of view expressed. The exchanges might have been heated but seldom caused enmity. Now these family get-togethers turned into bitter confrontations, with brothers, sisters, and parents angrily clashing with each other.

"Only labor and most of the agricultural workers remained steadfast in their support of the Allende government, and if anything they were moving to the left of the President, demanding that the opposition be controlled by coercive methods. But Allende would not hear of it. Most observers remained impressed with the fact that Allende, though on a collision course with the Chilean establishment as he pushed for a socialist society, was determined that Chile's social and economic transformation should come about without violence. Moreover, despite the fact that the opposition was escalating its campaigns and goading its followers to take part in hooligan provocations, the Allende government refused to tighten police constraints to maintain order. It was ironic that the Rightist terrorist campaign was coupled with dire warnings that the Allende regime would doom Chile's democratic traditions and bring about suppression and media censorship. The opposite was true."

According to the National Intelligence Estimates (NIEs), an American intelligence analytic unit which provides data for government policymakers, "Allende had taken great care to observe constitutional forms and was enjoying considerable popularity in Chile." In June 1972, about a year and a half after Allende became President, NIE said that "the prospects for the continuation of democracy in Chile appear to be better than at any time since Allende's inauguration . . . that the traditional political system in Chile continued to demonstrate remarkable resiliency. Legislative, student, and trade union elections continued to take place in normal fashion with pro-government forces accepting the results when they were adverse." All this, the NIE noted, despite the fact that the opposition news media "persisted in denouncing the government."

That was what Martner was observing at first hand. "While Allende continued to make sure that his administration adhered strictly to the constitution, his opponents used the same historic document to do the unconstitutional and rip apart the governmental structure. The Rightists had the best of both worlds. On one hand they charged that the government was in violation of the constitution because of its economic reforms. On the other, they called upon the armed forces to bring down the administration so that the constitution could be preserved.* The CIA-Rightist operations moved from mere propaganda to open insurrectionary preparations.** Patria y Libertad, as well as the National Party of the same Fascist hue, lured upper-class youths and middle-class professionals to their side, warning them that they could not look to a future as long as the Allende regime prevailed.

"Reactionaries were calling on Allende foes to join in an 'aggressive adventure.' The offer of free uniforms, helmets, and clubs and participation in motorcycle formations festooned with anti-Allende flags proved tempting to many. These youth brigades were taught how to provoke street fights in working-class

---

* In what amounted to an open call for mutiny by the armed forces, *El Mercurio* declared: "Army doctrine makes mandatory an unanswering loyalty to the Constitution and country, rather than to men, regimes or government. . . . It is necessary that the spirit of loyalty to the Constitution should not be used in order that they [the military] should remain still and unmoving while all other principles of the Constitution . . . are being violated."

** A seditious appeal signed by retired generals and admirals, calling on the population to disobey the government, was circulated within the military establishment.

neighborhoods and how to disrupt schools by insulting and attacking teachers."

At the same time, the plotting within the armed forces took on greater momentum. While the administration in Washington was concentrating on breaking up the country's economy by shutting off normal credit channels, the Pentagon maintained close, collaborative relations with the Chilean armed forces. Though Allende is credited with having been highly successful in thwarting earlier attempts at a military coup because of his close association with the armed forces high command, such as General Prats, the fact remains that much of the officers' corps was under the influence of anti-democratic elements. Many officers and enlisted men had been programmed to develop a disrespect for the Allende government and to regard Allende not as a Chilean patriot but as someone duped by a foreign philosophy: Marxism.

This is the view of Sergio Insunza, former Minister of Justice. "This ideological infiltration of the armed forces actually began long before Allende came to power. It was especially apparent among the generals, admirals, colonels, and many junior officers who had been trained in the United States or in American installations in Panama. Their technical training, whether with weaponry, aircraft, or tanks, was coupled with political brainwashing." Insunza pointed out that traditionally Chile's career officers and enlisted men were made to feel that they constituted "the first line of defense against potential intruders into the somewhat vulnerable territory of Chile, since it is bounded by Peru on the north, Bolivia on the northeast, and Argentina in the east."

Following the Second World War, the former Minister of Justice said, the emphasis began to change. "Under U.S. ministration," he said, "some of Chile's high-ranking officers began to perceive patriotism and defense of the country in terms of 'ideological frontiers' rather than 'territorial frontiers.' The frame of reference henceforth was 'the cold war,' and, therefore, the need to repel the philosophical enemy—Marxism—whether from abroad or within Chile itself. Much of the training was focused on repressive means to annihilate the domestic enemy.

'Counterinsurgency' rose high in importance in the training program of the military.* It was but natural," Insunza added, "that next to be tinkered with would be Chile's constitutional form of government. In the eyes of these generals and admirals the permissiveness inherent in a democratic regime made fertile ground for the growth of communism."

Insunza believes that while in training in the United States or Panama, this political outlook took root with the Chileans. "There were a number of pleasant, subliminal props that helped shape conservative thinking," he says. "There was the camaraderie between Chilean officers and their North American counterparts; special fringe benefits, such as side trips, parties, etc., the tabs for which were picked up by the Pentagon and, incidentally, the American taxpayer. In this anti-Red indoctrination process, the Chilean military were persuaded to suspect certain groups of fellow Chileans. They developed an intolerance for the shantytown dwellers and the constantly protesting Mapuche Indians and peasants—all of whom were tarred with the same Communist brush. Needless to say, supporters of the Popular Unity program fell into the same categories. This helps explain, to some degree, the enmity, the hatred of some of the military for the Allende people."

Insunza says that many of the Chilean officers have always suffered from a kind of inferiority complex. For the most part, they come from the middle class in the provinces. Generally they were looked down upon by the intellectuals or the Chilean upper-class social set. As a consequence, the military usually kept to themselves and were quite content to develop their own conceit and to wallow in their super-patriotism, their much-acclaimed readiness to shed their blood in the defense of their country. While such self-serving accolades might have raised a doubtful eyebrow among their betters—wealthy industrialists,

---

* According to the columnist Jack Anderson, the U.S. Army has been training Latin American soldiers for many years in a school tucked away in the jungles of the Panama Canal zone. As late as 1975, until Congress finally put a stop to it, about five hundred Chilean military people were given such training with the "emphasis . . . on anti-guerrilla warfare." The U.S. government, he charged, "was teaching the Junta's foot soldiers how to repel the 'dissidents' who oppose them."

doctors, or lawyers—their association with American officers gave them a special distinction and certainly extra prestige among their peers, since they had done postgraduate work in military schools of one of the most powerful nations in the world.

Insunza feels that this programming brutalized many of Chile's officers and enlisted men. "The brutality," he insists, "was demonstrated by the savage way they descended on Allende adherents when the coup got under way.

"The Rightists' ideological penetration of the army, together with the stepped-up sabotage and deterioration of the economy, exacerbated by the soaring inflation, made it apparent that the collapse of the regime was imminent," Insunza recalled. "So when the congressional elections were held on March 4, 1973, many people expected the Rightists to sweep the field. All they needed was to gain control of two-thirds of the seats in the lower house. Then they could impeach Allende and bring down the government without resorting to military means. What took place astonished friend and foe alike: The pro-Allende candidates won 43.4 percent of the representation in the lower house, 7 percent more than Allende's vote in the September 1970 elections. The Right was frustrated. Impeachment was out of the question. The strategy now was to turn to the use of brute force via cannon and machine gun."

Allende himself was overjoyed and overwhelmed. Popular Unity supporters waxed triumphant. Despite the sea of chaos that was engulfing the country, labor and the disfranchised would not be shaken from their conviction that the Allende regime was the only thing they could look to for a better life. Even the NIE, the CIA's collaborative unit, concluded ". . . the bulk of low-income Chileans believed that he [Allende] had improved their conditions and represented their interest . . ."

"In the ensuing six months before the coup," Martner says, "the Right and the CIA accelerated their efforts to overthrow the government. Not only were street fights more frequent, not only had the press campaigns become more shrill, but terrorism involving some of Allende's closest associates became the order of the day." A number of Martner's acquaintances were killed or wounded by Fascist gunmen. In his own case, a bomb was planted in his house. "The explosion ripped off the living room of the house and part of the staircase only moments after my son walked outside. Allende's naval aide-de-camp, Commander Arturo Araya, was murdered. The feelings of elation following the March vote were short-lived. Soon afterward the truck owners went on strike again, and this time stayed out until the coup."

What became very clear was that the nation's chief executive was the head of a government with diminishing power to govern. The major elements of state power were stacked against him, whether Congress, the judiciary, or the armed forces.

"The disorder in the city streets had a definite insurrectionary ring," Martner says. "Toughs belonging to Patria y Libertad rampaged through the cities assaulting pro-government activists, breaking into stores considered to be cooperating with government price control regulations, or dynamiting power plants. One evening while Allende was making a nationwide television address, a series of explosions rocked Santiago. Electrical power was knocked out, damaging the TV transmitters, disrupting Allende's speech and throwing much of the city into darkness. Even before the March elections the opposition made every effort to get the country to accept the notion that it was out of control and that the Popular Unity government no longer had legitimacy." On August 25, 1973, one conservative congressman declared in a speech before the (lower) House, that "the moment has arrived for the Congress to declare that the government has definitely lost its authority and the legitimacy of its mandate . . . nobody is obligated, either by law or morality, to continue obeying an illegitimate authority."

To some degree Allende's hopes were strengthened when a coup attempt made on La Moneda by a Colonel Roberto Souper on June 29th failed. Although not directly connected with the coup that toppled the Allende government, the Souper incident was reflective of the growing atmosphere of conspiracy fomented by the Rightists in the armed forces. Souper was involved with a military group of plotters, largely inspired by *Patria y Libertad*. Since there was no immediate solid proof of Souper's role, he was relieved of his post until an investigation could be completed. Anticipating the worst, that his career would come to an end,

Souper took it upon himself to lead several hundred men and a few tanks from an armored regiment in an attempt to seize La Moneda, the presidential palace. This rebellious exercise, which became known as the Tancazo Incident, was quickly put down by General Carlos Prats. The generals and admirals who had been working on the real thing, the putsch that eventually was to overthrow the Allende regime, didn't think much of the Colonel Souper adventure. But this incident obviously served as a kind of dress rehearsal. The speedy crushing of the revolt buoyed Allende's spirits and those of others. While holding the fort against his enemies, Allende continued to wrestle with the differences within his own Popular Unity coalition. There was growing demand that the government assert its authority over the military establishment. The need for a firmer stance, a Chilean observer reported, was made evident by the growing disaffection within the armed forces. Many of the officers became contemptuous not only of Allende but also of their commanders, such as General Prats. Officers' wives threw a picket line around the residence of the General and began shouting insults. It was probably the only time in Chile's history that the chief of the armed forces had been subjected to such indignity.

And so the next day, Prats resigned, leaving a gaping power vacuum in Allende's embattled administration. Prats recommended Pinochet be named to succeed him. A few weeks later Pinochet presided over the liquidation of Allende and his government and soon thereafter, it is believed, he ordered the assassination in Buenos Aires of his mentor, General Prats, and his wife.

After Prats' resignation many of the right-wingers in the high command moved against anyone in the armed forces suspected of having pro-Allende sympathies. They were charged with conducting political agitation in violation of military regulations.

At the same time the armed forces launched a search operation for weapons allegedly secreted by members of labor unions and pro-Allende slum dwellers. These search operations were conducted with the authority of an Arms Control Act (Ley de Control de Armas), a gun control regulation. As originally proposed in the autumn of 1972 by a Christian Democrat congressman, this regulation seemed to be designed to reduce the incidence of terrorism and was to be applied to any transgressor of the law. Actually, a former Allende advisor explained, it was a maneuver aimed at trade unions and parties of the Left, which the Right attempted to portray as the enemies of Chile. It was designed to associate the Left with violence and terrorism.

But Allende vetoed the bill, saying that its enforcement should be in the hands of the *carabineros* (the constabulary), who at that time were strongly pro-government and accountable to the Minister of the Interior, who was a Socialist. Allende made it clear that he did not want to have the army involved, unless there were emergency circumstances.

But the vetoed document never reached Congress. A Congressional commission, charged with the task of reviewing the veto, found a technical error in the document, but did not advise Allende or Congress of this fact. And so the bill became law.

As it turned out this regulation was not applied to such Fascist groups as *Patria y Libertad* but instead was used to terrorize pro-Allende supporters. These search expeditions were conducted in a brutal fashion. Doors were broken open; soldiers and naval personnel rushed into factories and the homes of working people, rifling every drawer and every shelf. In many instances defiant workers and peasants were arrested on trumped-up charges. In the province of Magallanes a number of workers were killed when they refused to let the military into their homes. Many workers resisted these search attacks and demanded that Allende stop them. They went further; they asked that they be given arms to defend themselves. But counteraction of any kind was impossible. Allende could no longer look to the army with confidence.

Fernando Alegría, then cultural attache to the Chilean embassy in Washington, arrived in Santiago about a week prior to the coup on one of his periodic visits. He said, "It was an unbelievable contrast to the cheerful atmosphere following the March elections in Chile [when he had visited the country at that time]. There was every sign that a coup was imminent," he told me. Alegría, one of the most important of Chile's contemporary poets and essayists, currently a professor at Stanford University in Palo Alto, California, had been a close friend of both Letelier and Allende. On the Saturday before the coup he lunched with the

Letelier family and was distressed at Letelier's tension. Despite the darkening political clouds that hung over the government, on hearing of Alegría's presence in Santiago, Allende made a lunch appointment with him for September 11th, the day on which he was to die. Later that day, Alegría was also scheduled to visit with Neruda. Of course, as it turned out, these appointments, "the most significant in my life, with two people whom I held in such high esteem, were cancelled for good.

"What impressed me especially on my return then," Alegría said, "was the passivity of some people, a kind of acceptance of the cataclysm to come. The country seemed to be grinding down, coming to a halt. There was a static quality in various aspects of life, economic, political, and social. It is true that one million workers and peasants marched by to mark Allende's election victory in 1970, still bravely affirming their will to stop a coup. They were greeting Allende, who was on the reviewing stand, but many of the people were asking that they be given arms to defend the government. But it was all too late." Alegría says that Allende would not and could not comply with the demand because of his fear that it would lead to a massacre on a massive scale. Alegria thinks it likely that instead of 30,000 people killed during the Junta takeover, there probably would have been more like a half million casualties had Allende acceded to his supporters' demands for firearms. Rifles and pistols, Allende believed, would not be a match for cannon and jet fighters. In any event, Allende did not have the arms to distribute.

Notwithstanding the adversities, despite the increasingly louder sounds of doom, Allende still hoped to chart a course that would allow him and the government to survive. Allende was convinced that even though the armed forces were shot through with discontent and treachery, a substantial section would remain loyal. And these loyalties, he felt, with help from workers stationed at the factories, would subdue the insurgents. His intended call for a national plebiscite on September 11th, he was sure, would elicit wide support for the government's programs and thus frustrate the perpetrators of the putsch.

"Having decided on this course of action," Alegría says, "Allende discussed it with some of his closest advisors, including

Pinochet. Originally the coup was scheduled for September 14th, but when Pinochet reported Allende's plans, the plotters decided to move sooner to prevent Allende's call for a plebiscite."

Not only was Allende unaware of Pinochet's perfidy, but he was also in the dark about the covert plotting of the Junta's Washington collaborators. July is the month when periodic, joint United States-Chile naval maneuvers take place as part of the hemisphere exercises, known as *Operación Unitas*. This time the exercises were postponed to September. A United States naval flotilla was supposed to have made a rendezvous with units of the Chilean navy off the coast of Valparaiso. But there were no maneuvers. The Chilean naval squadron steamed out of port at dusk on September 10th and dropped anchor once it was out of sight of land, while the American gunboats stood by at Coquimbo in the north. Needless to say, Nixon did not flash word to Allende that the Chilean navy had failed to keep its appointment.

While still at sea, the naval commanders involved in the mutiny began torturing and killing personnel suspected of being pro-Allende. In the middle of the night the Chilean squadron returned to Valparaiso. Naval and marine detachments set up road blocks, seized control of the police and power installations, and took over the city intact. Hundreds of sailors and marines who refused to go along with the coup were overpowered and brutally murdered. From then on, all events led to La Moneda.

Some hindsight analysts, not necessarily critics, felt that Allende's fall from power might have been averted if he had acted vigorously to purge the army soon after General Schneider was assassinated. As President and the Commander-in-Chief of the military he had the constitutional right to replace officers whose trustworthiness he questioned. But the Schneider incident took place before Allende's term began, when information was still lacking as to the overall character of the army. "Who was to replace whom," was the quandary facing Allende at that time, and, moreover, Schneider's successor was General Prats, who gave Allende little reason to suspect him. Prats repeatedly pronounced publicly the army's pledge to keep out of politics and to uphold the legally elected government. Further, because of the near-absolute rigidity of the army [a hangover from years of

German training before World War II] in which subordinates never questioned orders of their commanders, Allende felt somewhat secure. After all, he *was* the commander. Some among those close to Allende feared that his intrusion in military affairs might trigger resentment within the officer corps.

The early days of the administration, they insisted, were not the time for Allende to tussle with the armed forces considering his many other problems. There was the harassment by the multinational companies, the CIA machinations, and the U.S. spare parts blockade as well as cracks within the structure of his own Popular Unity Party.

Allende's critics felt that his greatest mistake was his overwhelming dependence on General Prats' appraisal of the armed forces. A glaring example of that, they insisted, was Prats' recommendation of Pinochet as his successor. In their judgment, Pinochet's personality was markedly different from what one would expect of a leader. Throughout the period that Pinochet served as Prats' second-in-command he seldom came forward with stimulating ideas or initiatives. He simply took orders from Prats and carried them out as directed.

As alert and sophisticated as Allende was with regard to the complexities about him, and especially with those within the armed forces, he still remained convinced that much of the army could be depended upon in a crunch. Even on the morning of the putsch this conviction was reflected in the three radio addresses he made to the Chilean people before the bombing of La Moneda commenced. In his first two speeches Allende still held fast to the possibility that as in the Tancazo Incident, some two months before, most of the army would stand behind him. There was still a spirit of resistance. He told the Chilean people, workers especially, to get to their factories and await further instructions. He still had confidence that the high command would be heading the attack to crush the insurrection. Later that fateful morning Allende became convinced that army support was out of the question, that he was betrayed. Thus in his final address when he bade the nation farewell as he reiterated his decision to fight and die to uphold the legitimacy of his government, Allende pleaded with the workers not to become needless victims. "The people should be alert and vigilant," he declared. "They should not permit themselves to be provoked or to be massacred."

Even in this last statement, Fernando Alegría believes, "Allende displayed his fundamental humanitarian quality. He knew that since there was no hope for his supporters to get arms there was no point in getting themselves killed. In my opinion Allende will emerge in history not as a revolutionary fighter, although he died fighting as a revolutionary."

On September 11th, at midday, the air attack on Chile's seat of government, La Moneda, got under way. A few hours later, Allende was dead and the Chilean state was a shambles. "And the Chilean Right as well as its American co-conspirators," Alegría observes, "succeeded in stopping socialism from coming to Chile democratically."

The military dictatorship takes over. General Augusto Pinochet, seated at left, with other members of the Junta and bodyguards, at a te deum in the Santiago cathedral soon after the coup. (Wide World Photos)

There are no monuments today in Chile commemorating Allende's martyrdom. Chilean school history textbooks refer to Allende only as a Marxist head of state who flung Chile into chaos. But, Alegría says, "neither censorship nor the iron fist of the Pinochet dictatorship will succeed in snuffing out Allende's memory. Whether in the hushed tones in shantytown conversations or in the world arena, the Allende phenomenon continues to spark debate."

3

Dawson Island:
Chile's Concentration Camp
near the Antarctic

DAWSON ISLAND is a speck among the fragments of land at the far end of Chile's long geography. Just west of Tierra del Fuego, south of the Southern Cross, it is about a one-and-a-half-hour flight from the Antarctic. On the map, Dawson is an upside-down question mark badly put together. It is desolate and bleak, about fifty-five miles long and twelve at its maximum width. Fierce, icy winds from the polar regions gust mercilessly across the stony terrain. The spiny brush sits permanently hunched and stooped, huddling for protection. Wet gales, edged with brittle sleet and snow, batter the island for weeks at a time. In January and February, a mix of spring and summer checks in and out as though through a revolving door. Hardly does the sparse vegetation begin to blossom than the leaves turn and are ripped off by the stormy autumn. The sun makes a few hesitant stabs through the leaden sky and then is banished for the long, hostile winter.

Surrounded by the Strait of Magellan on the north and west, by Gabriel Canal on the south, and by Whiteside Canal and by a body of water aptly called Useless Bay *(Bahia Inútil)* on the east, Dawson Island is condemned to perpetual dampness. From early morning a fragile, milky haze blankets the island's melancholy mountain range and empty valley covered by the tundra of the Antarctic regions. As the haze lifts toward midday, patches of forest reveal giant oaks, poplars, and larches. But relief from semidarkness lasts only a short time. With monotonous regularity the fog rolls back in toward evening, becoming one with the low-hanging clouds, blotting out everything.

81

During the dreary autumn months, snow and rain take turns in buffeting the island. At night it takes on a short-lived surrealistic beauty as snow at times a foot deep covers the earth's muddy warts. But because of the salt air from the surrounding waters, the snow begins to melt by daybreak, converting everything underfoot to slush and deep, muddy gullies.

Except for the Chilean military, which has long considered it an ideal place for artillery practice because there are no permanent inhabitants and therefore no risk to civilians, Dawson Island might have continued to the end of time as one of those geographical deformities that deservedly remain unheralded and unsung.

But in September 1973, Dawson Island became a concentration camp, the Junta's shelter for some of Chile's best-known political figures and intellectuals. There was Clodomiro Almeyda. There was José Tohá, Allende's Minister of Defense who had been forced out of office by a no-confidence vote of the Rightist-controlled Congress. There was Tohá's successor, Orlando Letelier, who had left his post as Ambassador to the United States to join the Allende cabinet four months before the coup. There were also political leaders, such as Luis Corvalan, Secretary General of the Communist Party, and Anselmo Sule, President of the Radical Party, as well as distinguished intellectuals: Dr. Edgardo Enriquez, former Minister of Education; Dr. Enrique Kirberg, rector of the Technical University, Chile's second-largest; Fernando Flores, an internationally known cybernetics theorist; Dr. Arturo Jiron, Minister of Health; Sergio Vuscovic, former mayor of Valparaiso, and before then, professor of philosophy at the University of Chile. And there were the Puccios, father and son, who had vanished in the spurious truce negotiations with the Junta general shortly before Allende was murdered at La Moneda. Thirty-five people were in the first group dispatched to Dawson Island.

They arrived at Dawson at four in the morning after a fifteen-hour journey: a nine-hour flight from Santiago in an old prop plane, 1,500 miles south to Punta Arenas, the southernmost city in Chile, and then by boat through the island channels for another six hours. The vessel was an American landing craft bought by the Chilean navy. It had been used during World War II assaults on the Normandy beaches.

As Professor Kirberg recalls, "We disembarked single file and were swallowed up by heavy mist. We were shivering in the cold; we had on lightweight suits and jackets, the usual clothes for a Santiago spring. Nobody was prepared for the frigid Antarctic blasts. We tried to walk close to each other to ward off the howling wind that cut into us as though with a hundred razor blades. We were terribly hungry, we'd had only one cup of coffee and no food for the whole trip. But above all we were bone-tired, simply overwhelmed with fatigue, our backs and legs in agony from the contorted positions we had been forced into on the plane, handcuffed and tied down to the seats."

Some had fared worse. Because of overcrowding in the small plane, some prisoners had to sit on the floor, with nothing to cushion the shocks to their bodies as the aircraft bumped its way through turbulence. "Stone-faced soldiers" took turns patrolling the aisles, pointing their rifles at the heads of the prisoners to make sure they did not talk to each other.

"Our ordeal began almost immediately, within hours of the putsch," Kirberg says. "Some, like Allende, were either murdered outright or first tortured and then done away with. Others, like me and especially high-level government officials and cabinet members, were seized at their homes or offices. And by the second and third day of the coup they were brought into the Bernardo O'Higgins Military School [Chile's West Point] in Santiago, the main collection center for high-ranking Allende officials. Almost immediately one sensed the attempt to break us down physically and psychologically. We were interrogated over and over about alleged conspiracies to subvert the armed forces and thus, presumably, keep the Allende government alive.

"Our inquisitors were insolent, vulgar, lacing their questions with profanity. This went on from the twelfth of September to the fifteenth. At night we were at the mercy of cadets, most of them scions of Chile's oligarchy or of the *buenas familias*, with hidebound anti-Allende prejudices. They amused themselves by banging at our doors or shooting off their pistols near our windows and threatening to murder us.

"And yet we felt that the Junta high command wavered on how to deal with our fate. Apparently the world outcry at Allende's assassination and the ensuing bloodbath all across Chile inhibited Pinochet and his henchmen from liquidating us en masse. This was evident when on the morning of September 14th we were shoved by the cadet guards into a big conference room. There the Junta's newly appointed Justice Minister, Gonzalo Prieto, offered us a plane on which to go into exile out of Chile. Our response was a unanimous 'No.' Our spokesman was José Tohá, who told the Junta representative that either we should be freed immediately or we should stand trial under the protection of the Chilean constitution. Prieto said he would consult with his colleagues, but he never returned and we never heard from him again. The whole scene reflected the topsy-turvy world in which we suddenly found ourselves. For right above the head table where Tohá and Prieto were conferring hung a great chart of Chile's governmental chain of command that had been drawn up only a few days earlier, when Letelier was appointed to his new post, and that the Junta had not had time to remove. At the top, in huge letters, the chart listed Salvador Allende, President and Commander-in-Chief, followed by Orlando Letelier as Defense Minister, and then, immediately below, the name of General Augusto Pinochet, head of the armed forces."

Next morning the prisoners were told to take whatever belongings they had and get ready for a journey. No destination was revealed. Heavily armed security guards herded them into jeeps and trucks and took them to El Bosque military air base. Ordered to walk single file they were searched once again. Each was frisked for hidden weapons. Shoes were removed and slit open at the heel to see if there were hidden messages. In the course of this examination whatever valuables had not been taken earlier, such as watches and cigarette lighters, were seized without explanation. Prisoners who resisted this robbery were beaten with rifle butts and threatened with summary execution.

At Punta Arenas, late that evening, the prisoners were pushed onto a windswept air strip. "There was an atmosphere of heightened tension," Kirberg says. "The moment we stepped off the plane we were blinded by the glare of enormous army searchlights that lit us up like targets in a war cinema. We stumbled along in the direction of a command post as soldiers armed with rifles with fixed bayonets kept harassing us to quicken our pace." Some were stripped naked, all were photographed and rechecked. They were then ordered to dress and steered toward a parking area jammed with personnel carriers, each with room for eight prisoners, an officer, and an enlisted man. "There was a lot of noise and commotion. Officers were shouting commands, sergeants were pushing us toward the vehicles, the searchlights never ceased their blinding assault.

"As we were about to climb into the truck, the officer in charge pulled out his revolver from the holster and screamed, 'Anybody who makes a move while in the vehicle will be shot.' And as we began getting in, a soldier blindfolded each of us by pulling a cloth bag over the head and face and tying it at the neck. Cold, exhausted, unseeing, some forced to lie face down on the floor of the truck, we were driven over bumpy roads for about an hour. Except for occasional curses from the officer in charge and the whir of the engine we were left to our own thoughts. But toward the end of the trip a shot rang out nearby and our lieutenant was quick to comment that there would be one less mouth to feed where we were going. We found out later that a guard had been carelessly waving his pistol around and had shot Daniel Vergara in the arm. Nobody did anything about it and Vergara almost bled to death on the trip. Despite the fact that the bullet remained lodged in his arm, the Junta refused to move him to a hospital where it could be removed. Dr. Arturo Jiron tended the wound with dressings made from torn up shirts and underwear, constantly rewashed. Not until a week later, when Vergara's wound was festering and nearly gangrenous, was he taken to a hospital in Punta Arenas to have the bullet removed. (Vergara's arm remained permanently maimed.)

"Once we reached our destination our blindfolds were taken off. The cold here was even more penetrating, a black sky ominously hung over us. But we didn't have to wait long to learn what was next in store for us. This was an embarkation dock, and we were pushed onto a gangplank which led to a seedy, grimy ship where we were forced to sit jammed against each other on the floor. 'Conversation and smoking strictly prohibited,' a Junta officer warned us. And so for six hours, jammed together in the old landing craft, we chugged along on choppy waters to what we eventually learned was our terminal point—Dawson Island.

"Heavy gray morning mist enveloped us as we got off the ship. Scrub and piles of rock littered the beach. We were ordered to fall into military formations and begin a march on a slippery dirt road, full of potholes. Occasionally the men broke ranks to bypass the frozen rivulets into which some of their less fortunate comrades sank knee-deep. And in so doing they almost bumped into what looked like mysterious, squat, nonearthly sentinels lurking in dark shadows at the sides of the road. It was only on closer inspection that they were discovered to be charred oak stumps four or five feet high. These were the remains of thousands of trees which fell victim to a forest fire that swept Dawson Island near the turn of the century."

Some of the group, men in their late sixties with heart problems, began to fall behind. But not for long. Junta soldiers, cursing, shouting obscenities, and from time to time jamming the barrel of a gun in a straggler's back, forced everyone to keep a quick pace, no matter how much the older men wheezed and panted in the attempt to keep up. This march was the beginning of a series of harassments designed to destroy the captives both morally and physically. They were compelled to trudge through the icy rain and muck for nearly two hours simply to have them undergo physical torment.

After what seemed like an interminable time, a hazy outline of their "home" hove into view. "A group of grim, bleak shacks huddled together on a sprawling military base was the sight that greeted us when we arrived at our destination," Kirberg recalls. "When we entered the compound we were ordered into a cavernous tent. There each of us received a cup of tea and a stale slice of bread. Some of us dropped down on benches, others had to make do with the earthen floor. We devoured our meager rations greedily. We were scarcely through with this repast when sergeants began shouting commands. 'Up on your feet and back into formation.' Once again the roll call and each of us was checked individually.

Dawson Island Concentration Camp. Here top-ranking officials of the Allende government spent nearly a year doing forced labor outdoors in a hostile, frigid climate. The island is about a two-hour flight from the Antarctic. (Wide World Photos)

"An army major, our base commander, jumped on a table and read us the riot act. 'You are all prisoners of war. This is to warn you that infractions of rules or insubordination, or any attempt to escape, will be punished with summary execution; in other words, you'll be shot on the spot.'

"'And now, all of you to your respective barracks,' he bellowed. Seven of the prisoners were assigned to a barrack which included Letelier, Dr. Jiron, Almeyda, Dr. Enriquez, Jose Cademartori, former finance minister, Hugo Miranda, and Kirberg. Because this group was made up of the highest-ranking

officials of the Allende government, the barrack was dubbed the
Sheraton Hotel. All the others were billeted in something that
looked like a warehouse. This was named the Tupahue, after a
second-class hotel in Santiago. In both, the space alloted for
each prisoner was about three feet square, and the bunks, which
were soon referred to as coffins, were so close to each other that
to get to the door a person had to flatten himself and walk
sideways.

"The barracks seemed designed to suffocate the occupants and
freeze them at the same time. There was one small, smoky wood
stove in each of them. A tiny, leaky window in the ceiling was
the only aperture to the outside world. While it effectively kept
out the fresh air, it was almost useless in keeping out the rain.
The water kept dripping inside."

Still hungry, crushed with exhaustion, nursing their weary
limbs, the prisoners dropped into their bunks and tried to relax
their taut muscles. Despite their fatigue, not everyone was able to
slide into the escape that sleep can offer. There was too much to
absorb. All of them had had the world collapse about them with
the suddenness of an earthquake. And most had already experienced the baptism of Fascist fury that descended upon Chile.

Only several days before, Orlando Letelier had been sworn in
as Chile's Defense Minister. Clodomiro Almeyda had returned
from a conference of nonaligned nations in Algiers and immediately gone into consultation with Allende about the president's
plan to call for a referendum in which the Chilean people would
express their support or rejection of the Popular Unity government programs. And early on the morning of the putsch Enrique
Kirberg was still being addressed by an army captain with the
usual respect accorded a leading intellectual. "Yes, professor,"
"No, professor," he said, in responding to Kirberg's questions
about an assault on the university the night before the coup.

It must have been particularly hard for Letelier because of the
sting of Pinochet's personal betrayal. Twenty-four hours before
the coup, at one of his meetings with his commanding general at
the Defense Ministry, Letelier had heard Pinochet hold forth on
his loyalty to Allende and his absolute resolve to defend the

legitimately-elected Chilean government against any attempts by
Rightist forces to topple it.

"Quite frankly," Letelier recalled, "in the time I knew General
Pinochet I had many doubts about his intellectual capacity.
However, there remains little doubt in my mind as to his talents
as a traitor." Indeed, after the coup, the Junta chief openly
admitted that forty-eight hours before the bombing of La
Moneda he had already endorsed a document circulated among
the senior officers that outlined the plans for overthrowing the
Allende government. And, presumably to reinforce his credentials for leadership of the Junta, Pinochet claimed that he had
initiated the anti-Allende plot as early as 1972.

An internationally respected economist who had served on the
staff of the World Bank for a number of years before Allende
appointed him ambassador to the United States, Letelier was
held in high esteem in Washington. Because of his valuable
international connections, Allende had asked him to leave his
post and return to Chile to help deal with the nation's worsening
economic situation. Soon after Letelier returned, his friend José
Tohá was forced out of office as Defense Minister and Allende
named Letelier to succeed Tohá. (These switches in cabinet posts
became increasingly frequent as the anti-Popular Unity majority
in Congress grasped at every opportunity to create new crises for
the government by accusing Allende ministers of incompetence
or violation of the law and voting them out of office.)

Letelier's personal ordeal began even before the bombardment
of La Moneda. With other ministers and high government
officials he spent the evening of September 10th with Allende at
Tomás Moro, the presidential residence, consulting on the
referendum speech the President was to deliver the next day. He
left the President with Carlos Briones soon after midnight. Once
home he continued to probe the earlier reports of the mysterious
troop movements. Given the increasingly tense political situation, rumors kept cropping up and in most cases they were just
that. On the other hand, none of them could be ignored, so
Letelier, as Defense Minister, began phoning the highest-ranking
officers to obtain clarification. The responses were most be-

wildering. Wives or aides answered, saying that the generals or admirals, as the case might be, were away and it was not known where they could be reached, or that they were expected home soon and would call back. A few of the generals did call back, but with a variety of fanciful explanations about the troop movements. They uniformly assured Letelier that nothing unusual or abnormal was happening on any of the army or navy posts across the country.

What made Letelier especially tense was that no one at the Defense Ministry answered the phone. Where was the usual night staff? It was not until 5:45 A.M. that the Ministry responded, and Letelier was dumbfounded when Admiral Patricio Carvajal, a top staff officer, answered the phone himself, and in Letelier's office at that. What was Carvajal doing there at such an early hour? And what was he doing at Letelier's desk?

Carvajal airily explained that he had arrived at his office early to deal with an inordinate amount of paperwork that had piled up on his desk. And he happened to be walking by Letelier's office, he said, when he heard the phone ring; so he picked it up.

Letelier was now convinced that something serious was afoot. Soon after, Allende called him with the news of the Valparaiso rebellion and told him to go to the Defense Ministry to check out the situation there. When Letelier got to the ministry, two armed security guards barred his way. "How dare you!" he shouted. "Don't you know I am the Defense Minister?" But the verbal scuffle didn't last long. A booming voice from inside said, "Let the Minister in."

Scarcely through the door, he was seized, hit with fists and rifle butts, then dragged to the basement of the building and beaten again. All around him was chaos: men were being pounded savagely by soldiers and officers. Letelier was then taken to Regimiento Tacna, a military post in Santiago, and pushed into a room overlooking a large walled-in compound. For most of the afternoon Letelier was to hear again and again an officer's order to fire and then the short, barking noise of a dozen rifles in the compound. The window of the room was blacked out, and so was the glass section of the door that led to the compound. But there were tiny gaps in the masking material and so Letelier put his eye close enough to them to see the bodies of those executed dragged out. He counted seventeen corpses. Toward the end of the afternoon, guards began tormenting him by banging on his door, laughing and shouting, "You're next!" And then it really happened. The door opened and six men burst in, carrying a big towel, "which I quickly surmised was to be my blindfold when they put me up against the wall. 'Let's go,' they yelled as they dragged me out of the room."

But Letelier put up a fierce struggle. The scuffle was loud, with shouts and the stamping of feet. The noise attracted the attention of a lieutenant on the next floor who insisted on his right as commanding officer to decide who was going to the execution grounds. He said that it was a long day and he was tired, and he ordered the men to hand Letelier over to him. Accompanied by military guards, he took Letelier to a jeep and drove to the O'Higgins Military School. It was from there that Letelier and thirty-four others were taken to the airport for the flight to Dawson Island. A few hours prior to their departure, Letelier was given permission to call his wife Isabel to tell her that he was about to start on a trip, with a destination unknown.

Now on Dawson Island, tired and still nursing the bruises from the beating two days before, Letelier somehow kept his innate optimism intact. As his comrades at Dawson recall, "his attitude was that of a man who says, 'OK, here we are. How are we going to deal with the new crisis here?'" It is ironic that Letelier's life was spared when he was seized on the day of the coup, and that he afterward survived Dawson Island and other concentration camps, only to die at the hands of Pinochet's assassins when he was finally at liberty in Washington, D.C.*

Clodomiro Almeyda was another inmate of Dawson Island's

---

* As it later developed, Letelier became more dangerous to Pinochet when he was sent into exile than if he had remained in Chile. For it was because of his persuasion of certain European officials at the highest levels of government—people he had come to know when serving with the World Bank—that a number of governments began cutting trade with the Junta, thus endangering the Chilean economy.

"Sheraton." Once a professor of political science, he looks the part to perfection. Serious, with heavy-rimmed glasses, a high domed forehead, and a gravelly, authoritative baritone voice, Almeyda is not, however, the absent-minded variety of academician. He is precise and articulate, quick to respond and explain.

On the day the Junta struck, however, he might have been somewhat foggy. He had arrived the evening before from the nonaligned nations conference in Africa, and gone straight into a meeting with Allende. The jet-lag malaise was still with him when his phone rang at about 7:00 A.M. and the President told him about the Valparaiso developments and summoned him to La Moneda.

After taking leave of his family, Almeyda drove to his mother's house for another hasty farewell. "We'd become very realistic about the critical situation in the last few months of the Allende regime," he said. "So when we said goodbye to each other, we didn't embellish it with outpourings of emotion, but we didn't take it lightly either. The immediate future looked dark and at best unpredictable."

Strangely enough, en route to the palace, the streets seemed normal, with no evidence of unusual police or military traffic. It was only at the palace that the *carabineros* (the national police), still loyal to the government were out in large detachments around La Moneda, with several tanks at the entrance. "Within an hour or so after my arrival, however, the situation changed dramatically. The police switched sides and withdrew the palace security guard, taking the weaponry with them. My conference with Allende was of the briefest. He was already deeply involved in organizing the defense of the palace against the impending attack."

Though Allende asked all those inexperienced with firearms to leave the palace and try to carry on resistance against the Junta on the outside, Almeyda as well as the brothers Tohá (José and Jaime), Carlos Briones and Anibal Palma, a top Allende advisor, chose to stay with the President. They removed themselves from the scene of battle because of their inexperience with firearms and walked down to the subterranean passages that connected the palace with the Foreign Ministry wing. There in a tiny storeroom they remained for most of the bombardment. They heard the muffled detonations of the bombs and cannonfire. The earth and the building shook with every direct hit on the palace, but the basement they were in remained unscathed.

Soon their phone connections with the main buildings, where Allende and his young guards hoped to repel the assault, were cut off by the destruction of the intercom system. Oddly, their phones to the outside world still functioned. They could talk now and then with their families, who sat mesmerized at their radios, and thus learned more about the state of La Moneda than they themselves could determine.

The conversation among the five officials centered on the emergency at hand. "This was scarcely the moment for us to undertake a deep analysis of the political situation in which we and the other Popular Unity people found themselves," Almeyda says, smiling a little. "We were involved with survival. Once the bombardment began, even though we were not in the direct line of fire the smoke began to infiltrate our little shelter. We started to cough and choke. Then the Junta pilots dropped tear-gas bombs, so in addition our eyes became acutely irritated.

"We then decided to move from the storeroom to an office on the floor above, still in the Foreign Ministry. We were now exposed to shelling and instant obliteration had the Junta military decided to make an attack on this side of the palace. But we really had no alternative. The smoke and gas in the basement were no longer endurable. Our phones to the outside stopped functioning, and it wasn't until late in the afternoon that we learned of Allende's murder. A Junta patrol broke into our refuge. With guns and bayonets pointing at us, we were taken before one of the Junta generals who had been directing the palace attack. At first his behavior and that of his officers was correct, even polite. We were then escorted to a personnel carrier and driven to the O'Higgins Military School, where other high-ranking Allende people were being brought in.

"In the first day of the putsch a lot of catastrophic, life-changing experiences were crammed into a matter of hours. I felt stunned, groping for leads to what the future held. The scene around us was horrendous. We were all in profound anguish.

But perhaps there was nothing more painful than to look out the windows of the military school and watch the continuous sorties by Junta bombers over the working-class shantytowns as they bombed the defenseless populace. Again and again we saw them zoom in and unload their bombs and machine-gun the streets. These attacks were followed by plumes of smoke rising into the thin blue sky, as the rickety shacks burst into flame like stuffed matchboxes set on fire. Hundreds upon hundreds of people—men, women, and children—were put to the torch in this precisely organized exercise, so terribly reminiscent of the films of B-52 bomber attacks on the Vietnamese."

The murder of Allende, the destruction of La Moneda, and the attack on the shantytowns continued to beat at Almeyda's mind as he lay down on his bunk in his new home at Dawson and watched the little window in the ceiling streaked with rain.

On September 11th, the day of the coup, Professor Kirberg got up early, since this was one of the days when he would go to the school gym for a workout and relax in the sauna before starting his day at the university. Kirberg, about six feet tall, now in his middle sixties, walks with a firm step. His well-chiseled face with high cheekbones and a lofty forehead, lights up with a friendly smile when in conversation. But that morning there was little to smile about. At 6:45 the university custodian called to tell him that five men in civilian clothes armed with machine guns had broken into the administration building, overpowered the security guard, and attacked the university radio station, smashing the transmitters. It was a quick, hit-and-run operation, obviously the work of technically trained marauders, not merely mischief by a gang of hooligans. As they left, with some of the university night staff screaming and pushing toward them, they fired several rounds to intimidate the few pursuers. "There was little doubt in my mind that it must have been the work of cadets stationed at a marine base close to the university," Kirberg says.

"I immediately drove to my office, and soon afterward my wife joined me there. I was appalled at the violence with which the radio station had been ransacked and destroyed. I called the police and within minutes several officers arrived and in a very businesslike manner jotted down all the details and descriptions from some of the people who were on night duty. They promised to begin work on the case immediately. This was about seven o'clock. Still shaken, I called the *carabineros* again at about eight with a few more details I thought would be useful in their search for the culprits. But no one answered the phone. I tried several times but there was no response. I didn't know that was the hour when the *carabineros* had switched sides and gone over to the Junta."

Despite the early-morning rumors and reports spreading across Santiago, confidence still prevailed that, as in previous attempted coups, the armed forces would stand fast and defend the government. The perils of bloody confrontation did not inhibit the thousands of students who came to the university that morning. Kirberg recalls: "The students arrived in droves, probably the best attendance we'd had in months. Both curiosity and a desire to participate in whatever action there was to hold back the Rightists were the motivating factors."

At midmorning Kirberg called a meeting in the administration building of representatives of the faculty, the student organizations, the employee trade unions, and the political party student groups. Even the Christian Democratic Party faction, whose leader, former President Eduardo Frei, had helped pave the way to the coup by joining with the extreme Rightists in demanding Allende's abdication—"they too wanted to be part of whatever fight the university was going to put up against the putsch."

The meeting was tense, with many strongly expressed opinions about what to do. Some advocated making a stand at the university if the military attacked, but others pointed out that the buildings had enormous glass facades that could never hold up against gunfire.

"Our deliberations went on while contradictory bulletins were flashed on the radio about Allende's situation at La Moneda. And even when it was announced that the battle for the presidential palace had begun, it was not clear whether pro-Allende sectors of the army were helping to defend the government. Rumors also spread that pro-Allende forces had over-whelmed the pro-Fascist military in other parts of Chile. Our mood would swing from hopeful optimism to profound depression, depending on the latest rumor.

"By about four o'clock, however, the Junta's radio announcements made it abundantly clear that the Popular Unity government had fallen. And then the thunderclap—Allende was dead. Among the Junta's first acts was to order a curfew, effective that afternoon, and to warn that anybody caught in violation would be shot. Many of the students began making their way off campus, filtering back home. About a thousand students and faculty members chose to remain, some in the administration building, others in the arts building.

"At five o'clock a military patrol appeared at the university entrance. I met them on the steps. It's amazing how cocksure we were of the Chilean tradition that the university's autonomy was sacrosanct and could not be violated by the military. And, indeed, the commanding officer, although speaking sternly about observing the curfew, addressed me respectfully as 'professor.' Since the curfew was already in effect, he told us to spend the night at the university. In the morning, he said, he would dispatch special buses to take us home.

"We settled down as best we could for the night. Some slept on benches and chairs, others on the floor. A watch was set up, with students taking turns. But as it turned out sleep was out of the question. The night was shattered by continuous gunfire. It wasn't directed at the university itself, it was largely designed to terrorize us and the community as a whole."

Come what may, Kirberg began the next day by making himself presentable. He shaved, changed his shirt, and was about to open the door of his office, "when I was suddenly lifted off my feet and deafened by an enormous explosion. A cannon shell had made a direct hit into the communication Telex room, only about fifteen feet away from my office. This was followed by volleys of heavy machine-gun fire, the staccato accompanied by the ear-splitting sound of splintering glass and the whine of bullets ricocheting from marble pillars."

Both he and his wife dropped to the floor. Then, keeping his body as low to the floor as possible, since the bullets were coming close to the window level, Kirberg crawled to a small table near his desk that held a phone and a directory. He found the number of the police and dialed. "I was able to get through to the captain who shouted insolently, 'Rector, you and your rebel students better get out fast before you're all blown to hell.' 'But, captain,' I argued, 'we were told that we'd be bused out of here this morning. Why this attack?' 'Well, things have changed,' he screamed and hung up.

"After that, the shooting continued to pin us down." Unless some move could be made to indicate surrender, everyone would be killed as more and more of the walls were torn away by the cannon and machine-gun fire. Kirberg decided on one last gamble. He took off his shirt, tied it to a ruler, sidled to a window and lifted his improvised white flag of truce high enough to be seen outside. It seemed to work. The Junta men shouted orders to come out of the building with the flag.

"As I walked out I was stunned to see the concentration of troops and firepower scarcely 150 feet away from the buildings. Some of them were already demolished. There were cannons, heavy and light machine guns, and rifles. A military officer yelled, 'I'll give you five minutes to go back and tell the rest of your miserable crowd to get out on the double. Everybody leave the building with your hands up.' I ran back inside and started shouting to everyone I could find that we had a chance to survive if we left at once. I tried to call the other buildings but the switchboard was out. The people there had no way of knowing what was going on because their windows faced the back of the campus and they had no idea of my negotiations with the Junta soldiers out front.

"The five minutes were up and we had to leave. Some of the women among us were particularly brave. They were among the first to file out with my wife and me. Even though we did as we were ordered, firing was still going on, with bullets screaming a foot or so above our heads. As soon as we reached the gate we were ordered to drop to the ground, face to the pavement. I suddenly felt a heavy blow on my back and heard a voice bellowing, 'So you're the university rector!' 'Yes,' I replied, as I half-turned my face upward. There stood a colonel, gun in hand. 'Now you'll see what an autonomous university looks like.' As he spoke he swung the butt of his machine gun against my arm and started kicking me in the lower back. He then forced me to stand up by twisting my arm and pushing me against the wall. He stepped back and said, still bellowing, 'I'll give you fifteen seconds to tell me where the hidden arms are stored. We know you have an ammunition dump somewhere. Now remember, only fifteen seconds.' I heard the sound as he cocked his rifle. I shouted back that there were no arms and no ammunition at the university. He ignored me and began counting out loud, 'One, two, three. . . .' Suddenly he stopped, turned to a soldier and said, 'I'm much too busy for this nonsense. If this man doesn't speak up in the next fifteen seconds, you know what to do.'

"The soldier was a youngster from the northern sierra. Round-faced, dark, scarcely twenty, he was obviously in dread fear of the colonel, overwhelmed by what was going on and basically gentle. Since he hadn't exactly been ordered to shoot, the soldier waited fifteen seconds and then lowered his gun. I smiled and he smiled. But he didn't say a word. For a moment we were an island unto ourselves. On all sides officers were shouting orders, pistolwhipping the students and professors. My sentry seemed relieved at not being forced to execute me. At the same time, he was unsure of what to do next. Suddenly we were approached by an officer, who said, 'I know you, Professor Kirberg. I took some of your courses last year. I'm going to talk to my commanding officer and make sure you are looked after in keeping with your rank,' as though I were a general.

"And sure enough, a jeep soon drew up with a lieutenant and an enlisted man in it. As I got in I glimpsed my wife and several other women walking under guard away from the campus. I was driven to an army post in downtown Santiago, where I was left in a small room with a sullen-faced soldier who kept his rifle pointed directly at me, not saying a word. After about half an hour the oppressive quiet was shattered by rifle fire that seemed to be coming from the courtyard. It was not the sound of guns used for target drills. It was the sound of maybe a dozen rifles going off at the same time, following a shouted command that I couldn't make out. It dawned on me that executions were going on just outside.

"I was convinced that my turn would soon arrive. The resounding volleys were all too near, all too personal. I was overtaken with anxiety. Was I to be marched to the execution area? I tried to reason with myself that the ordeal would be brief, that I should try to be calm. But just how calm can one be when death is so close at hand? I didn't feel either chilled or hot, but my body was covered with perspiration. I had a compelling urgency to write a farewell note to my wife and family, but I had neither paper nor pen. And so I sat and waited, my sentry sitting opposite with cocked rifle in hand.

"Suddenly the door swung open and one of the captains who had commanded the shelling of the university walked into the room and said that the battle for the campus was still going on because the people in one of the buildings were still holding out. 'But why don't you stop the shelling so they *can* get out?' I asked. 'I can assure you,' I insisted, 'there are no guns at the university.' He then asked whether I would talk to the students by loudspeaker to persuade them to surrender. 'But of course,' I said. 'Let's go at once.' He went off to get his helmet and pistol, saying he'd be right back.

"I felt momentary relief for two reasons: I was not to be shot right away, and I might help prevent a massacre at the university. But five minutes later the officer returned to say our trip was no longer necessary; the students had just given up.

"Shortly afterward I was taken by jeep, under guard, to the Defense Ministry. But as we got near the building a gun duel developed between the Junta soldiers guarding the ministry and some sharpshooters on the roof of a higher building close by. Despite this fusillade my guards said we were to make a run for the entrance. I dashed toward the door with two soldiers, pistols in hand, right behind me. Once again death was very near. I felt certain that either I would be shot in the back by my escorts or from the front by the resistance fighters, who could scarcely distinguish friend from foe at that distance. But I made it safely and was pushed and shoved through a subterranean passage into a room where I was ordered to stand with my arms outstretched and my chin against the wall. Within minutes I experienced a terrifying sensation of fatigue and body tension. Fortunately this didn't go on long. I was taken into what looked like a cave, where a number of people were on their knees, faces touching the wall, each separated from the others by a distance of about six feet. I too was ordered to the wall, a nastily damp one. But in about half an hour I was on the move again, this time to the infamous stadium. There I was interrogated again and then again made to stand facing a wall with arms outstretched. It is an extraordinary sensation. As one's eyes focus on the wall, nausea develops and the body goes into spasms of pain.

"While in that position I heard a raucous noise at the door and saw from the corner of my eye a rather big man, a prisoner, shoved inside and brutally knocked to the floor. As he was being kicked and beaten with a rifle butt an officer kept shouting, 'So you are the revolver-carrying bastard!' Another officer burst in and, with a stream of profanity, proceeded to shove a pistol into the prisoner's mouth. He threatened to shoot him then and there, but for some reason he didn't. He allowed the prostrate, semi-conscious body to slump to the floor, and walked out.

"At about this time groups of students and professors began arriving from the university. Some already showed the telltale signs of Junta treatment. Many had their clothes torn, their shirts ripped. Streaks of dried blood encrusted cheeks and foreheads. Because I was near the entrance, many of the arrivals recognized me and nodded sympathetically. Among them was Victor Jara, with his famous warm smile.

"Then, for the fourth time that day, I was suddenly grabbed by the arm and taken to a waiting jeep, and whisked to the O'Higgins Military School, which turned out to be the last stop before my journey to Dawson Island."

And now, after the tumultuous events of the past four days, Kirberg lay back in his bunk and contemplated the future, as a biting wind howled outside and rain mixed with sleet beat down on the thin walls of the barracks.

The following day the Dawson Island prisoners were startled by a furious banging on the doors of their barracks. Marine guards shouting obscenities unlocked the doors and ordered the prisoners to get dressed and get ready for work.

As former Senator Hugo Miranda remembers it, "At 6:15 it

was still very dark and beastly cold. A hard rain mixed with sleet swept down upon us as we stood outside, bewildered, shivering in our wet spring suits. Some of us pleaded with the guards to let several of the older men stay inside—they looked very sick—but the answer was, in their military jargon, 'Negative,' followed by shouts of 'No excuses, everyone out.' Only Vergara, with the bullet in his arm, was allowed to remain inside and ordered to sweep the floor.

"Like soldiers we were ordered to fall into squad formations and answer to our numbers during roll call. In the meantime blinding searchlights swept across the prisoners. We had to do about thirty push-ups *(puchados)*, as part of our 'physical fitness exercises.' Our hands were blue from cold and the rain formed pockets of water in our shirt collars, then cascaded down inside our shirts.

"Still out of breath from the push-ups, we were told to begin jogging. We skidded on the muddy, half-frozen ground, slipping and falling while desperately keeping pace around the perimeter of the camp grounds. This was to go on for about half an hour every day. We were then ordered to sing the 'Hymn of the Americas,' which was composed during the Second World War and contained the names of all the nations of the western hemisphere. However, we were forbidden to include the word 'Cuba,' and instead supposed to hum—*mmmm*—at that spot of the script. This musical rendition over, we were marched to our dining room, a huge, drafty tent, where for about half an hour we had our breakfast, a cup of watery tea and a piece of stale bread.* We then returned to the barracks to clean up and make our beds.

"Our work day began with 'welcoming' remarks by the camp commandant. He said, 'You are to forget who you were. Look at what you are today. You certainly don't amount to much. One army recruit is worth a hundred times more than all of you put together. Chile needs soldiers, not intellectuals like you. And we

* Because Dawson Island was a marine facility, and since for many years the Chilean marines and navy were British-trained, the tradition continues to be British, so far as tea drinking is concerned. Coffee was never made available to the Dawson prisoners.

shall make soldiers out of you, no matter what the cost. And now to work.'

"With that sendoff we marched to our place of work—a five-mile trek to a rocky beach where we crushed huge boulders with extremely primitive tools. These five-mile marches, first in the morning to work, and again on the late-afternoon return to the barracks, involved us in a struggle with sixty- and seventy-mile Antarctic winds. In between, we had no protection against the hazards that accompany rock-breaking operations. We had no helmets, no gloves or goggles to shield us from rock splinters as we attacked the stone with mallets and pickaxes."

The prisoners scooped up the crushed rock and carried it in bags on their backs to marked places where the telephone poles were to be erected. They had to dig the holes in the frozen ground, then dump the rock to prepare the foundation for the

At Dawson Island, prisoners always worked under the command of armed marines. (Wide World Photos)

heavy oak timbers they cut in the oak forests on the island. It was a backbreaking operation and the weather was an implacable part of it.

Like everything else on the island, the forest too had an awesome, doomsday quality. An oppressive, deathly stillness hung over it throughout the year. The prisoners couldn't get over the fact that unlike the usual wooded area, the Dawson Island forest was devoid of any sign of life except for an occasional woodpecker tapping out its staccato solo. Otherwise they saw no rabbits, no other birds nor anything else suggesting the presence of animals. But the forest did offer temporary protection; it was considerably warmer there because the giant trees were a shield against the wind. This was a mixed blessing. This natural warmth combined with the speed-up enforced by the yelling guards made the prisoners sweat profusely. But as soon as they left their wooded shelter, the abrupt drop in temperature produced an astonishing change: The subfreezing wind transformed their foreheads, cheeks, and mustaches into icy, glistening surfaces.

"I am not ashamed to tell you that there were times when the cold was so bitter we were moved to tears," Benjamin Teplisky recalls. Of medium height, baldish, round-faced, in his late forties, Teplisky was the Vice President of the Radical Party which, despite its name, is a centrist party. An easy conversationalist, Teplisky's comments on his experiences voiced in a deep baritone adds a sobriety to his lasting sense of outrage.

In the eight months the prisoners spent on Dawson Island they put up dozens of telephone poles along thirty-five miles of the island's territory. They also built roads, dug tunnels, and hauled timber.

The first few months were especially difficult. In addition to the hostile climate, the psychological disorientation, and the cruelty of the guards there was poor nutrition and threatening hygienic conditions. Almost immediately the prisoners developed heavy colds and high temperatures. But most menacing was the water problem. The prisoners were dependent for their water, whether for drinking or washing, on a narrow little creek running down from a hill where the security guards were quartered. And so at all times of the day, bits of fecal matter or soapsuds would come floating down toward the area where the prisoners were billeted. "It was a near miracle that we didn't have an intestinal epidemic," Teplisky says. "No doubt there would have been if the Red Cross had not demanded a change when its officials visited Dawson several weeks after we had arrived."

The food was so poorly prepared and so lacking in basic nutrients that most of the inmates suffered severe weight loss. Every prisoner lost about fifty-five pounds during the eight months on the island. Tohá—an extremely handsome man of forty-seven, tall, slender, about 6'6"—lost sixty pounds in the first few months. As his colleagues put it, he literally began to waste away. *

Teplisky remembers the food in painful detail. "Our main meal, dinner, consisted of a sort of onion soup—hot water and a few strips of onion, but no cheese—a slice of bread, and a bowl of lentils. Scarcely a day passed without lentils. Twice a month our soup contained a sliver of meat, the size of a chicken liver, per prisoner. And there was also watery tea. Except for an occasional bit of fish which we were able to catch, thanks to a friendly guard, the above menu scarcely ever changed for the duration of our stay at Dawson."

Former Foreign Minister Almeyda again: "From the outset Dawson Island was intended to be a kind of living graveyard. The Junta may have been inhibited about killing us in one big swoop; nevertheless, our gradual annihilation was very much on its

---

*News of his condition became known abroad, and several important international leaders expressed concern. Tohá was transferred to a military hospital in Santiago. But once there his condition was not only ignored but considerably aggravated, as the Junta began to pressure him for information about hidden weaponry that Allende was suspected of having had stashed away in case of an emergency. After all, Tohá had been a Defense Minister and consequently might have been in possession of such information.

In Santiago his wife was permitted to see him several times. She was shocked by his wasted appearance and his weakness, so serious that he could not get out of bed. When the Junta announced one morning that Tohá had committed suicide by hanging himself in the lavatory, Señora Tohá charged that this was impossible; he would not have had sufficient strength to walk to the bathroom, let alone strong enough muscles to shape his trouser belt into a loop, attach it to the ceiling, move a chair into position, then step up and place his head in the noose.

Sharing lentil soup, the mainstay of the prisoners' diet for months on end, in a military tent on windswept Dawson Island. In the foreground, with glasses, is former Foreign Minister Clodomiro Almeyda. Across from him, left to right, are Socialist Party leaders Julio Palestro and Ancieto Rodriguez, and former Education Minister Anibal Palma. (Wide World Photos)

agenda. We were thrust into a world of harassment and terror, both physical and psychological. We were supposed to feel that we were forgotten, exiled to a kind of frigid vacuum, where the temperature averaged 20° F., where even the sun, in the rare moments it would peek through the clouds, was cold and unfriendly. We were forced to give up our identities, no longer allowed to call each other by name. We had to address each other by our prisoner numbers.

"But most depressing was the fact that we were swimming against a tide of hate from our own countrymen. Most of the officers and enlisted men who had become our custodians had been brainwashed into thinking that we were murderers, traitors, conspirators. And they treated us accordingly.

"I doubt if I'll ever forget the young sergeant who pointed a machine gun at several of us and said with a venom that is absolutely indescribable, 'God, how I hate you all. I see fear and hatred in your eyes too, but believe me, I hate you a lot more.' It was not until some time later that we discovered that the guards who expressed the greatest animosity toward us had special anti-insurgency training in U.S. military camps in Panama, under special arrangements with the Chilean armed forces.

"But still another factor contributed to this kind of animosity, something we were not aware of until some weeks later—the so-called Plan Zeta. According to the Junta propaganda machine a few days after the putsch, this was a diabolical project conceived by the Allende regime that called for the mass assassination of the top officer corps of the armed forces as well as thousands of private citizens suspected of being hostile to the Popular Unity government. Since it no longer had confidence in the military, the Junta contended, the Allende coalition was determined to hold on to power by liquidating any group or individuals who threatened its existence."

As Almeyda later learned, the Junta claimed that an elaborate strategy was laid out to launch this sinister plan on September 19th, Chile's independence day. The Junta charged that the car that was to carry the general staff to where the armed forces were to parade early that morning, was to have been blown up, thus beheading the leadership of the military. "The question is," Letelier subsequently asked, "how could that have been possible, since I, as Minister of Defense, would have been expected to join the chiefs of staff and thus be inside the ill-fated car? Still another question, if this indeed was the plan, then why would I not have been discussing the preparations of such a parade with Pinochet or other high-ranking officers as late as one week before the plot was to have taken place?"

Letelier has also pointed out that in the initial interrogation following the coup, both in Santiago and in Dawson Island, Plan Zeta was never brought up. From every indication, he said, it would appear that Plan Zeta was a last-minute brainstorm by the Junta to justify the putsch and to whip up hatred against the "treasonous" Allende supporters. And for several weeks it worked.

Every day the Junta-controlled newspapers published lengthy lists of individuals purportedly targeted for execution by the Allende people. Since there was no longer an independent press to question or reject these calumnies, the force of these "disclosures" had the desired calamitous effect. Readers were stupefied, outraged when they saw their names in print as potential victims had the putsch not taken place. The Junta newspapers, radio, and TV vied with each other in trotting out gory accounts about Plan Zeta under hysterical headlines, such as SIX HUNDRED FAMILIES SLATED FOR EXECUTION IN CONCEPCIÓN or HUNDREDS OF CIVIL SERVANTS SLATED FOR DEATH IN VALPARAISO.

When middle-class bank tellers, store clerks, or professionals who had been only marginally involved in politics read these stories they naturally began to clamor for revenge, Almeyda notes. Whatever initial sympathy they might have had for some of their co-workers or colleagues who had been hauled away to the Junta's "interrogation" centers, thawed overnight. The Junta played this macabre Plan Zeta game to the hilt for several weeks. But when foreign correspondents tried to pursue the story to its source it began to fade away with the suddenness with which it first surfaced. But in its wake, anger and doubt, certainly among the upper-middle class and the aristocracy, remained strong. The Junta made special use of this maneuver within the armed forces, which helps explain the brutal and even murderous manner of many of the officers and enlisted personnel in their treatment of pro-Allende prisoners.

"On a number of occasions," Teplisky says, "especially in the nightmarish first few weeks at Dawson, some of the military amused themselves by sneaking up behind a prisoner to box his ears repeatedly, but with such force as to damage the eardrums. Apart from the extreme physical pain, the victim vomited and would fall to the ground. It was what the guards called the 'telephone' game. Several of the prisoners became partially deaf.

"Dawson personnel was given a lesson on how to treat us," Teplisky recalls, "when a military intelligence unit flew in from Punta Arenas to reinterrogate us, a few days after our arrival. They descended on us like a storm late one evening, herding us outside the barracks like animals ready for branding. One by one we were ordered to undress, were frisked for hidden arms, questioned, and hurled bodily toward the entrance of our barracks. Some of the men smashed heavily into the walls or against the floor, bruising their bodies, wounding their heads and faces.

"As if to underscore what additional horrors might be in store for us, the goings-on in a barracks close to those we occupied were even more terrible. About a hundred and fifty young men, some only eighteen or so, were in this building, and they did not have the privilege of our dubious VIP status. There was nothing to inhibit the sadism of the torturers. These young men were political militants, workers and students from the neighboring province of Magallanes, who were rounded up after the putsch and tortured continuously. Their cries and moans haunted us far into the night. From time to time we were able to catch a glimpse of them. Some had broken jaws and arms; many underwent electric shocks to their genitals and other torments that became accepted methods of torture in the effort to extract information about other pro-Allende suspects."

To make sure that no camaraderie developed with the prisoners, the security guards were changed every fortnight. Thus the quality of their lives would depend on the degree of brutality of the commanding officer. Most of the time, especially at the start of their confinement, the Junta command directed its energies at creating an atmosphere of imminent physical extermination. Many of the officers found great delight in setting up situations in which the shadow of death was omnipresent.

One night, soon after the prisoners' arrival at Dawson Island, the barracks doors were flung open and a squad of marines with fixed bayonets rushed in screaming insults and shouting, "None of you will get out alive." "We stared at them, trying to make out what it was all about," Senator Miranda recalls. "It didn't take long. Our sadistic captain, his mulish jaw opening and closing like a trap, strutted in screaming, 'We know you made contact with the Soviet submarine that is now prowling about in the waters around us. This is your final warning. Anybody trying to make a getaway when the sub lands and begins the attack will be shot on the spot. You and your commie friends will never succeed. Our cannons are ready to blow them to pieces, and our reconnaissance planes are on the watch.' And as he was speaking guns emplaced on beaches close by opened up with roaring salvos, further intensifying our tension. Of course there were no submarines and there was no attack, but this crazy story served as yet another excuse to terrorize us."

Sergio Vuscovic, who joined his Dawson Island colleagues late in September, remembers a scene that would be more appropriate in the Theater of the Absurd.

"This happened one evening when we returned from work— all half-frozen, aching with fatigue and pining for our so-called supper, the usual lentil soup, tea, and a slice of bread. It wasn't much but it was something to help get the chill out of our bones. As we entered the semidarkened tent, our 'dining room,' we saw our commander, justly called 'Crazy Valenzuela,' sitting at a table, continuously throwing something and catching it as it was about to hit the floor. As our eyes became accustomed to the murk we were able to make out that it wasn't a ball the commander was playing with. It was a grenade. Up and down, up and down it went, each time his hand darting out to seize the deadly object as it was about to land. We carefully sidestepped our commander on our way to and from the chow line, but our uneasiness was obvious and he enjoyed it. A missed catch and dozens of us would become casualties.

"Finally, no longer able to contain his anxiety, one of the prisoners walked over to the commander and said deferentially, 'Lieutenant, may I have permission to ask you a question?' 'Affirmative,' the lieutenant barked in reply, and went on playing with the grenade. 'Would it be possible for the lieutenant to be tossing the grenade outside, perhaps at some distance from this place where so many of us are gathered?'

"'Are you out of your mind?' the lieutenant shot back. 'Don't you know it's raining and sleeting out there? Do you want me to catch cold?' he railed, still toying with the grenade. Then he shouted, 'You are impertinent. You owe me thirty.' And so the supplicant set aside his soup and began doing thirty push-ups while the lieutenant went on tossing the grenade."

"There was an especially sadistic episode about two months after we got to Dawson," Vuscovic says. "Our guard reported to the commandant that Osvaldo, Jr., the nineteen-year-old son of Osvaldo Puccio, and Teplisky had been overheard talking about using grenades for an attempt at a breakaway. They were taken to the camp headquarters and accused of mutiny. Regardless of their denials—for any such conversation would have been madness—they were told to expect a court-martial within the next day or two. In the meantime they were returned to the barracks.

"But about three o'clock that morning a detachment of marines smashed into the barracks and ordered Osvaldo, Jr. and Teplisky to get dressed and proceed outdoors. As they left, the marines shouted at the shocked prisoners, among them young Puccio's father, who has chronic heart trouble, that they would now understand that 'warnings of maximum punishment are not idle threats.'" When the two men were hustled out of the barracks, and the doors once again locked from the outside, the prisoners ran toward the thin walls, trying to listen to what was going on outside.

"We suspected that Osvaldo, Jr., Teplisky, and the guards were somewhere in a small scrub woods a couple of dozen feet from the barracks, and so we listened intently. For the first half hour or so the suspense was deadly. Several of us were sitting with Puccio, wordlessly sympathizing and hoping that somehow the outcome would not be what we all expected. But then we heard the clicks as soldiers cocked their rifles, and then the command, 'Fire!' and the ring of rifle shots. A shiver ran through the barracks. Puccio sat up on his bunk, mechanically running his hands through his hair, breathing with difficulty. We mumbled words of consolation to him but there was no comfort, just mumbles. We sat quietly, thinking of these first deaths among our little group.

"Then suddenly the barracks doors were once again flung open and the commanding officer marched in with our 'executed' fellow prisoners. The grinning commandant said, 'As you see, nothing happened. But it is all for your own good, so no one gets the idea of taking up arms against us or trying an escape.'"

Teplisky's side of the story is that he and Osvaldo were indeed taken to the little woods and each was tied to a tree. "There were all the ceremonies of a formal execution. We were even offered a last cigarette. Then they blindfolded us and the soldiers stepped back to make up the firing line. Whether or not it was twenty minutes or forty minutes before the shots rang out is hard to tell. But when you're tied to a tree and blindfolded you think a century has gone by. Then there was the order to fire and the whine of bullets. And then nothing.

"After what seemed like another period of endless time we were untied and our blindfolds removed. We stood there stunned, scarcely able to take in whatever reality there was about us. But our captain and his marine detachment were all smiles, telling us it was only a little private joke. They offered us more cigarettes and in a very kindly way one of them asked, 'Why do you people hate us so much?' We feebly tried to dissuade them of that notion, and they continued to assure us that this little execution exercise was for our benefit. 'Try not to get involved in any kind of mischief that might lead to such a disaster,' the captain said. And he added 'And now let's not hold any grudges against each other.'"

"What always rattled our guards most was the way we handled their acts of provocation," Miranda says. "We didn't panic and we tried not to ask for mercy when we were tormented. But our stony stares, our way of looking past their faces rather than meeting their eyes—our guarded, subtle, but unmistakable disgust, more than made up for the outward passivity we had maintained. This wasn't planned; most of us had that attitude from the beginning.

"Late one evening Captain Mario Zamora, one of the more sadistic officers, burst into our barracks demanding to know if Alejandro was the man who had given the clenched fist salute to a group of prisoners just arrived from Punta Arenas. 'No, captain,' said Alejandro. 'For not telling the truth you owe me thirty, to begin with,' said Zamora. Alejandro immediately began doing his thirty push-ups. As soon as he finished, the captain said 'And for your attempt to stir up an insurrection among the new prisoners, you will spend the night in the punishment cell.' Before Alejandro could open his mouth, two husky marines grasped him by the arms and dragged him outside.

"The punishment 'box' was about three feet square and a little less than six feet high. Some of us got to know it well. It was flimsily built with almost no protection from the brutal, cold winds. Since sleep was impossible, Alejandro kept himself from freezing by doing exercises. At six the next morning, the guard told Alejandro that Captain Zamora 'in his compassionate way' would allow him to rest an hour before work. 'No thanks,' Alejandro snapped, and he added, 'Extend my appreciation to the captain for his solicitous consideration.' With that, Alejandro joined the rest of the group in the national anthem and then marched off to cut timber for the rest of the day."

Life took a minuscule turn for the better, for a short while, following a one-day visit by the International Red Cross several weeks after the prisoners' arrival at Dawson. "But the chicanery with which the visit was stage-managed was sickening," Miranda says. "Toward midmorning we were told that we'd have a day off. As a matter of fact we were told to go to the parade grounds and play soccer instead of doing our exercises. So there we were, running about on the soggy, frozen grounds but getting a definite lift.

"Suddenly a military entourage arrives with the Red Cross people and press photographers, who get to work recording our 'blissful life' in pictures. The Junta made maximum publicity use of this reportage abroad but it didn't fool the Red Cross officials, especially when they examined us physically and noted the hematomas—bloody swellings—on our bodies, evidence of beatings and torture many of us endured before being sent to Dawson.

"The Red Cross visitors listed our names and promised that the world and our families would learn of our whereabouts. This improved our morale substantially. Some part of our identities had been returned to us, for it was the first time since our incarceration that we were referred to by names and not by serial numbers.

"For several days after the Red Cross came, the men in charge here were more restrained in their harassment. But not for long. They soon came up with new ways to depress us psychologically. Since we had no access to newspapers, the Junta command offered us newspaper clippings every few days. They always had stories with the names of those arrested and those executed, many of them our lifelong friends or colleagues. From time to time there were articles attacking us personally, as well as our wives and relatives, for 'misappropriating government funds' or 'black marketeering.'

"Caged animals that we were, we had no way to defend ourselves against these obscene lies, and the clippings had their intended effect. Several of us were driven into a kind of depression. You could tell this was happening: People would sit in their bunks, in whatever free time they had, obviously brooding and reluctant to join in any kind of conversation. But somehow there was always a helping hand from someone else. Whoever was feeling stronger would dream up morale-bolstering activities to coax the melancholy ones to reenter the group discussions. One time there'd be a birthday party, with funny takeoffs of alcoholic toasts; another time we'd celebrate a wedding anniversary; and so on."

Miranda was smiling now. He was amazed, he said, "at the cooperation and good will among the prisoners, considering the lack of creature comforts and the close quarters. The most impressive example of our concern—respect—for each other was the total absence of political recrimination about why the Allende regime was overthrown. Despite the fact that all of us belonged to the Allende coalition—the Popular Unity Party—we were nevertheless members of parties with different political orientations. We also came from different professions, and for that matter even from different economic levels. But everybody joined the effort to avoid controversy that might divide us. Above all, there was an instinctive desire to help each other in every way possible. When the rare food packages would arrive from families or groups abroad, the recipient would divide the contents into halves, quarters, and even eighths, trying to have everyone in the barracks share equally.

"And on the positive side I must mention the one member of the Dawson Island military who proved to be a human being. This was the army chaplain, Father José Luis. When he came to our barracks for the first time, in November, fear was written all over his face—fear that we would seize him as a hostage. 'Come in, come in,' one of us said as he hesitated at the door. Once he did venture inside, he seemed shocked to discover that we actually belonged to the human species and were not the loathsome band of murderers described by the Junta command.

"It was because of his intervention that for a short while the command began to allowed us to conduct so-called cultural activities. In the little free time after work and dinner, we tried to rekindle the intellectual atmosphere long denied us by the Junta captors. We actually set up what can be fairly described as lecture seminars. Fernando Flores, an internationally respected authority on cybernetics, discussed his subject and took questions. Dr. Edgardo Enriquez, a famous neurologist, guided us through the mysterious neural pathways of the cerebral area.

"Former Foreign Minister Almeyda and Vuscovic exchanged views on the theories of knowledge. Dr. Jiron introduced us to basic medical theories, and Professor Kirberg of the Technical University, who is also an electrical engineer, brought us the fascinating history of artificial illumination. Jaime Tohá, former Minister of Agriculture, discussed Chile's forestry and Orlando Letelier exposed us to the skullduggery involved in international finance. Letelier also conducted an English language course. French and German were taught by Sergio Bitar and Dr. Jiron, respectively.

"For these classes a Junta officer always came to the barracks to make sure we didn't stray into any seditious or conspiratorial plotting. But the concepts were so much beyond his grasp that in the first quarter of an hour he'd begin to nod and after that he usually fell into a deep sleep. Sometimes a lecturer would be moved to cite 'seditious' theories, for instance those of Karl Marx. But that was easily handled by referring to Marx as 'the man with the big beard.' And on the rare occasions when the officer was still awake, he took no notice because he had no idea what we were talking about."

Late in December 1973 the prisoners were transferred to Rio Chico, the new concentration camp, appropriately enough one of the first public works projects of the Fascist regime. "This was a significant accomplishment for the Dawson Island command." Miranda explained. "Leading members of the Junta, with the press and photographers and even a few foreign correspondents, came from Santiago for the opening ceremonies. Modeled after a

Nazi concentration camp, Rio Chico was ringed by an electrically charged barbed wire fence; heavy machine guns were mounted on its four turrets; and, of course, it was equipped with enormous searchlights that poured their blinding beams across the compound. The visitors cheered mightily. Everyone enjoyed the prisoners' humiliation as they were marched into the new camp.

"One of the majors could scarcely contain his delight," Miranda recalls. "We saw him rush over to a British correspondent, to the latter's obvious disgust, and gleefully exclaim, 'Look at it. Look at the design, look at the fence. See the turrets? Exactly like the German camps in the movies. Isn't it marvelous? And we did it all ourselves.'

"He did not mention what we had learned, that one of the chief designers of this piece of architectural grotesquery was Walter Rauff, a former Nazi Gauleiter." (After Hitler's death, Rauff had made his way to Southern Chile, in the Magallanes province, where he became the manager of a lumber business. When the Bonn government tried to have him extradited to face charges for his Nazi crimes, the reactionary-minded majority in the Chilean judiciary sabotaged the extradition request. Rauff and his son now hold important posts in Pinochet's secret police.)

Rio Chico was somewhat more comfortable physically than the ramshackle Sheraton and the Tupahue whose "guests" were now under one roof. But it was also more depressing because it looked every bit the concentration camp. It had a quality of permanence; a foreboding of long-term incarceration.

As it turned out, because the camp now also accommodated other groups of prisoners, the nucleus of former Allende officials were able to learn about developments on the mainland through occasional clandestine contact with the new arrivals. And when one such group brought them a small shortwave radio smuggled in from Punta Arenas, their spirits soared. They hid the radio in the top section of the chimney of the woodburning stove that stood in the center of the barracks. Late in the evening they would take turns standing guard at the door in case of sudden Junta spot-check, while the rest hovered about the smoky stove, smothering their coughs and straining to hear the news.

They could pick up broadcasts from powerful transmitters in London, Moscow, Bonn, Havana, and other faraway capitals that frequently mentioned events in Chile. In February 1974 the prisoners were stunned to hear that even in the United States, whose government was so closely identified with the creation of the Junta, a congressional conference was held to discuss the Junta terror. And when they heard congressional critics of the Nixon Administration and American academic experts denounce the policies leading to the putsch, the excitement was heady. Locked away for months, with the nagging feeling that the world had all but forgotten them, this newsflash bearing directly on their role in history and on their predicament, Kirberg says, "rekindled hope in all of us."

But except for the high moments of news from abroad, life dragged on as usual—the same lentil soup dinners, the same work assignments in the forest, on the road and on the rock pile. And the same bitter, unrelenting wind battered the prisoners every day as they trudged through the mud to and from work.

Then one morning, about eight months after their arrival at Dawson, they were wakened at five o'clock, told to pack their essential belongings, such as socks and underwear, and get ready to leave in fifteen minutes. Whatever books—such as novels—they had been allowed to receive were to be left behind. They were given their usual breakfast and then told to wait, still with no explanation as to their destination. As an hour dragged by there were those who thought the whole episode might be one more cruel hoax concocted by the new commander. But not so. Suddenly they were ordered into formations and told to begin marching toward the airport, ten miles away. Whatever the eventual destination, everyone held on to the hope that it would be a march toward freedom, and all proceeded with a spirited step.

But it was still Dawson Island. "Soon we were forced to walk through a long stretch of road that was partially flooded," Professor Kirberg says, "and the worst was yet to come. We were ordered to take off our shoes, socks, pants, and underwear and negotiate a frigid stream with blocks of ice floating around us.

We made a kind of human chain, passing our bundled clothes and shoes from hand to hand until they reached those already on the other side of the river. While we were trying to hold on to each other, losing our footing, blue with cold, barely able to breathe, the camp officers drove by in large personnel carriers smiling and making obscene gestures at us.

"But we made it. Shivering, drying ourselves as best we could with handkerchiefs or extra shirts, we stumbled on toward the airport, now, of course, on the double. Once there we were put inside two small planes for the short flight to Punta Arenas, where we were reprocessed again, searched, then transferred to a Hercules transport. We were handcuffed and chained to the seats, and ordered not to talk. And this is how we made our nine-hour return trip to Santiago. We let ourselves dream of freedom—whatever that would have meant then—not able to imagine that once back in the capital we would all be split into small groups and sent to other concentration camps, some in the high Andean plateaus, others in the desert areas; some for six months, others for another two years.

"However, our Dawson Island stay had come to an end."

4

Chile's First Ladies
at the Mercy of General Pinochet

WHEN ALLENDE rushed from his home to the presidential
palace, his wife, Hortensia, was still asleep. Though the early
bulletins on the Valparaiso uprisings were ominous enough,
Allende continued to be confident that the odds were still on his
side. He therefore decided not to awaken his wife, who was still
trying to restore her strength following a long flight from Mexico
the day before. Señora Allende and her daughter Isabel had just
returned from an official courtesy visit to Mexico to convey
Chile's gratitude for Mexico's aid after the devastating earthquake
of 1970.

Señora Allende had been out of the country only a week, but
she was confronted at once with a dramatic change in the
political climate. "When we landed at the Santiago airport on
the afternoon of September 9th," she said in an interview in her
modest apartment in Mexico City, "we were met by my
husband, several government officials, and a group of friends.
Having been away I wasn't fully aware of the latest developments,
but I sensed almost immediately that my husband looked very
tense, nervous, not his usual self. And as we walked through the
airport lounge toward the exit, I was appalled to see small groups
of young toughs, members of the fascistic Patria y Libertad
organization, shouting at us, 'Down with Allende.' Hooliganism
from this group, as well as other Rightist gangs against the
Popular Unity government was something we had come to live
with. But I had not yet seen them attack so close to the person of
the President. Our security guards were about to scatter the
hoodlums, but Allende signaled to ignore them.

"This close-up demonstration of hate was frightening, and in
sharp contrast to the mood in Chile when I left the week before.

Hortensia Allende, widow of the slain President Salvador Allende, at a rally in London where protesters condemned the Junta coup. She is seen here with a bouquet given her by sympathizers. (Wide World Photos)

Then millions of workers were preparing celebrations to mark the third anniversary of Allende's election on September 4, 1970. Economic sabotage and deterioration of the economy had been going on for many months, but there was still tremendous enthusiasm, almost euphoria, across the country though mixed with growing anxiety. I was in Mexico on the anniversary itself, but I knew there had been huge parades all over Chile. In Santiago alone a million people shouted slogans in support of the government as they marched by the reviewing stand where Allende and leaders of the coalition parties were standing.

"The airport scene was also painfully different from our receptions on the trip. In stopovers in Bogota, Colombia, and Panama, large groups of newspaper reporters met us, all wanting to know how the Popular Unity government was faring and about the various social programs we had started. I realized from their questioning that the word 'Chile' had become a symbol of hope for all of Latin America's forgotten people. I encountered nothing but genuine sympathy and applause when people heard how the Popular Unity government was bringing about a New Deal for the Chilean people through constitutional, democratic means.

"The day after I got back I held a press conference to report on my experience in Mexico and on the warmth and respect with which Latin Americans regarded Chile. The conference was very well attended, and everything seemed quite normal. That evening, the last time I was to see my husband alive, we had dinner at home. Allende arrived with several cabinet ministers and aides, to continue the day's discussion of immediate problems facing the government. Orlando Letelier, just shifted from Foreign Minister to Defense Minister, Carlos Briones, and Augusto Olivares, among others, were there, as well as our daughter Isabel. I keep remembering one small thing that happened that evening. When my husband came home I went with him to our bedroom where he changed into casual clothes. He put on a new sportjacket, which seemed to fit him very handsomely. I complimented him on his appearance. He looked at himself in the mirror, paused for a moment, and as if in reply said, 'I wonder if *they* will let me wear it.' Shocked, I asked him, 'Are things really that bad?' He didn't answer, just thought for a moment and then said we'd better go down and join our guests. There was a bit of small talk as we sat down around the table and then, inevitably, conversation turned to the governmental emergencies. At one point Allende said, 'We have discussed my proposal several times. But now I have to make a decision. I will be speaking to the Chilean people tomorrow on national radio and television. I am going to tell them there will be a national referendum, a plebiscite to allow them to indicate their support or rejection of our programs. The present situation cannot continue. And if the people respond in the negative, I shall resign.'

"After dinner," Señora Allende said, "the President and ministers went to the study to consult on the text of the speech that Allende was to deliver the next day. Since I was still exhausted from my trip, I said good night and went to bed. And I knew nothing more about succeeding events until the next morning, when Allende called me from La Moneda. He still expressed confidence in the outcome but at the same time he urged me to phone our daughters and have them bring their children to join me at our home, which he thought would be the safest place for the moment. In that brief conversation, he urged me several times to speak to our daughters at once. A small group of security guards stationed at the gates of Tomás Moro Street around the clock, and a tank unit positioned at the entrance, did indeed add a feeling of security. But while I was talking, I didn't know that the military had already withdrawn both the tank and the guard.

"I immediately phoned my daughter Beatriz, but I couldn't reach her because she had already left for the presidential palace to be with her father. I did reach my younger daughter Isabel, as Allende had urged. But Isabel too felt that she should be with him. I tried calling a number of my friends that morning but apparently some of their phones were already no longer functioning; and some of them were continuously busy. A little while later I tried to phone my husband. Every time I called a different person would answer— 'The President is not at his desk,' or 'The President is in conference with his ministers.' I finally did reach the secretary of Daniel Vergara who told me that Vergara was with the President. It somehow reassured me to know that Vergara was there. He was a very direct and valiant individual. And it was under his direction and that of General Prats that the earlier attempt at a putsch—a tank attack on La Moneda on June

29, 1973—had been put down, with all the assailants taken prisoner.

"As you can see," Señora Allende said, smiling bitterly, "in the three years Allende had been in office, we had become accustomed to living with life-and-death emergencies. Only two days before the attack in June, the President's naval aide-de-camp Arturo Araya, whom Allende regarded with great affection, was assassinated. In the middle of August, there was another attempt at a putsch in Chillan. Perhaps you know this is the birthplace of the great patriot Bernardo O'Higgins, and several important government officials had gone there to participate in the celebration of his anniversary. The conspirators attempted to use air force units to behead the government then, but the coup was quickly squelched by loyalist forces.

"This time the situation seemed to me very grave indeed. I felt completely isolated—very much alone and very uncertain what I should do next. But there wasn't much time to ponder. Suddenly the house was shaking as though from an earthquake. The Junta's air force pilots were on a reconnaissance overflight. I called out to our driver and asked if the tank and the guards were in place. 'Señora,' he shouted back, 'there is no tank, nor for that matter are there any military at the gate.' He had hardly finished his sentence when the planes were over us again and this time they were dropping bombs. In seconds our lovely house was engulfed in flames, rubble and chaos. Coughing and choking from the pulverized masonry and staggering from shock, I recovered somewhat when our driver materialized at my side and said, 'Let's get out of here immediately. This is an inferno.' I owe my life to that driver. With him and a man from the guard contingent who had managed to stay behind out of loyalty to us, I left the house and the three of us drove toward the rear of the grounds adjacent to a neighboring nunnery. When we finally got out into the street, the driver turned to me and said, 'Now, Señora, where are we to go?' He answered his own question by suggesting that we take refuge at an embassy, but I wouldn't hear of that. I wasn't going to flee to seek asylum abroad while my family and country were under attack. Instead I asked him to drive to the home of a friend who lived close by, the former president of the Chilean Development Bank.

"Except for my purse, I had left everything behind. I had no passport, no money, and no clothes except what I had on. As I was leaving the house I could perhaps have retrieved a few of the personal belongings, such as family photographs, but I could not convince myself that it was all over. Somehow I felt that just as in the past, this catastrophe too would be overcome and I would be back."

On the advice of her friends, who called the Mexican Embassy, and on the insistence of the Mexican ambassador who sent his personal car for her protection, Señora Allende did go to the Mexican Embassy that afternoon. There she learned of her husband's death, which the Junta announced on radio and television as a suicide. The following day, Hortensia Allende, with her daughters and a nephew, was allowed to accompany a sealed coffin that contained Allende's body on a flight to Valparaiso to bury the President in the family plot. The Junta guard refused to open the casket, despite Señora Allende's insistence that she was entitled to see the body. The day after, she left Chile on a Mexican plane. From Mexico City, she carries on a campaign that, she believes, will one day lead to the overthrow of the Pinochet regime.

While Señora Allende was desperately trying to reach friends from her home, a number of them were trying to reach her. Two who were very close to her, Moy Tohá, wife of José Tohá, and Isabel Letelier, the wife of Tohá's successor, Orlando Letelier, were especially anxious when they heard that the Allende residence had been bombed. Despite overwhelming anxiety for their husbands, who they believed were with the President in La Moneda, each kept trying to contact Señora Allende, something which was no longer possible because of the bombing.

Both women had already been traumatized by what they had experienced on the morning of the coup. The Tohás learned of the rebellion on the radio at about seven in the morning; the Leteliers were alerted to the impending catastrophe by the President. As Señora Tohá recalls it, "As soon as we heard the news, José called La Moneda and talked directly to Allende. He then turned to me and said, 'I'm leaving for the palace at once.' First he drove both of our children to his mother's home, which we thought would be safer than ours. He also left a small pistol there for me, with the appropriate permit. We Chileans have always been very law-abiding," Señora Tohá added with a smile. "Then he went on to La Moneda, and I tried all morning to get him on the phone. But ironically enough, at the time of the first bombing attack he called me saying that he and his brother Jaime, Briones, and Foreign Minister Almeyda were still un-harmed because they were in the foreign ministry wing of the palace, which remained unscathed. The brunt of the attack, he said, was on the area closest to the President's office. Then there was complete silence, and finally the phone went dead. I heard nothing more about what had happened to him and the others until four o'clock that afternoon. I tried calling several top-ranking officers of the military in the various departments, but to no avail. In the many months that my husband was Defense Minister, before he was forced out of office by the Rightist majority in Congress, I had come to know admirals, generals, and air force commanders on a very personal basis. They and their wives were often in our house. But now I couldn't get past their secretaries.

"I finally did get to a Commander Merrick who said, 'Señora Tohá, don't worry, your husband is all right. He, Briones, Almeyda, and Jaime are now safe and under guard in the Ministry of Defense building.' And that was all. I continued my telephone assault on just about everybody that I could possibly have met during my husband's Defense Ministry tenure. It was not until about eleven that night that I finally reached Admiral Carvajal, who in a very friendly fashion addressed me by my first name: 'Moy, don't be alarmed, your husband is perfectly well.' I screamed at him, 'But where is he? What is being done to him?' I demanded. Except for a few generalities I could not get any further information out of him. His replies were scarcely reassuring after what I had heard and seen earlier that evening, when the four leaders of the Junta appeared on television to tell the people that they were now in command."

Señora Tohá's eyes blazed with anger when she talked of personal as well as political betrayal by the people who seized the government. A strikingly good-looking, spirited woman in her early forties, highly articulate, she sketched the personality changes of the Junta leaders—people who had been her acquaintances and even her friends. "I swear," she said, "these individuals who I had come to know so well socially, who played with my children and who, so many times, showed such personal concern over José's pressure of office or about an occasional illness, were almost unrecognizable on television that night. It was not only because of their rantings; they seemed to have transformed physically. Their total appearance was different. They appeared demented; their eyes bulged; they shouted their wild charges against the Allende regime. Most vociferous was Pinochet, who really was like a madman. At times he was incoherent. It became obvious that his crazy accusations were

Moy Tohá (left) widow of former Defense Minister José Tohá, strangled to death by Junta agents while hospitalized in Santiago, and Isabel Letelier, widow of Orlando Letelier, Tohá's successor in the Allende cabinet, who was murdered by Junta assassins in Washington, D.C. in 1976. (Photo by Peter Helmich)

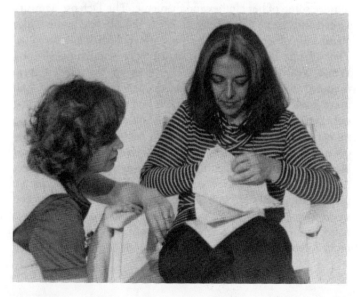

attempts to justify his betrayal of trust. 'For every soldier killed by a Marxist,' he threatened, 'there will be at least ten executions.' It was impossible to imagine these people as heads of any government. One assumes that in the launching of a new regime, its leaders would want to pacify the country, calm its inhabitants, bring about some kind of order as soon as possible. But the Junta was doing just the opposite. Rancor, the venom of revenge, and the promise of death were the leitmotifs of the new order.

"The next day the Defense Department phoned to tell me to pack a suitcase for José, who, I was told, was about to be banished from Santiago. Late that night there was a knock at the door and an officer said he was there to pick up the suitcase. He also gave me a note in which José asked me to include a coat, some cigarettes, and some sweets. He said it was extremely cold where he was going and perhaps chocolates or sugar would help keep up his body heat. 'But where are they sending my husband?' I demanded to know. The officer claimed ignorance and wanted to get on with his assignment.

"Early the next morning I finally heard from Señora Allende, who was safe at the Mexican Embassy. She asked me to speak to the Junta officials to authorize me to go to Tomás Moro to retrieve some of her clothes and medicine. The Defense Ministry agreed and the next day I was driven to the Allende home under guard—an officer and two soldiers armed with machine guns. The Allende home was a sad war casualty, something out of a World War II battle scene. The trees in the garden were uprooted and the lawn was slashed open by the bombs. The house itself took two direct bomb hits and some of it was burned out, and yet sections of it were still holding up, including the staircase. The inside was littered with rubble. As I climbed the circular stairwell, I saw the remains of a beautiful statue, its head blown off and one of its arms hacked away. I learned that after the bombardment, soldiers sent to stand guard had ransacked the place. The Allendes' clothes were literally bayoneted to pieces: sleeves were torn off dresses, jackets, and coats. There was scarcely anything I could salvage that would be of any use. I went on to Allende's study, where Señora Allende had told me I would find about five hundred dollars in a metal box. The box was there but the money was gone.

"Nearly all the works of art, a collection made up of gifts to Allende by admirers from many countries even before he became president, were broken or torn to shreds. Among the paintings that were totally destroyed were those by Diego Rivera, Picasso, and Guyasamin. Strips of canvas and broken frames fluttered in the wind that blew in from the smashed windows and the broken walls. All the bookcases were empty; many of the books were ripped apart and all were in mad disarray. A cloud of death and despair seemed to hang across the room. I leaned against the table, traumatized by the havoc about me, and looked around like a mourner at a wake. Somewhere I heard a noise like a moan. I picked my way across the rubble toward the adjoining room. And there, on what remained of a sofa, was a scene that put me in tears. There lay Allende's dog with a litter of newborn pups, whimpering and nestling close to it. In a way, my tears were tears of joy. Within this context of hell and death, there was an affirmation of life. I walked over to this little family, petted the pups and stood helpless, unable to provide them with either milk or food.

"I filled the suitcase with whatever I thought might still be useful (I did find the medicines), and we drove off to the Mexican Embassy. The next day Señora Allende flew to Mexico as a guest of the Mexican government, and that was also the day my husband, and the others who were in the first contingent sent to Dawson Island concentration camp, left Santiago.

"Several of us whose husbands were in that contingent kept almost hourly telephone contact trying to find out where they were being banished. Isabel Letelier, frustrated like I was with the inability to reach any one of the former acquaintances who were now in power, said to me, 'We must take a firm stand. After all, we were known as the first ladies, since our husbands were cabinet ministers. Why don't we try to use what remains of that privilege to go to talk to Pinochet directly and find out once and for all what they are doing to our husbands?' I quickly agreed. It scarcely occurred to us that we too would be running great risks by going to the Junta headquarters. We were the wives of the top

Allende associates, and that could have been enough to indict us as anti-Junta accomplices. Already we were hearing rumors that many women were under arrest and some had been executed, but that didn't stop us.

"Before going to Pinochet I suggested we try to see General Bonilla, whom I knew very well. He and his wife had been our dinner guests quite often. But when we reached his office at the Junta headquarters we were told that he could not be disturbed, he was in conference. I became quite impatient and told the receptionist it was imperative that he speak to us. The receptionist said, 'Why don't you leave your phone number, we'll be in touch with you.' I snapped back, 'General Bonilla knows my phone number better than I do.'

"At that moment, as we were about to leave, I suddenly saw Pinochet coming down the corridor. He hastened his step and rushed over to us with a big smile on his face. As he approached us Isabel whispered to me, 'Moy, I have a feeling he is going to embrace you.' I was mortified. The waiting room was full of newspaper reporters and photographers, TV cameramen, foreign correspondents. I had the awful feeling that he would throw his arms around me as a photographer snapped the picture, and the whole world would see the Junta chief embracing the wife of the former Defense Minister, now exiled to some God-forsaken hellhole. I took a kind of diagonal stance, with my hands in front of me to ward off that possibility. But there he was, strutting toward me like a king, with all the television lights on him. And once again Isabel said, 'Moy, he's going to embrace you.' And he did in fact fling his arms about me and even tried to kiss me. I forcefully held out my arms and threw myself back and at the same time I said, 'I have to talk to you immediately about José.' Pinochet replied, 'Don't worry, your husband is fine. I will see you tomorrow and we'll talk.' There he was, as informal as usual, with the same affable smile, as though nothing had happened.

"The next day Irma Almeyda, the wife of the Foreign Minister, joined Isabel and me. There was a change in the ministry guard from the day before; the soldiers did not know us and were quite arrogant as we were about to enter the building.

But when we identified ourselves, the names of Letelier, Tohá, and Almeyda, which had dominated the headlines of the Chilean press for the past three years, had an electrifying effect. The lower rungs of the military still didn't quite know how to cope with the new situation and were confused about who was and wasn't persona grata. It was ironic how the guards' attitude changed on hearing our names. They snapped to attention and one of them shouted to the receptionist, 'The wives of three cabinet ministers are here to see General Pinochet,' and they saluted as we walked inside.

"When we were ushered into the presence of Pinochet he seemed to be totally different from the day before, with none of the geniality he had displayed then and before the coup. At first he was aloof, a stranger. 'Good morning, ladies. What is it you want?' he asked as though he were meeting us for the first time. 'Well,' we replied, 'we came to talk to you about our husbands.' 'Your husbands are perfectly well,' he barked. Then he suddenly went off into a harangue about our husbands' 'Marxist involvement.' As he continued with what became a tirade, especially against Allende, whom he called 'that horrible creature now six feet under,' he became more and more agitated."

As Isabel Letelier recalls that interview, "Pinochet became quite abusive and shouted at us for about twenty minutes. The veins on his neck swelled, his face alternately turned red and purple. There was obviously guilt and embarrassment which he tried to mask with this rowdy scene. He was 'General Almighty.' We three, who had spent so many social evenings with him and his wife, now had to undergo the humiliation of being stopped and searched for weapons before being admitted to see him. He had all the planes, all the tanks, and all the firing squads. And we, his former friends, with our husbands in jail or worse, stood utterly defenseless.

"I couldn't quite believe," Isabel says, "that this was the same Pinochet who would fawn over his superiors, practically grovel before them. I remember Orlando telling me how uncomfortable he felt dealing with Pinochet. He said Pinochet was always obsequious, always rushing to help him on with his coat, or carry his briefcase when walking through the corridors. Orlando said that Pinochet often reminded him of a barber-shop attendant armed with a whisk broom, waiting for a tip.

"We didn't quite know how to react to his shouting," Señora Letelier says. "We were calm, but terribly apprehensive as he continued his diatribe. 'It's a shame the way Allende ran this country; the way he and your husbands ran it into the ground; the way they tore its economy to pieces. We didn't want to take over but we were compelled to do it by the will of the Chilean people.' Finally Moy gently interrupted him, saying, 'General, each of us here has an immediate problem which you can help resolve. Can we write to our husbands?' And again he began to sputter and shout, 'No, no, no.' His behavior was that of a psychopath. He continued to insult and berate Allende and his counselors. 'Even though the traitor is now buried deep in the ground, we're going to prosecute him nevertheless. He is not going to get away with it.'

"Moy tried again. 'General,' she said, 'my children—you know my little José pretty well—want to send a letter to their father and would like to receive an answer.' I believe she touched something of what remained in Pinochet that was human. He obviously remembered the times he had brought toy soldiers to the little boy when Tohá was still his boss. At this point Pinochet, somewhat more controlled, said, 'All right. Bring the letters here to me and they will be forwarded to José.' So Señora Almeyda and I asked whether we too could send letters to our husbands. He grudgingly agreed. And we went further and said, 'How about all those others now jailed with our husbands, could their wives send letters to them?' He snarled, 'Enough, enough,' and marched out of the room.

"We gathered as many letters as we could and brought them back to Pinochet's office the following day. And I must admit he kept his word. Almost, that is. They were delivered to our husbands four months later."

5

Sweden's Heroic Ambassador
Saves 1,300 Lives

I AM THE SWEDISH AMBASSADOR! You're violating Swedish sovereignty! You're violating international law!" This was Harald Edelstam, shouting at a dozen Junta soldiers and policemen. "They were beating us with their fists, and sometimes with their pistol butts," the Swedish diplomat recalls. "We tried to fight back, but there were only four of us, myself and three of my staff."

This was one of Edelstam's many confrontations with the Pinochet government as he tried to rescue Chileans and foreigners from torture or execution. In this instance, the altercation developed when Junta soldiers came to abduct a woman, a suspected anti-Fascist, from a private clinic, where only an hour before she had had an emergency operation for a bleeding ulcer. Edelstam and the Junta military agreed earlier that the woman was to remain under Swedish jurisdiction.

Edelstam's first skirmish with the Junta began with the very first day of the coup. As was his habit, he began the morning with a brisk walk from his home to the embassy. When he was about to enter the building, some of his staff members ran out to meet him. "The army is marching toward Santiago, and Valparaiso is reported to be in the hands of the navy," they told him. "I could scarcely believe it," Edelstam said. "Only ten days before I lunched with Allende and we touched on the ever-growing political and economic crises in Chile. And despite the panicky feelings of many that the Rightists were involved in all kinds of conspiracies to topple the government, Allende was confident that there were enough important generals within the military who would not permit this to happen. But now, obviously, the putsch was indeed here, with the generals and admirals in the forefront."

The news of the Junta putsch was broadcast at 8:15 A.M. An hour later the roar of military aircraft deafened Santiago. Helicopters were buzzing the city. Telephone and Telex communication with the outside world began to break down. Edelstam was able to keep in touch with Stockholm by means of a powerful two-way radio. Strangely enough, in most of Santiago itself the local phone service was normal throughout the coup.

At noon the Junta radio began warning that a curfew would start at 3 P.M. and that anyone on the streets would face summary execution. Soon after these announcements the embassy staff began rushing home and Edelstam started to return to his house. But on reaching the immediate area he was stopped by soldiers who told him it was out of bounds. He protested vigorously, asserting his rights to get to his home. Finally allowed to proceed, he quickly realized that the dozens of armored personnel carriers and heavily armed Junta soldiers were there to surround the Cuban Embassy, only two blocks from where Edelstam lived. (Because of Fidel Castro's strong sympathy for the Allende regime, the Junta generals considered the Cubans their archenemies.) He was scarcely inside his own house when he heard machine-gun fire. He hurried out again, and saw about 150 soldiers advancing on the Cuban Embassy, some of whom were sporadically firing away. To his experienced eye it looked like an assault that would end in a massacre. Edelstam pushed his way towards the officer in charge, showed him his diplomatic credentials, and demanded to enter the Cuban Embassy.

There was a good deal of arguing, but Edelstam's 6'4" height and his no-nonsense manner finally seemed to cow the officer who let him go through. Almost stereotypically a diplomat in appearance, or what people expect an ambassador to look like, Edelstam is a slender, handsome man. Although by nature a mild, serene person, with none of the pomposity so frequently associated with diplomats, he is also capable of presenting a stern, implacable facade which on this occasion got him onto the Cuban grounds.

There Edelstam was confronted with a chaotic scene. The

Harald Edelstam, Sweden's former Ambassador to Chile,
addressing a Stockholm meeting in support of Junta prisoners.
Edelstam was outsted from his Santiago post by the Fascist regime
because he gave asylum in his embassy to about 1,300 Chileans
fleeing from Junta terror. (Fotograf Reidar Holmen)

embassy building was pockmarked with bullet holes. Embassy automobiles had been shelled and were now aflame in the parking area of the courtyard. Inside, the Cuban ambassador was at his desk with a huge bandage on his arm covering a gunshot wound from the first assault. Other staff workers had been cut by flying glass from shattered windows, or had less serious bullet wounds. Everybody, including those who had been hurt, was working—destroying documents, packing suitcases, keeping vigil at doors and windows, and occasionally returning the fire with small arms. The shooting subsided, however, when Edelstam went inside. The Cubans asked Edelstam to get in touch with the Junta leadership and remonstrate with them, reminding them that such a violation of diplomatic immunity was an act of war. For a starter Edelstam went out to the military surrounding the Cuban grounds and warned them of the serious international consequences of their actions. Somewhat uncertain in the absence of instructions from the Junta high command, they promised Edelstam there would be no more shooting.

But late that evening Edelstam heard rifle fire again, and some of the stray bullets hit his own residence. Early the next morning Edelstam found the Cuban embassy surrounded by many more soldiers than the day before, and they now had cannon emplacements and armored cars. "So I said to myself," Edelstam recalls, "I really must do something to stop this impending carnage. The military were clearly preparing for a knockout blow.

"This time when I tried to get over to the Cubans the military kept pushing me back. It seemed as though most of my energy was being spent in persuading the Chilean officers to let me go through. Suddenly I recognized a huge bear of a man, an artillery captain I had met some months before at a reception. I succeeded in getting to him and saying hello. When he saw me the man's eyes almost popped out of his head. He practically screamed at me, 'Are you crazy, Ambassador? Don't you know there is a curfew, and that we have the right to shoot you on sight?' His huge frame was shaking with anger. 'Yes, I know all about it,' I said. 'But my Cuban colleagues are in danger and I have the diplomatic right and obligation to see how I can help them.'" Angry but somewhat taken aback by Edelstam's persistence, the officer grudgingly agreed to let him through, on condition that he stay only a couple of minutes. "He followed me to the door," Edelstam said. "I knocked and the Cubans let me in and shut the door behind me.

"Fifteen minutes later the military began shouting, 'Ambassador, get out!' I shouted back that I had no such intentions. The officers were furious. They had actually been planning a cannon assault on the Cuban Embassy. My being there prevented them from carrying it out." In the meantime the Cuban ambassador and Edelstam were discussing what to do next. Several hours went by without incident. Then at about 2 P.M. they saw a small man on the street, running toward the officers in charge. He waved a piece of paper and they made way for him as he ran up the stairs and knocked at the door of the embassy. There he waved the paper again and yelled that he was an official from the Junta protocol office. When he was allowed in, he began without further ceremony to read a statement from the Junta government that Chile had broken relations with Cuba and that the ambassador and all his staff were ordered to leave Chile by midnight. Buses would come for them precisely at 11 o'clock that evening to take them to the airport.

"Considering the fact that the Cubans had less than twelve hours to evacuate their personnel and whatever property, I told my Cuban colleagues that I would take charge of the Cuban interests even though I had not yet conferred with my government. But there was no other way to help defend the Cuban embassy from violence and vandalism," Edelstam explained, shrugging his shoulders to indicate that it was obviously the logical step to take. He had one of his secretaries drive over from the Swedish Embassy with a huge Swedish flag, wrapped in paper, and placed at the entrance of the embassy. That night, as the Cubans began boarding the buses for the airport, the Junta soldiers surrounding the embassy grounds were obviously preparing to move in and take over the premises. But as the last Cuban quickly lowered his nation's colors and ran with it toward the bus, Edelstam rushed out, alone, unfurled the Swedish flag, and began hoisting it up the flagpole in the courtyard.

"Stop that, stop it!" the commanding officer bellowed at Edelstam. But here was this tall man, determined and impervious to threat, continuing to run up the flag and shouting back that this was now Swedish territory. As the Chilean officer made a move to enter the grounds, the Swedish diplomat warned him formally that he was violating Swedish sovereignty. The captain drew back, confused. The soldiers milled around, thwarted and enraged. With the chain of command not yet fully set, the officers at the Cuban chancellery didn't know where to get immediate instructions, and therefore didn't know how far they could go.

"I was quite alone; almost, that is. For with me was my first Chilean refugee, Max Marambio, a young man who had been with Allende at La Moneda the day before, and had managed to escape and find his way to the Cuban embassy.

"It was a dark night. Huge army floodlights were poking at the embassy buildings, constantly sweeping across the grounds or pausing for a moment at a door or a window, as though hoping to uncover some unusual development. And Max and I, for our part, were scurrying about inside, bolting doors and securing the shutters of the windows. And so that night passed without incident."

Early in the morning Edelstam phoned his office and one of his secretaries, a sturdy, husky man in his thirties, volunteered to come to his relief. Edelstam then left for his own embassy, where he was greeted with the spectacle of nearly two hundred people, mostly women, with a sprinkling of men and some children, all pressing against the locked gates trying to get in for asylum. Edelstam was in a quandary. Like most European nations, Sweden has no reciprocal conventions with other countries to provide sanctuary to political opponents of existing governments. At first Edelstam tried to persuade the crowd to go to the Latin American embassies, which do have such reciprocal arrangements.* But both the Chileans and the anti-Fascists from other

* With their histories of political instability and the frequency of government changes in their respective countries, asylum agreements among various countries have been convenient expedients for those fleeing from persecution.

Latin American countries argued frantically that they could not depend on the embassies of Chile's neighbors, with their reactionary governments.*

Even though he had not yet had time to confer with Stockholm about the diplomatic legality of offering asylum, Edelstam opened the doors of the embassy and the refugees piled in. "It was a heartbreaking scene, the anxiety and terror on the faces of these people, many of whom saw their neighbors bayoneted, or were forced to look on as their relatives were beaten, kicked, or shot down before their eyes."

Word spread quickly and dozens more refugees besieged the embassy pleading to get in. Many jumped over the fences surrounding the chancellery and forced themselves into the building. By the third day of the putsch the embassy had become a hostel for some 300 people. "We were making sandwiches all day, heating milk for the children and trying to improvise sleeping accommodations," the Swedish ambassador said.

Edelstam had to account for these developments to the Swedish Foreign Office. "It was, as you would say, the cart before the horse. I first allowed the refugees in, and then I cabled my superiors for permission to do so. The word from Stockholm came three days later. In effect the message said: 'We approve your refugee asylum action. But don't do it again, at least not before you confer with us.' But by the time the message arrived I had two hundred more people seeking protection."

Rescuing people fleeing from Fascist dictatorships was not exactly a novel experience for Edelstam. His first such involvement dates back to 1943, when he was a junior member of the Swedish Embassy staff in Norway. In a variety of daring operations he smuggled Norwegian and Danish resistance fighters to the Swedish border and into freedom, since Sweden was neutral during World War II. The Swedish government yanked him out of Norway, and just in time. It was only a matter of hours before the Nazis raided the place in which he was

_____
*Only Mexico was helping in the first days of the coup, and the Mexican Embassy was quickly swamped. The Mexicans were taking in hundreds of refugees each day and flying them out of Santiago on Mexican transport planes.

monitoring German radio communications. The Swedish press at once began to call the dark-haired diplomat, "The Black Pimpernel."

His life was saved but his career was seriously compromised. The Swedish Foreign Ministry took a dim view of Edelstam's anti-Nazi activities and reacted even more harshly to his own criticism of Sweden's neutrality as Hitler swept over Europe. This hostile attitude continued for some time, even after Edelstam was decorated for bravery by the Danish and Norwegian governments. Edelstam was broken in rank and relegated to performing routine tasks in the home office. But fortunes shifted, a new administration came in, and Edelstam was quickly promoted. He served as consul general in Turkey and Poland and then as ambassador to Indonesia, Guatemala, Chile, and Algeria.

Despite the painful personal setbacks after his Norwegian exploits, Edelstam stuck to his credo, to extend a helping hand to those fighting against injustice: "I may be my country's official emissary but I am also a human being." When he was in Indonesia soon after the CIA-supported takeover by the Suharto government, which slaughtered some half a million people suspected of being Leftists, the Swedish diplomat once again was in the middle of things. Sometimes he would drive alone for two days across the huge island to keep a secret rendezvous and rescue somebody slated for execution.

His Chilean activities exposed him to even greater dangers than he had faced in Norway or Indonesia. His efforts to provide asylum at the Swedish embassy could scarcely be kept secret, considering the scope of the rescue operations. In little more than three months the Swedish embassy enabled some 1,300 anti-Junta refugees to flee Chile and find a haven in Sweden and many other countries.

His pro-Allende sympathies were a matter of public knowledge. This was not especially surprising. Even though Sweden is a monarchy, its government in the seventies was Socialist, headed by Prime Minister Olaf Palme, who is Edelstam's personal friend. When Edelstam came to Chile in October 1972, a little less than a year before the putsch, Allende's reform programs received enthusiastic support in Sweden. Edelstam found his new assignment exciting; he felt he was to witness the transformation of a semi-colonial territory into an independent country with a Socialist program. He felt particularly fortunate that his role was not only to be that of an observer but also of someone who could offer Sweden's economic assistance to help Chile fulfill some of its projects.

On his arrival in Santiago he was received by President Allende at La Moneda, where he presented his ambassadorial credentials. As he came out of La Moneda a military band struck up the Chilean and Swedish anthems, but immediately behind the band, out in the open square some distance away from the palace, was an ominous portent of the future. Members of Patria y Libertad, which received financial and organizational aid from the CIA, were shouting obscenities and pushing forward to disrupt the ceremony for Edelstam. The police opened up with a water cannon to disperse the crowd, while the band began playing faster and faster to wind up the ceremony as quickly as possible. And as Edelstam was being escorted into the official car to return to his embassy, a strong gust of wind picked up some of the cannon water and dropped it directly on Edelstam and other officials. "This was my baptismal into troubled Chile," he recalls with a chuckle.

During his first visit, Edelstam had asked Allende what in his opinion was the most important accomplishment in the first two years of his administration. Allende thought for a moment and then said: "The best thing I have done so far is to give every Chilean child half a liter of milk daily." Having done his diplomatic homework, Edelstam knew that Allende's preoccupation with Chile's infant malnutrition began when he was Minister of Public Health, many years before he became President. Allende said as early as 1940 that if ever he became President the first thing he would do would be to provide children with free milk. The Swedish milk industry had developed a fish-protein additive for milk that did not change its taste, and Allende told Edelstam that the first project he would ask the Swedish government to help with was building a huge dairy plant to produce special protein-reinforced milk for children.

"This was the great humanitarian side of Allende," Edelstam says. "Among his primary objectives was to help children attain their full potential; and to place emphasis on human needs in general, with defense spending and other such commitments way down on the list of the nation's priorities."

Considering his very special concern for Allende and the people around him, it was not entirely unexpected that Edelstam would throw himself into the rescue activities as energetically as he had. He and his staff worked around the clock organizing ways to feed their guests and devising plans to speed their departures under Swedish protection. To augment the normal embassy staff strength of fifteen people, Edelstam enlisted the support of some thirty Swedish volunteers who were semi-permanent residents in Chile.

The volunteers would venture out on various food patrols to forage for vegetables, flour, and bread, to feed the ever-growing refugee guest roll. Despite a rather spare diet, with fish or meat available on rare occasions, nobody went hungry. Because of the crowded quarters people ate in groups of twenty. Some did the cooking and some the serving. There were shifts of those cleaning the embassy and the kitchen. There were no petty squabbles over duties. Anxiety and grief seemed to cement the bond among the refugees.

It was not uncommon, Edelstam recalls, for people to awaken from nightmares as they relived their horrifying experiences. But there were unexpected morale builders, too. When a baby was born to one of the Chilean women, the procedure went off without a hitch; there was no doctor but plenty of expert midwives. Even those who had seen their husbands or sons murdered, or seized at gunpoint and carried off in army vans, found some comfort in this symbol of continuity of life.

The Swedes organized amateur concerts or even dancing parties. "At times," Edelstam says, "these terrorized people would sing and dance, while stony-faced Junta guards stood around the embassy listening, armed to the teeth, itching to blast us out of existence."

It was not exactly a continuous party, of course. Edelstam's guests were in a state of constant mental anguish. From time to time there would be the dreadful news that someone's father, husband, or brother had been shot or tortured to death, or had simply disappeared.

By the fourth day of the coup the refugees were coming in droves. And so Edelstam converted the Cuban Embassy and later the Cuban trade offices uptown into shelters, under Swedish jurisdiction. Edelstam depended on two expedients to lessen the refugee population pressure. One was to secure safe conduct passes from the Junta so that he could have them flown out of Chile to Sweden. Since most of those at the embassy were Allende activists, Edelstam and his staff would dream up new names for them which were submitted to Junta authorities for exit passes. It was slow going. The Junta would provide only about twenty such passes a week. The other means of reducing the guest load was to transfer small groups, and sometimes only one person at a time, to friendly embassies which in turn would try to transport them out of Chile. By this time, in addition to Sweden and Mexico, Venezuela, Costa Rica, and Finland were also taking people in small numbers.

But Edelstam's smuggling of the refugees to other embassies was a nerve-wracking procedure. Junta police and soldiers were ever on the lookout, searching automobiles and challenging passenger identities. Many people underwent dramatic cosmetic changes in the embassy before starting out on their trips. Men would frequently take on the appearance of women and vice versa. Clean-shaven youths would suddenly sprout beards and curly-haired women plastered down their hair with gel creams.

That same week, Edelstam was confronted with yet another problem. He learned that about thirty Swedes were detained at what had become Santiago's "house of horrors," the football stadium jammed with thousands of Chileans as well as foreigners suspected of being pro-Allende. These Swedes were mostly young teachers, agronomists, or technicians who had come to

Chile to contribute their skills to some of the Allende government-sponsored development programs.

When Edelstam hurried down to investigate, a Colonel
Espinoza, who was in charge of the hastily set up "interrogation"—meaning torture—facilities, appeared flattered at having
an ambassador call on him. He lied politely that there were no
Swedes on the premises, and then tried to shake off the
Ambassador by making appointments, presumably for further
discussions on the matter, at weird hours. Edelstam was obliged
to show up at 7 A.M. or at 11 P.M. or just sit and wait in the
reception area for endless number of hours. A few days later,
while waiting for Espinoza, Edelstam saw some Red Cross
people come in. "So I walked over to these elderly girl scouts and
said, 'Look here. You must help me. This is indeed a scandalous
situation. The Swedes have never done any harm to your
country. You must prevail upon this man to see me and release
my countrymen.'" The Red Cross people were impressed, went
to Espinoza and eventually pressured him to respond to
Edelstam's demands.

The immediate result was that Espinoza discontinued the so-
called interrogation of the Swedes and agreed to begin processing
them for exit visas out of Chile. But this was done at the rate of
two or three a day, so that Edelstam invariably had to spend a few
hours each day at the stadium to speed the procedure.

Burdened as he was with the growing refugee population in his
embassy, and now taxed with the urgency to protect his own
nationals at the stadium, Edelstam nevertheless became even
further involved by trying to rescue individuals who were still at
large but faced certain death if apprehended. Every day there
were phone calls or messages from someone on the run urgently
pleading to be picked up. After carefully evaluating each call
with some of his Chilean guests at the embassy, Edelstam would
take on these missions and go out with his chauffeur, a trusted
and dedicated staff member. At times, to make sure he was not
being followed, Edelstam would have two cars leave the Swedish
garage at once, both at top speed, so that the Junta guards would
not be sure which car to pursue. If the trick didn't work and if the
Edelstam car was followed, the Ambassador would drive around

for a while, return, and then try the same thing all over again a little while later.

Most of Edelstam's lonely forays were at night, through the semi-lit deserted streets of downtown Santiago. Shutters were drawn over store fronts and apartment windows. Chile's traditionally gay and cheerful capital was a ghost city. Occasionally the eerie stillness was shattered by the crackle of machine-gun fire as Junta troops raided a home or factory suspected of hiding Allende sympathizers. Every so often there would be the sound of shells exploding in the hilly outskirts of Santiago, evidence of pockets of resistance that refused to yield to the Junta takeover.

Once Edelstam was able to elude his pursuers his car would begin weaving its way to some out-of-the-way rendezvous where a man or woman was hiding in a doorway or an alley awaiting rescue. Trigger-happy Junta soldiers stationed at street intersections, brainwashed into believing that Cubans or Russians were about to invade their homeland, were only too ready to summarily execute anyone even faintly suspicious. Edelstam's only shield against such a finale was the slender Swedish pennant attached to the hood of his car, and his diplomatic credentials.

Edelstam's explorations were usually successful, but the military were increasingly suspicious of him. They also precipitated a series of provocative situations, making Edelstam's life ever more difficult. There were at least three incidents in the very first week of the coup that resulted in international headlines concerning Edelstam's efforts in rescuing Chilean refugees.

On the fifth day following the coup, Edelstam got word that there would be a new attack on the Cuban chancellery, now packed with refugees, protected only by the Swedish flag still flapping in the breeze. He felt that his only means of defense would depend upon the cooperation of some of his colleagues from the diplomatic corps. He asked several ambassadors but only India's ambassador agreed to help. And so on the day of the expected assault, the Indian diplomat and his wife drove up to the Cuban Embassy. In clear view of the Chilean soldiers they were greeted by Edelstam at the door and escorted inside. The Indian couple spent the night in the embassy, thwarting the Junta's plan to take over Edelstam's fortress.

"It was a very brave act by the Indian couple," Edelstam says. "For that night, more so than usually, there were many hair-raising activities aimed at destroying the morale of those inside the Cuban compound. There was periodic shooting around the embassy grounds. Helicopters continuously buzzed overhead, and blinding army floodlights swept across the buildings."

No sooner did he succeed in getting the Cuban situation in hand, thanks to the help he received from his Indian colleague, than he faced an ever more serious development in his own embassy, one in which his ambassadorial status was threatened.

An attractive Uruguayan woman, about thirty years old, was among several dozen refugees crowding the embassy doors hoping to get asylum. Scarcely inside, she collapsed; she was running a high fever and in extreme pain. An attempt at first aid by the embassy staff didn't work. "We thought her condition was critical, that she would not survive," Edelstam says. "So I phoned various doctors, pleading with them to come quickly; it was a matter of life and death, I thought. No matter how I implored them, of the first twenty-six doctors that I was able to reach, none dared to show up. Finally, on my twenty-seventh try, a physician on the staff of a private clinic nearby agreed to make the call." Following a quick diagnosis the doctor said she was suffering from an acute ulcer accompanied by massive hemorrhage. Immediate surgery was imperative. After an hour of thorny negotiation, Edelstam and the captain of the Junta security guard stationed at the embassy reached an agreement to extend Swedish jurisdiction for the woman, while she remained at the clinic. "So we placed her in my car and drove to the clinic, with a military jeep right behind us. The Junta officer in charge," Edelstam explained, "actually thought the woman would try to make a getaway."

However, the Junta broke the agreement scarcely an hour after the surgery was completed. Edelstam received a telephone call from someone at the clinic, who in a hushed, panicky voice said that a group of soldiers had arrived to arrest the patient. Edelstam and three of his staff raced to the clinic. A heated verbal exchange between the Junta soldiers and Edelstam and his aides over custody rights soon took on a more physical character as the soldiers attempted to wheel the bed, with the patient on it, into the corridor on the way to a police van outside.

"We were trying to hold on to the head of the bed," Edelstam says, "the soldiers and policemen were at the other end, straining to drag the bed out of the room. Sometimes they managed to get the bed out into the corridor, but we then succeeded to drag it back."

While this bizarre tug-of-war was under way, the Ambassador managed to place a number of phone calls to other members of the diplomatic corps to come to his aid at the clinic. But this being Sunday many of his colleagues were not to be reached, and those who were refused to cooperate. The Peruvian Ambassador said he was about to go to the country for the day. The Ambassador of the Vatican said he would not engage in anything as "undiplomatic" as what Edelstam proposed. "No, no, no," he told Edelstam, "I cannot get mixed up in this. This would be meddling into the internal affairs of Chile."

Edelstam tried the Chinese Embassy, but there too he was turned down. The Chinese would have nothing to do with refugees because "we are not allowed to do so," Edelstam was told. "We have instructions not to become involved." And he couldn't look to the Soviet or other Eastern European Socialist countries because they had already severed diplomatic relations with Junta Chile.

The only diplomat who responded to Edelstam's appeal was the Ambassador of France. As he entered the room he beheld a drag-out fist fight between the Swedish Ambassador and the Junta police. His serene, mildmannered colleague was exchanging blow for blow with the soldiers. "You can't do this," the Frenchman shouted at Edelstam. "Ambassadors don't fight with soldiers." But at that moment Edelstam fell to the floor and several of the soldiers jumped on top of him. "This so enraged the French Ambassador," Edelstam recalls, "that he completely forgot about his own diplomatic reservations and he too jumped into the fray. Now it was the French diplomat who was shouting at the Chileans: 'You can't do this; you are not allowed to beat an ambassador.' Infuriated, totally forgetting diplomatic niceties, he chased some of the military into the corridor." This reinforce-

ment from the representative of the Republic of France seemed
to stun the soldiers and their officers, who suddenly left the clinic
to seek further orders. It was something of an anticlimax,
Edelstam recalls with a chuckle, when the Frenchman, still
breathing hard, sweat glistening on his forehead, suddenly ended
the scene with: "I am really tired and put out. I think I'll go
home now and have some lunch."

But Edelstam and his aides remained at their ward's bedside.
Sooner or later, they thought, the Junta people would come to
their senses and realize the folly of their tactics, but meantime
the Swedes held fast. The small room in which the patient lay,
anxious, pale, in considerable post-surgical pain, was now
crowded with terrorized doctors and nurses. (Among them was a
young nurse who had helped shield Edelstam from serious injury
during the brawl. When a husky Junta officer was about to land a
knockout punch to the Swedish diplomat while he was down on
the floor, she managed to get close enough to whack him over
the head with a heavy ashtray. Edelstam's assailant went
momentarily limp, enabling the Ambassador to get up.)

The respite from the battle was brief. Suddenly the parking lot
in front of the clinic became alive with noise. Three jeeps with
Chilean officers and a huge army personnel carrier full of
soldiers drove directly to the entrance of the clinic. Their captain
rushed into the room. "He was like a tiger. His face was purple,
apoplectic with rage, and he threatened to shoot us right then
and there if we continued to block the arrest of the woman. I still
tried to argue, when he suddenly lifted his machine gun and
pointed it directly at my chest. 'We've come here to take this
woman,' he screamed at me. 'You can do nothing about it. If
you try to resist, we will shoot you.' We were physically
exhausted, nursing painful bruises. But above all, the barrel of
the machine gun made all further conversation useless. There
was nothing more we could do. The representative of the U.N.
Commission on Refugees who had come soon after the French
diplomat left stood in the corridor and took no part in the
arguments. He was a man with a big stomach who smoked a
heavy pipe and said nothing."

The Junta people took the woman out of the bed, threw her

into a jeep, and took off. One of the Swedish Embassy staff jumped into his car and followed the convoy, which eventually came to the women's prison where the patient was carried inside.

Frustrated but not beaten, Edelstam immediately called a press conference and telephoned the major newspapers and wire services across the world, informing them of the incident. The press abroad reacted vigorously. The Swedish Foreign Office filed a protest with the Pinochet Ambassador in Stockholm. This led to a prompt Junta response. About a week later Edelstam was informed that he would be issued a safe conduct document to enable the woman to get out of Chile. *

This latest incident scarcely improved his already strained relations with the Pinochet government. Soon afterward, however, Edelstam was involved in an action which topped in audacity and daring all his previous Chilean exploits and which, incidentally, led to his expulsion as ambassador. This operation took place under the nose of Colonel Espinoza, the sadistic Gauleiter of the Santiago sports stadium concentration camp. Edelstam's visits to the stadium to negotiate the release of some

---

* Although virtually neglected medically, at least the woman was not tortured while in the prison. To make sure that there would be no foul play, a staff member of the Swedish Embassy accompanied the woman on her flight to Stockholm, where she was taken directly to a hospital. After several months of treatment she was able to recover. The Ambassador saw her again on his return to Sweden. She eventually slid out of public view. It is assumed she returned to Uruguay to rejoin the resistance against the dictatorship there.

Mirtha, as she came to be known, had fled from the repression of the Rightist-Fascist military regime that seized power in her country some five years before the coup took place in Chile. She and hundreds of her compatriots found a haven in Chile. There were also many young Brazilians, Argentines, and Bolivians in the same fix, having been hounded by the military dictatorships that govern their respective countries.

Allende flung Chile's doors wide open to all of these people. His Popular Unity government offered them sympathy and jobs. Generally these refugees were young men and women who took active part in the resistance against the tyranny of their governments. Mirtha had managed to make a getaway from a Uruguayan jail through a tunnel which she, her husband, and a group of others had been able to dig out of their concentration camp. She was among those who were able to make it. The rest, including her husband, were killed while trying to escape.

Because of their strong democratic commitments and willingness to fight for their beliefs, such refugees were of course special targets for extermination by the Junta. Pinochet and his henchmen spread the word among the military that these exiles constituted a special advance task force, to subvert the Chilean armed force.

of his fellow Swedes and other prisoners, had almost become routine. He would wait in the vast reception area where dozens of women were milling about, weeping, wringing their hands, as they tried to get information from brutal-faced officials about the fate of their relatives. Often they were ignored; sometimes they were told to report to the city morgue to reclaim the body of someone "shot while trying to escape."

Busloads of newly arrested people were jostled into the stadium by rifle butts. Other groups were shoved out into trucks to begin the trip to remote concentration camps—Dawson Island near the Antarctic, or an isolated outpost in the Andean highlands. Unable to help, Edelstam watched, horrified, as hundreds of people were "processed" each day. He became even more horrified when he learned of the tortures that went on in the subterranean passages of the stadium. By now it was an open secret that many of the prisoners were hooked up with electronic gadgetry through which electric shocks were administered to the nostrils, nipples, or genitalia. Others were mowed down by machine guns, individually or in groups. This had become a daily occurrence.

His long hours of waiting for a meeting with Colonel Espinoza made it possible to strike up an acquaintance with a Major Lavandero, who was directly in charge of incoming and outgoing prisoner traffic. "He seemed to be quite pleasant personally," Edelstam says, "and he appeared to be doing the job with little enthusiasm, more like a soldier forced to carry out orders from his superiors." Occasionally Edelstam and the Major would exchange bits of conversation.

One day as Edelstam stood about in another hopeless wait, while the usual crowd of anxious relatives crowded the reception area, a man walked over and asked him for a light and at the same time offered him a cigarette as he winked. An old hand at spotting a signal, Edelstam took the cigarette and went into the lavatory, where he carefully unraveled the wrapper and, as he had expected, found a message. Written in a small, shaky hand, the word was that fifty-four Uruguayans were scheduled to be shot the next morning. Edelstam carefully crumpled the piece of paper, flushed it down, and walked back to the main corridor to collect his thoughts.

The prospect of the scheduled mass slaughter of fifty-four young people was more than Edelstam could bear without taking action. But how? It was already late in the afternoon; there was not much time to decide. His first plan was to approach the people at the highest level of authority. After all, he had got to know Pinochet quite well during the Allende period. On various occasions they had met to work out details of a visit to Chile by Sweden's army chief-of-staff. Edelstam had also enjoyed a friendly relationship with two others now in the Junta, Air Force Marshal Leigh and Admiral Montero.

The idea of reaching them was tempting, but Edelstam had to dismiss it. Once the putsch took place the Junta leadership had cut off all communication with him; they would not help him now. In his typical spontaneous, fearless fashion, Edelstam walked over to Major Lavendero's office and asked to speak to him. The two sauntered toward the corner of the vast corridor adjoining the reception room and there Edelstam took the gamble. He put it to him directly. "Look here, Major. I don't think you are particularly happy with your job. Suppose I can help make it a bit less odious by relieving you of a group of fifty-four people who are to face a firing squad tomorrow morning?"

The major was speechless. He drew back as though from a madman, eyes riveted on the graciously smiling face of the diplomat, who continued to argue the matter in his softest voice. Tall and lean, wearing a tweed sports jacket, Edelstam towered over the muscle-bound officer who ironically looked as if he were about to go into disorderly retreat, side arms and all. But Edelstam kept pursuing the issue. He wasn't trying to beguile the major with phony rhetoric, he explained. He honestly felt that Lavendero was not so much a villain as a cog in the military machine, that he was simply carrying out orders and was therefore open to reason.

"There are some 7,000 prisoners in this stadium," Edelstam said. "With all the goings on, with all this traffic, your commanding officer Espinoza will never notice the absence of a few dozen people." At first, Lavendero was positively outraged when he heard Edelstam's proposal. Grudgingly he began to listen. Edelstam went on and on and on. Obviously he had made an astute judgment of Lavendero, for the major began to weaken. "Believe me," he admitted, "I really don't enjoy killing people. But I am a soldier so I have to do what I am told to do. But you are right. Espinoza will probably never miss those Uruguayans. I'll do my part. And good luck to you if you can get away with it, once they are outside these walls."

While Lavendero was making out the appropriate release documents for the fifty-four Uruguayans, Edelstam telephoned his embassy and told one of his assistants to get a bus and drive to the stadium at once. As he had predicted, the huge traffic of army trucks and vans arriving and departing with their doomed human cargo made the transfer of the Uruguayan group all but invisible. One of the group, a nun, was approached by Lavandero, who said, "Please pray for me." Half an hour later the Uruguayans were safely ensconced in a three-story building, the Cuban Trade Center, in Santiago's uptown area, over which the Swedish government had extended its jurisdiction.

Before he left the stadium that afternoon, Edelstam had the distinct impression that if he went back the following morning Lavandero would turn over to him another group, this time half a dozen Brazilians who were to be executed the next afternoon. Early the next day Edelstam arrived at the stadium, almost ebullient at having saved the Uruguayans and looking forward to rescuing six more people.

But as he entered the reception area there stood Colonel Espinoza. This time it was Espinoza who was waiting for Edelstam. At the sight of the Ambassador, Espinoza burst out at the top of his voice, "You've overstepped your bounds as a foreign diplomat. You thought you were so smart. But you know what you did? By persuading Lavandero to release these criminals, you had him break the rules. And I had him punished accordingly. This morning, an hour ago, Lavandero, together with the six Brazilians you were going to sneak out of here, were executed by a firing squad. And now, Mr. Ambassador, leave this place immediately and do not dare to return."

*Aping the Nazis, Junta soldiers began "purifying" Chilean culture
through book-burning sprees. In this instance, not only books
but also a poster of Ernesto (Che) Guevara went up in flames.
Edelstam managed to salvage many valuable Chilean works
by shipping them out through his diplomatic pouch. (Wide World Photos)*

For days afterward Edelstam struggled with his guilt at having been directly responsible for Lavandero's death. Arithmetically, perhaps, it could have been an acceptable equation: one death weighed against fifty-four young people who survived. But as Edelstam remembers it, this logical calculation was no solace for the soul. Under ordinary circumstances Major Lavandero might have been a perfectly decent fellow, and he had lost his life directly because of Edelstam.

About two years after the coup, Edelstam was on a worldwide lecture tour raising funds for the Chilean refugees. In Mexico City, when he finished speaking to a small gathering, a young woman in her early twenties rushed up to him and said: "I am the daughter of Major Lavandero. May I have a word with you?" Edelstam excused himself from those surrounding him and stepped aside with Lavandero's daughter. "Please tell me, was my father really bad?" Edelstam looked into the anguished and yet hopeful eyes of the girl and said at once, "You should be proud of your father. You should always honor his memory for what he did for the fifty-four Uruguayans." The young woman breathed a sigh of relief and left abruptly. He later learned that she, along with her mother and brothers, were now living in Mexico as exiles.

In the three months that Edelstam carried on with his rescue operation more than 900 people were either spirited out of Chile to Sweden or else to other embassies for exile to Mexico, Costa Rica, or Europe. 400 more refugees were evacuated by the Swedish government after Edelstam had left Chile. By the third month the Junta was determined to get rid of him one way or the other. The anonymous telephone threats became more frequent, and one day the Paraguayan ambassador, an avid supporter of the Junta, suddenly paid a call. He had word from responsible sources, he said, that Leftist elements were planning to assassinate Edelstam. "Why the Left?" the Ambassador asked. The Paraguayan was somewhat confused. Why indeed? It was obvious that the threat came from the Junta.

In the meantime, whatever contact he had with the new regime was one of recriminations. The Junta Foreign Minister repeatedly complained to Edelstam, charging him with behavior

Santiago National Stadium, where many thousands of pro-Allende suspects were tortured and executed. Victor Jara was among those who was murdered here. (United Press International Photo)

inconsistent with the role as ambassador. His heresies were many. Via his diplomatic pouch Edelstam managed to ship out of Chile books by Chilean writers and historians which otherwise would have found their way to the Junta book burnings, a fiery ritual designed to purify Chilean history, which the Junta copied directly from their Nazi precursors. (Many libraries, both private and public, which contained literature considered suspect by the Junta, were destroyed. Even the vast book collection of Chile's most distinguished literary figure, Nobel Laureate Pablo Neruda, was demolished.) Edelstam even sent out some film footage of the Junta's storming of the presidential palace, which was later used in the famous documentary *The Battle of Chile*.

The Junta's charge was that Edelstam was involved in conspiratorial arms smuggling, which was not the case. Ugly encounters with the police and the military were becoming ever more vexing. The Junta never tired in its attempts to invade the former Cuban Embassy grounds, and with every such incident, in which the Swedes held fast, Edelstam was called down to the Foreign Office. Then one day the Junta's protocol chief phoned to say he was on his way to see Edelstam at the embassy. "Immediately on sitting down," Edelstam says, "the man took out a document from his portfolio which declared that I was persona non grata and that I was to leave Chile immediately. No formal explanation was provided. No charges were lodged against me. After some negotiating the Junta allowed me to stay on for another week to wind up my affairs."

And so Edelstam, to the very end of his stay, made sure that the remaining refugees on his premises were either flown to Sweden or transferred to such friendly embassies as those of Mexico, Finland, Venezuela, or Costa Rica. It was a near miracle that throughout his Chilean rescue operations there was only one serious incident involving his refugee guests, and that took place after Edelstam had already left Chile. Allende's Minister of Culture was hit by a sniper's bullet through the window in the Swedish Embassy. Though seriously hurt he eventually recovered when treated at a hospital in Stockholm. Agile, continuous screening made it possible to eliminate infiltration by provocateurs. There was one occasion when a

Chilean was suspected of wavering and becoming an informer; somehow he was talked out of it.

When Edelstam left Santiago International Airport on December 9, 1973, there were only three foreign emissaries to see him off—the *chargé d'affaires* of Finland, and the ambassadors of India and Romania. (Romania and China were the only Socialist countries that continued to have normal relations with the Junta regime.)

Immediately after Edelstam left, the newspaper *La Tercera* named him "the most degenerate" of the year, but lauded Pinochet and Henry Kissinger as "the most outstanding." Chile's most prestigious pro-Pinochet newspaper, *El Mercurio*, said that Edelstam's interventions on behalf of the anti-Junta people made it clear that he was "mentally unbalanced." His actions, it went on to say, were obviously "in violation of the most elementary norms of international conventions."

It was a different story at home. This graying "Black Pimpernel" was lionized. He spoke about the Chilean tragedy before a packed house in the Swedish Parliament, and most of Swedish society considered him a national hero. Premier Palme, labor leaders, artists, writers, and human rights representatives praised him. He went on a national fund-raising tour to aid the anti-Junta resistance fighters, and one of his most gratifying moments was when he, with Premier Palme, headed a mammoth parade through the center of Stockholm honoring Allende. This was climaxed with Palme's handing over several hundred thousand kroner to Allende's daughter, Beatriz, for the support of the Chilean refugees. These contributions came mainly from Swedish trade unions.

While awaiting reassignment to another diplomatic post, Edelstam traveled to many lands to describe the Pinochet atrocities and to stimulate solidarity with the opponents of the dictatorship. In the United States, in February 1974, he accepted an invitation to take part in a congressional conference titled "Chile: Implications for United States Foreign Policy." The Junta's ambassador in Washington, who was to appear as his regime's spokesman, withdrew from the conference when he learned of Edelstam's participation. Instead he issued a press release damning Edelstam for the acts for which he had been commended throughout the world.

Edelstam's heroic undertakings in Chile were in sharp contrast to the half-hearted efforts of most of the other ambassadors when called upon to offer their protection to the besieged refugees. It certainly was shockingly different from the attitude of the United States mission, headed by Ambassador Nathaniel Davis. It not only ignored the pleas of men, women, and children who were targeted for extermination, but also backed away from giving protection to some of its own nationals.

Americans who made it safely home have testified on numerous occasions to the shabby treatment they received at the hands of the embassy staff. There were instances when some of them would push into the embassy in panic after having received death threats, asking for temporary haven at the embassy or for help in getting out of Chile. What they got was the cynical advice to take their complaints to the Santiago police, who at that very moment were hounding and torturing foreigners as well as Chileans. Most tragic were the cases of Charles Horman and Frank Terrugi, two Americans who were murdered by the Junta because of their sympathies for the Allende regime. The U.S. authorities not only failed to assist Horman and Terrugi but may also have been implicated in their destruction, according to recent charges by Horman's father.

Both Edelstam and Davis knew each other quite well. Both served as ambassadors in Guatemala at about the same time, shortly before being assigned to Chile. Both got to know each other even better when Edelstam happened to be on the same ship with Davis and his wife, while on a cruise to the south of Chile. The trip was pleasant and leisurely, with conversation for the most part nonpolitical. Once, however, the two emissaries discussed the Chilean situation. Edelstam maintained that the Allende program, if successful, was not only of local significance but had worldwide ramifications. "Using a democratic process to change a capitalistic system into one that was democratic-socialist," Edelstam contended, "would open a new page in world history." Davis disagreed. "Allende will not succeed," he said. Since it is not likely that Davis was totally ignorant of U.S.

plans to disestablish the Popular Unity government, he was obviously in a better position than his colleague to predict the future course of events.

Following the putsch, relations between the two men were not only strained, they simply didn't exist. Edelstam received only one telephone call from the U.S. Embassy in the three-month period before being forced out of his post in Chile. That was to inquire about the identities of five Americans whom Edelstam had managed to put aboard a plane on a flight out of Chile. Edelstam acknowledged having helped some Americans escape but he would not disclose their names.

Thus Edelstam, the representative of a kingdom—the Swedish monarchy—tried to help the Allende regime establish a Socialist economy. And Davis, the emissary of the United States—the first country to become a democratic republic and break away from a monarchical form of government—was involved with an all-out effort to destroy the Allende regime, paving the way to the seizure of power by a Fascist dictatorship. Edelstam came from a Swedish noble family. His father was chamberlain to the Swedish king, and young Edelstam spent much of his youth in the royal court. Davis sprang from a middle-class family in New Jersey.

It is true that Edelstam received backing from the Prime Minister of a country whose policy it was to favor Allende and, later, the victims of the Junta atrocities. But it was basically Edelstam's own code of ethics, his conscience with regard to injustice, that impelled him to stick his neck out, regardless of consequences, whether in Chile, Guatemala, Indonesia, or Nazi-occupied Norway.

Davis simply followed his government's policy.

6

The Shantytown Dwellers
Make a Last-Ditch Stand

On the day of the putsch I found myself crying like a baby."
The man saying these words looked old, burnt out, although he
was only forty. His eyes were deep pools of pain and fatigue. He
spoke haltingly. From time to time a hacking cough parted his
lips to reveal three missing teeth. "A souvenir from my Junta
torturers," Felipe Hernandez explained.

"I just could not accept the fact that our government—I could
say 'my personal' government—was no more; so I wept. For me
the Allende regime was like a fairy tale come true. But then it
went crashing down on me and millions of other Chilean slum
dwellers who crowded the country's *poblaciónes*, and who, for
the first time, got a taste of what it is to be human. It is not only
that we began living better; having regular jobs and real pay; and
that our kids went to school on a regular basis. It is not only
because we were able to see real doctors at free clinics, not some
quacks as before, simply because we couldn't raise the money to
pay a trained physician.

"Perhaps most important was that for the first time we began to
count for something. Not only did the newly organized neighborhood committees listen to our complaints and suggestions
about our living conditions, but we could actually go to La
Moneda, the presidential palace, and discuss our problems with
high government officials. Until Allende, we were not even a
statistic. Nobody came around to find out how many of us lived
in the *poblaciónes*. We were always referred to in 'approximate'
numbers. I was just a cipher.

"So on the first night that the Junta seized power, the people
in my *población* (some 1,500 families) rushed out into the main
street to build barricades, as though this little pocket of resistance

would help stop the enemy. We piled up boxes, chairs, tables, bags of pebbles, and rocks. Everybody took part in this so-called defense, men, women, children. It was a desperate effort to hold on to something that was so dear to us, something as personal as breathing. It was a last-minute attempt to hold off an enemy made up of fellow Chileans who were Fascists. If they could do away with Allende, we knew they would kill us just as easily.

"We kept scurrying about, shoring up our flimsy defenses under the cover of night. When you think about it, this was not really resistance. It was tantamount to a kind of decision, though we didn't vote on it, to commit mass suicide rather than surrender and die without a fight. Although in the back of our minds there was also the faint hope that some of the military would not go along with the Junta and put down the revolt. There were no commanders telling us what to do and how to do it. We just did it."

Hernandez (that is not his real name) said, "Early the following morning about twenty army vehicles, including a few small tanks, appeared on the road leading to our shantytown. A voice from the lead armored personnel carrier rasped through a loudspeaker. It ordered us to leave our homes, and all our belongings, and promptly report to a registration center immediately outside of the town, while the Junta soldiers conducted a house-to-house search for guns.

"Our response was immediate, as though on command. It was a fusillade from several dozen pistols, rifles, and shotguns, some dating back to World War I. It all sounded like a bunch of firecrackers going off at the same time. But some of the bullets did reach their mark. Several of the armored cars tried to smash through the barricades. But because the street was narrow and crooked, they made their way slowly. For the next half hour or so they contented themselves with spraying the whole area indiscriminately with machine-gun fire. Dozens and dozens of our people were killed or seriously wounded in the few hours of resistance. Others, however, still continued to blast away at the enemy that was methodically routing our makeshift troops.

"Men and women were dropping like clay figures in a shooting gallery. On either side of me in a shallow hole that was supposed to pass for a trench, two of my neighbors were hit the moment the soldiers opened fire. One died instantly. The other, a mother of seven children, mortally wounded on her right side, her face twisted in pain, managed to hand me her gun, saying, 'Give it to them hard, hard,' and died a minute later.

"As our skimpy resistance fighters fell back, some of us filtered through the debris and made our escape to an adjoining *población* where better fortified slum dwellers were putting up a stiff fight against the military. After contributing our bit there, we made our way to a wooded area where we joined a small group of men and women who were already at work planning clandestine activities against the Junta. But my clandestine involvement lasted only two days. On September 14th, I felt somewhat proud that I was able to distribute about a hundred leaflets calling on workers not to lose heart. The leaflet was headlined FRIENDS, WORKERS, THE BATTLE IS NOT OVER, ALLENDE CONTINUES TO LIVE. FOR US HE WILL NEVER BE DEAD. I was proud for the simple reason that I was not caught. I had only one leaflet when I ran into a bit of bad luck. I was suddenly caught in a brief crossfire between Junta police and a group of resisters whom I did not know. I quickly turned to get out of the area, crumpled the last leaflet in my hand, and began chewing on it as fast as I could. Hardly done with my last swallow when two policemen grabbed me and began pulling me toward a wall of a building adjacent to a hospital complex, while others made ready to raise the machine guns for the execution. At that very moment I heard shouts, 'Why don't you let him go? Why don't you let him go? You're a bunch of assassins.' I looked up and saw dozens of nurses and other hospital employees standing at the entrance of the hospital defiantly shouting at the police. For some reason the Junta men wavered, gave me a hard shove, and let me free without even frisking me, which was lucky because I had a gun in my pocket, a sure passport to execution.

"I made my way around to the rear of the hospital grounds where several of the hospital staff led me into a cellar hideout. I stayed there in very cramped quarters several days because the area was under constant surveillance. It was frustrating; I was impatient to rejoin my group. But even more oppressive, now that I was out of the battle itself, was my anxiety about my wife and son who remained at home. I finally decided I would take my chance. I reentered my *población* at night and made my way through the mountains of rubble to my house, which miraculously was still standing, and found my little family inside. The joy of seeing them suddenly triggered within me a feeling of overwhelming fear that this reunion wouldn't last long. While I was under fire at the barricades, and then in the woods, I somehow was too busy to think of fear. But now in the presence of family warmth and love, the reality of danger enveloped me, immobilized me and for good reason.

"Scarcely an hour after my return there was a deafening rumble of military vehicles invading the night. Within minutes Junta soldiers armed with machine guns broke open the door, seized me without even asking my name, pushed aside my terror-stricken wife who was holding our infant son in her arms, and drove me to a small plaza where I was transferred to a waiting helicopter. I soon arrived at a prisoner collection center on the grounds of the former International Fair in Santiago. I was led to an office on the third story of a building where I was questioned for about an hour. I was told to remove my clothes and then forced to run down the three flights of steps and across the fair grounds, and then up the stairs in a kind of warehouse which was half-opened at the ceiling. There, completely naked, I spent the night shivering.

"The following day Junta guards threw me some dirty clothes, ordered me to dress and then took me to the headquarters of the Air Force building. A woolen sack was thrown over my head to blindfold me. And now the questioning was accompanied by savage threats. Again and again these questions: 'So where were you in the days that you were away from home? What resistance group were you with? What were the names of the others in the group?' Again and again, for about six hours this interrogation continued. I was then pushed onto a chair where my clothes, my shoes, my socks were removed. My hands were tied to the armrest of the chair. Wires were hooked up to my chest and the electric shocking began. This went on for maybe a half an hour while I screamed and screamed. At different intervals the current was turned off and the questions rained down upon me like bullets—what was my role in the resistance, and who were my accomplices. I gave them my name, told them where I had worked, but denied having anything to do with resistance activities. After shocking me several times more and getting the same answers from me, it seemed as though my interrogators might have become weary of me. But one of the officers had second thoughts and argued that it was important to question me in greater depth.

"They now put me into a spread-eagle position on a kind of metal bed that had no mattress, inserted an electrode into my anus, and began shocking me all over again. This time, the pain was much worse, absolutely unbearable. In between the shocks they'd resume the questioning, and always the same: 'Where did you go into hiding? Where were you in the two weeks that you were away from the house?' I can't tell you how long this torture went on, whether an hour or three hours, but it was horrendous. I lost consciousness many times. I began to hallucinate. I remember seeing a huge swimming pool filled with beautiful azure water, that I was reaching out for it, but never getting to it. Every night since that experience, after two or three hours of sleep, I wake up with a nightmare, reliving the torture and the swimming pool episode in which I'm never able to reach the beautiful azure water.

"My tormentors removed the electrodes and threw me to the floor from the improvised bed. I must have been seriously injured because when I came to I was in a hospital, where I remained for nearly two months. But this was not a hospital to help me get well. As soon as I began to feel somewhat better, they began torturing me anew. At times they injected air into my veins and eventually succeeded in precipitating a thrombosis. After a so-called recovery, they tried something new. They forced me into a small closet with a metal floor and half filled it with water. I had to languish there several days; toward evening they would take me out and threaten to execute me.

"One night they stood me up against the wall and somebody who was dressed in a cleric's habit said to me, 'Look, my son, you are about to go to the other world. So why don't you confess everything? Tell me of your sins, of your accomplices in the resistance against the Junta and I promise I will pray for you and help send you off into a better world. I am blessing you now in the name of the Father, the Son, and the Holy Spirit.' I must admit that I was near the breaking point. I wept and I could not control my bowels. And yet, at the same time, I looked to death almost with pleasure, as a way out of my hell on earth.

"Not having succeeded in getting out of me the information that they thought I might have had, and somehow sure that they would eventually extract it from me, they proceeded to subject me to even greater torture. This time they inserted an electrode into my penis. Until then I was able to hold out and not name names, but at this point I must confess I did name names, but of people I knew were dead. For a few days they let me be, while they checked my confession, but then they came at me with a savage fury. On discovering that I had fooled them, they gave me more of the electrode treatment. By this time I must have lost approximately eighty pounds. I was just wasting away. Probably because of that I was transferred to the care of the security police where things were a little better. There, there was no more shocking. All they did was beat me and punch me directly in the mouth while they were interrogating me. But they did not blindfold me. And to this day I remember each one of my tormentors and I know their names. And one day they'll hear from me.

"I remained there for fifteen days and at no time was I or any of the other five hundred prisoners allowed to wash ourselves. From there I was transferred for about six months to a concentration camp in northern Chile. I was no longer tortured, but the effects of the lacerations on my genitalia produced a serious infection with continuous discharges of pus. I was taken to a local hospital and there I underwent surgery for removal of tissue section from the penis. In order for me to have a normal sexual act, I have to prepare for it three or four months in advance, mostly psychologically. But I don't want to discuss it.

"Following my hospital stay I was transferred to a prison. After a four-month stay there they decided that I could go free since they could produce no evidence that I had taken part in the resistance against the Junta. This was at the end of 1974, nearly fifteen months after I was taken prisoner. Seven days after I went home, they went looking for me again. They took me to the Marine Corps headquarters in Valparaiso. But they had second thoughts. They saw that I was in a pretty hopeless, battered state and probably would die if pressed any further. My legs were swollen, my body spotted with hematomas, my metabolic system all askew. So they let me go and I took refuge in the Italian Consulate.

"For the present, I'm living here in Italy with my wife, my son, and my mother. I cannot do any heavy work, my arms ache constantly; my legs don't seem to support me for longer than a few hours at a time, and I have constant, unexplained crying spells. There is scarcely a night that I don't have a nightmare. People tell me that I look amazingly well considering the horror that I've experienced. But I can assure you that inside of me I'm like a rock. I feel very little. Well, not quite," he half-smiled, as his very sad eyes suddenly lit up. "Yes, I feel strongly about wanting to get back to Chile. I want to return there and denounce the people who tortured me and thousands of my comrades. But I want to get back because Chile is my country and not the Junta's. I'm not that educated, so I can't tell you how Allende should have dealt with the United States when they were engineering the overthrow of my government. But I can tell you what the Allende regime meant for me and others like me.

"I'm a true son of Chile's poor. I was born in a shantytown, and I was raised there, or maybe I should say I managed to survive there. My mother was born in Italy and she came to Chile in the early thirties, to escape Mussolini fascism. She married a poor Chilean laborer. They settled down in a shantytown near Santiago, and she began producing a lot of children—eleven all told, seven of whom died as infants because they starved to death. I began to work at the age of six as a shoeshine boy. I did other things as well. I'd rush to wipe windshields on cars while the drivers waited for the lights to change. I also delivered and carried packages for women who were marketing. I had only one year of schooling.

A scene typical of shantytown life near Santiago
or any Chilean urban center. (Liberation News Service)

"My father died when he was thirty-five years old. Cirrhosis of the liver got him. I remember him always looking for work, always preoccupied with how to feed the family, working hard at all kinds of jobs, such as loading freight, or anything else that came along. But there was never enough work, and out of desperation he would rush to a bar and drink up the occasional wages he would earn. We were always hungry. At times the only way I could still my hunger pangs was by rummaging for *pan duro* [bread found in the garbage pail]. Other times I begged for food, but I must admit that I did some petty thieving. I would steal a knife or a spoon and then try to sell it.

"I got my first regular job at the age of nine in a glass factory. It was very hard work and hazardous to one's health because boys like myself had no shoes and had to walk barefoot on floors covered with splintered glass. There were no protective devices covering the cutting machines and so the air was full of fine-ground glass dust. I worked at this job and others like it until I was about fifteen, and the wages were less than enough to keep one alive. But then I had a break. I became an apprentice in a machine shop. The men there were very kind to me. They were politically conscious and tried to explain things to me in a way that made me aware of why I, and others like myself, were so hard up. This was in 1949.

"Because it was a union shop, my salary was quite decent; it seemed wonderful to me. It made it possible to help my family get out from a very primitive type of existence. We never had any furniture. The table, the chairs were boxes. The house itself was made from flattened tin cans and pieces of wood and stood on an earthen floor. From time to time we had coffee cups, but when some broke, we took turns in using those that were still serviceable. Of course, on many days it didn't matter whether one had a coffee cup, or a plate, for food was not always available. I can say that I seldom had breakfast with which to start the day when going to work. The lunch and dinner were always the same. If we were lucky we had a piece of bread and some beans and maybe some coffee, but we never saw any milk.

"It was in this machine shop that the older workers began to open new windows into the world about me. It was through them that I began to understand something about the politics of the country. Until then my life's concentration was on survival, sheer personal survival, how to try to get food from one day to the next, without stopping to think why life was so hard. It is strange that although my mother had suffered so much under Mussolini repression, especially because several of her brothers and sisters were either killed or were in prison, she scarcely ever discussed fascism with me. She was in dread fear that political involvement of the other children would lead us to the fate that befell her family in Italy.

"I made considerable progress on my job. I now worked only eight or nine hours a day. To improve my earning power, I would remain at the shop for an extra two hours to learn how to operate a lathe. But more than that, I began to thrive on politics. I was now a member of the trade union. I took part in political discussions; I became very active in the Socialist Party. And I began to read a lot, although slowly and with a lot of difficulty. And at the age of thirty-three or so, I married, and believe it or not, my bride was an elementary school teacher. I married late because I had to help with the family. (My mother is now quite old and I'm afraid she is seeing her native land only through the window of a hospital where she's been for the past six months.)

"My life until I became a lathe operator was not very different from those around me in the *poblaciónes*. Any of the people in the *poblaciónes* who were able to eat fifteen days out of the month were considered lucky. But in addition to that, we didn't know anything about nutrition; we had no idea as to the importance of whatever food was available. Seldom did we have meat throughout my childhood. On rare occasions, we'd manage to buy some beef bones to make soup. What struck me in Italy was that bones which we had to buy in Chile at what seemed to us a considerable cost are thrown away here as garbage. Fish was more available, but we didn't know enough about it and scarcely developed any taste for it. With what little earnings we had, many of us would go to the local bars and take two or three glasses of wine which would somehow still our hunger but gave us very little nutrition. With a few salary raises our lifestyle improved considerably. I bought my mother a couple of chairs, some forks and knives, and regular plates and soup bowls. Things really began looking up. We never had a mirror until then.

"Of course the important change in our lives came with the arrival of the Allende regime. We had a good wage rise. Children in the *poblaciónes* began getting daily a half liter of milk. Don't forget that we had thousands and thousands of children who had never tasted milk until the Allende election. Poor children began attending school regularly and in great numbers. And not only that, they had their notebooks and textbooks supplied to them free if the parents hadn't the means with which to buy them. To us, all this was a miracle and Allende made it happen. He said that going to school was not a privilege, but everyone's right. But it wasn't only the children; older people like myself grabbed at the opportunity, for hundreds of classes were open to adults. But there were also other miracles as far as we were concerned. Lots of new housing was going up and it was for poor people at very low rent. And as I said before, we ate a lot better and lived a lot better.

"But all this began skidding downhill because of the intrigue from the Chilean oligarchy and their friends in the United States as they tried to torpedo our little miracle. It sounds contradictory. With Allende we had more wages and more opportunity, but as time went on, life began getting harder and harder because of the scarcities of food and other goods. But despite these difficulties and despite the fierce propaganda against Allende and the Popular Unity government, faith in Allende among the people would not be shaken. And so in the March 1973 congressional election, when the Rightists were confident, cocky in their belief that they'd get enough congressmen elected to guarantee a vote to impeach Allende, the poor and the working people stuck by the regime. Not only were the Rightists stopped in the move to impeach Allende, but our side increased its vote.

"Allende, in many ways, was a father to us. We never had a President who was not only respected because of his high office, but who was actually loved by at least half of the population. But many of us feel that Allende made a big mistake when he would not give arms to the people to defend themselves against the possible coup. Allende argued, and so did many of his advisors, that by giving arms to the people the putsch would have arrived even sooner. He thought that we would have never had a chance, even if we would have had rifles and machine guns, standing up against an army that had cannon and bombers. He thought hundreds and thousands of us would have been massacred. But I feel that I would rather have died fighting than become a prisoner as happened to me. Yes, I think it was a big mistake. But I don't think it is all over. Allende has become one of our greatest heroes. And the people in the *poblaciónes* will never forget what his government did for them."

Carlos Echeverria, another *población* resistance fighter, came through his ordeal with the Junta in much better shape than Felipe Hernandez. He seems physically restored, and, as he says, "I'm even okay psychologically," as his genial, attractive, bronzed face breaks into a friendly smile. "Oh, sure, there are times when I wake up in a cold sweat as I relive several of the simulated executions that I was forced to go through. But it's only a nightmare." He again grins, as though to reassure me that his state of health is good.

Like Hernandez, he got his early education in the *población* school of survival. But because he went to work in a large plant sooner than Hernandez and was, therefore, exposed to labor consciousness early, he became worldly-wise early in life. Because of his attractive personality and natural gifts of oratory and organization, he received special attention in his trade union.

He rose quickly as a union spokesman. By the time Allende became Chile's chief magistrate, Echeverria had been elected one of the vice-presidents of a union local at the Sumar textile complex which employed approximately six thousand workers. Sumar was one of the eighty large monopolies that were nationalized by the government. After nationalization much of the management responsibility was handed over to the employees and their unions.

"On the morning of September 11th, at 7:00 A.M.," Echeverria recalls, "I was already at my place of work. At 8:00 we received a phone call from CUT (Confederacion Unica de Trabajadores—Confederation of Labor) that there had been a navy rebellion in Valparaiso, and that we should remain at the plant and await further instructions on how to defend ourselves against possible attack from the Rightists. Men and women were congregating in small groups: talking, questioning each other, all quite dazed.

"In the attempt to ease the deepening anxiety we called a meeting. Several of the union speakers were still holding forth on the possibility that as in previous attempts at a coup, some of the army divisions would refuse to go along with the rebels and thus turn the tide. For a short while there were murmurs of hope. People wanted to be optimistic even though reality was increasingly discouraging. 'Since there is a remote possibility that things may return to normal once the putsch is put down,' a union leader said, 'why don't we take this opportunity to discuss how we can expand our textile production and improve the distribution?' I must say it was somewhat bizarre. While our real world was tumbling and the sound of gunfire was growing closer, we were talking about better efficiency and expansion of textile output. But this talk was becoming quite ridiculous; some of those at the meeting shouted, 'Let's cut out this nonsense. Where are the weapons? How are we going to fight? And let's get the women out of here.'

"The move to get the women out of the plant took on urgency. There were a number of women there whose children were being taken care of in the day-care areas of the plant. And even though some of the women were fierce in their demand to participate in the defense of the plant, they were finally persuaded to go home. All of us at the plant—men and women—felt strongly about our factory complex since it was nationalized. We carried out a variety of improvements which had a direct effect on our lives. We introduced day-care facilities for the children of the working mothers. We installed machinery safeguards. We issued work uniforms rather than expose our normal wearing apparel to dust and dirt as before. We also opened an infirmary staffed with doctors and nurses on the premises. All these changes boosted worker morale tremendously, and as a result Sumar increased its production output to unprecedented levels.

"By 1:30 P.M. it was evident that the likelihood of getting armament or getting word from our union was most remote. So we held another meeting at which it was decided that those who wanted to leave the plant were free to do so and as quickly as possible. Soon nearly all the workers began making their way to their homes or to those of their friends in the immediate vicinity of the plant. Only about forty men—mostly union officers— remained, still hoping that reinforcements would arrive. Then to our great surprise, at about 2:00 P.M., a mini-bus dashed up the driveway and hastily unloaded about thirty rifles and a few machine guns. The two drivers were in a great hurry to get on to their next destination and all they could tell us was that a few of the shantytowns were putting up a stiff fight. But they had no idea of the overall situation in Santiago.

"We looked at our arsenal; it was a paltry haul indeed. Some of us felt that any attempt at resistance would prove suicidal. We had little time to ponder the matter because, as though on cue, an army helicopter began buzzing our plant. Once it spotted our lone guard atop a water tank, it began spraying the area with machine-gun bursts. We returned the fire and a few of us actually scored direct hits but the copter kept coming back again and again. Then it suddenly flew away, probably to refuel, but we decided that it was our first combat victory and we practically jumped for joy. Our triumph, however, was short-lived. We learned that an infantry unit with tanks was headed our way. This time we were quick to agree that we didn't stand a chance. A getaway was clearly indicated. Most of the group departed for neighboring La Legua which was known for its strongly disciplined adherence to the Allende program. Its inhabitants were all working people, always at the forefront of those calling for greater militancy in defending the government.

"From a distance the noise from La Legua sounded like ominous thunderclaps, but as we neared the town, we could distinguish the sound of cannon and machine guns. We took a circuitous route and presently were in the battle zone. It was a sight I shall never forget. The entire population seemed to be on the firing line. Men, children, and even women, some obviously pregnant, were rushing about with machine guns, rifles and pistols, firing away at the military who seemed to be stuck at the entry gates of town. It was amazing to see housewives, elderly men, and even twelve-year-olds suddenly emerge as warriors. Except for the younger men who saw army service, these people had no previous experience with weapons. Our Sumar group quickly joined the defenders of La Legua. Some of us took up positions in the firehouse. Others were in the small church rectory.

"It was a ferocious battle with many, many casualties. The Junta forces armed with heavy weapons took a heavy toll. The streets began to look like an open grave. I was traumatized for days after having seen so many of the dead and so many rivulets of blood that seemed never to stop flowing. I've read a lot about Nazi concentration camps and about the horror of people being exterminated. But it is another matter when you yourself are part of so gruesome a scene.

"La Legua's population, between 4,000 and 5,000, relatively well armed with light machine guns and rifles, continued to resist the military successfully for nearly three days. But then the town's defenders ran out of ammunition and the Junta soldiers broke through. People were shot down right on their doorsteps. Entire families, children, wives, husbands, were killed with bursts of machine-gun fire. Those who remained alive were ordered out of their homes, which were vandalized or in many instances set afire.

"On the first day of the battle of La Legua, in which I and the others from Sumar took part, the fighting lasted until dark. It then came to a sudden halt with scarcely any exchange of fire. Several of the Sumar group, including myself, took advantage of the lull and left to find shelter and perhaps something to eat. We were exhausted, battle weary and terribly hungry. Carefully making our way in the direction of Sumar by way of side paths, we found some deserted chicken coops and settled there for the night. Early the next morning we decided that somehow we must get some food. We hadn't eaten for twenty-four hours. One of our group went out on a reconnaissance mission in the direction of Sumar. He soon came back and said that, as best as he could judge, the plant was not occupied. He and others urged that we

Shantytowns that resisted the Junta were treated savagely. Here two youths
suspected of being snipers were thrown to the ground by army soldiers
and then taken for interrogation, followed by jailing or execution.
Note the soldier pulling the youth's hair. (Wide World Photos)

get back to the plant, sneak into the kitchen cafeteria and grab what we could from the well-stocked refrigerators. We toyed with that proposal for only several minutes and agreed to take the chance.

"About twenty of us made our way to the factory. And just as we settled down to what looked like a hearty breakfast, the military broke in and began taking prisoners. Several of us were able to elude the roundup and get out of the area. Our adventure was obviously foolhardy regardless of how hungry we were. But in a crisis all kinds of utterly senseless things are done by perfectly normal people. Since the Sumar plant was still unoccupied, we somehow felt that we had a chance.

"When I was out of reach of the military, I waited until nightfall in a clump of bushes all the while holding onto my machine gun. And then I began feeling my way through back roads to my house which was about five miles away from the plant and in the opposite direction from La Legua. When I arrived, my family was virtually in mourning. My father was convinced that I was dead. My wife and children were in tears. I immediately hid my machine gun outside the house. By then I had grave doubts whether I'd ever be able to use it against the Junta. The dark shadow of the new era had already thickened, and the reality of our defeat was fast growing upon us.

"I remained at my house until September 18th. It was somewhat of a miracle that I was not arrested right away, because the neighborhood, including the local police officer who had known me ever since I was a child, knew of my union activities. Obviously something of the human, interpersonal relations still remained with him, for he made no effort to finger me. I remember sitting with my father at the TV set listening to one of the three top Junta generals—Gustavo Leigh (later deposed by Pinochet), saying 'All Marxists, all Leftists shall be dead. There's no better Commie than a dead Commie,' as he pointed his finger at the audience. I broke into a nervous guffaw and said to my father, 'My God, it looks as though he is pointing at me.'

"Day after day the Junta decrees were read over the radio and on television. Among these was an order that all workers report to their respective plants. I knew that I probably would be arrested

When workers were ordered to return to their factories following the coup, they were stood up against the wall, searched for weapons, and then questioned. (Wide World Photos)

once I showed up at my plant, but I decided to go nonetheless. Why? Because I felt fully responsible as a union leader. After all there were many rank and file workers from my plant who were already behind bars, many who had depended upon me and other union officers for direction and guidance. I felt that they would find it strange that I was out of jail while they were in. It may have been foolish on my part to present myself for what looked like certain imprisonment but it was a matter of conscience, so I went. A number of other union leaders did the same entirely on their own, without previous agreement among them. In general, workers began to present themselves to the new managers of the plants where they had been previously employed, although many would have preferred to continue resistance against the Junta. But the clandestine operations were still uncoordinated, so they had no idea where to go. Also, many labor and political leaders had already been executed or thrown into concentration camps. Workers felt that there was very little else they could do except report back to their places of work since failure to do so would have been interpreted as insubordination leading to quick arrest and possibly the firing squad.

"When I presented myself at the Sumar plant I decided there was no point in trying to deceive anyone, so I identified myself and also my status in the union. After some preliminary questions, I, together with about sixty-five others, were told we would have to undergo further interrogation. The questioning was along the classic Junta lines: Are you a Communist? Have you helped hide weapons and munitions so as to fight the Junta? What underground activity were you involved in? Give us the names of your accomplices? And so on. For two days and two nights this questioning went on with the accompaniment of beatings by soldiers armed with rubber clubs. Every denial on our part elicited intensified assault. I was clubbed across the body and across the face. My nose was broken on the first day of questioning. I lost consciousness several times. Each of us was questioned separately and ordered to inform on the others.

"From time to time they'd stop the beating and suddenly very solicitously ask, 'Why are you stupid? Why don't you talk? You'll be dying for naught. You're protecting people who have fled and are in hiding, while you are here taking the rap.' But we kept mum. I must say that the orientation we received from the union before the putsch, in anticipation of the questioning which we were undergoing, proved helpful to us. Not everyone, of course, was willing to abide by the pledge not to name names. But many of us did. After three or four hours of torture and interrogation, each of us, separately and totally nude, was led past the others who were next in line for this ordeal.

"Late the first night, we were told General Benavides, who supposedly was the man who gunned down Allende, was coming. 'And he will shoot you all, you bastards,' one of the officers threatened. Exactly at midnight, General Benavides arrived. When he was told that we would not turn informers, he let loose a stream of profanity. He screamed, 'You'll not be long in this world.' He was outraged at our determination, despite the obvious signs of torment that we had already undergone, such as torn faces, broken jaws, broken noses, blackened eyes. His big, pimply, hostile face turned purple, and his heavy frame quivered as he harangued us with insults and threats. There was a smell of death about him. 'For the last time,' he said, 'is there anybody here who will cooperate?' And when our response was stony silence, he ordered that our executions should begin immediately. He pointed at me as the first to be executed. I was pushed to an adjacent room which was separated by a thin wooden wall from the room in which the others were waiting their turn. I was shoved against the wall under a platform loaded with sacks of salt [used in the processing of textile materials]. Once again I was asked whether I was going to talk. And when I said no, the preparatory steps for my execution got underway. They tied my hands in the back and put a blindfold over my eyes. And in my case, at least, it was very much like what I've heard or read about the last moments of a person who is about to be shot. My entire life seemed to rush by as though on a film. I saw my father, the anxiety and tension that he always showed when coping with the family's poverty, much of my early life, and the courtship days with my wife. But then I heard the guns being cocked, the order to fire and then the rifle shots. There was a rush of what seemed like splinters against my face; actually it was the salt into which they fired which came tumbling over me.

"It was indeed a strange sensation. I seemed to feel nothing—anesthetized. I knew that I was not dead; that I was alive; however grim, my situation was not as bad as those of my comrades who heard the shots and knew they were next to be executed. And the thing that made it especially ghoulish was the death cry, which was simulated by a soldier standing close by. I was then led away with my friends standing in deathly suspense in the next room. One by one, they went through the same harrowing experience. But that wasn't the end of it. The military staged the execution scene three times to each of us on the next two nights. In the second and third go around, they threatened to shoot us en masse. Once again we were blindfolded and put against the wall. And mind you, this was in addition to the constant beatings. What clothes we had clung to our bloody, battered bodies like torn sails on a mast, yet we did not give up; we did not talk.

"On September 21st, they took us to the Estadio Nacional [National Stadium] which was turned into the infamous concentration camp. Here we entered a protracted period of electronic torture, beatings and psychological terror. I was in the Estadio Nacional for two months. I was then transferred to another camp in northern Chile, where I was imprisoned for a year. There was no torture there. The camp was used as a showplace of acceptable conditions of servitude to impress visiting Red Cross groups and other human rights agencies investigating prison conditions in Chile. I was then set free.

"Here in Mexico we found a warm welcome as refugees. I have a pretty good job as a technician and I'm also studying at night. We're all studying—my wife, and my two children, a boy of thirteen and a girl of eleven, who take their schooling seriously. We want to get as good an education as possible because when we get back to Chile we want to be useful in lifting the country out of its Fascist morass. I don't know how soon we'll be back or how we'll get there. But I know that the Junta is not going to last for too long. I'm convinced of that. I promise you, we will be back."

7

Chile's Women Divided:
The Supporters of the Coup
vs. the Jailed Resisters

About a week after the coup, when the Junta ordered everyone to return to work in factories, stores, and offices, twenty-three-year-old Carmen D. decided to go back to the law office where she worked part-time. A senior at the law school at the University of Chile at Valparaiso, Carmen was an enthusiastic Allende supporter and student activist, but had no party affiliation. She was stunned when a detachment of six marines surrounded her as she went into the office building.

"Why are you arresting me, and where are you taking me?" she asked, a bit scared but indignant. The officer in charge said that everything would be explained when she went with them to naval headquarters. She had known that going back to work might be risky—all pro-Allende people were suspect now. "But after all, I wasn't a political big shot, or for that matter even a little shot," she says with a wry smile. A tiny woman, maybe five feet tall, with deep, dark brown eyes, she talked to me in a small town in southern France, where she is now living in exile. "Sure I was involved, but as a representative of the student association, working with the faculty to revamp our very antiquated curricula." The marines hustled her into a jeep and drove off. "I still thought my detention would be only a matter of a day or two and then I'd be released.

"When we got to the naval base out at the edge of town, an officer took down my name, my address, and the fact that I was a law student. He said I was to be interrogated about charges that I was involved in smuggling arms and helping 'subversive elements' resisting the Junta. Before I had a chance to reply, I was pushed out of the office and into a big room to await my turn for the questioning.

"It was a dimly lit room and it smelled of vomit and blood. Dozens of men were lying on the floor. Some were moaning. Their clothes were torn, blood-drenched, their hair disheveled. Some were motionless. I couldn't tell whether they had fainted or were dead. Toward the far end of the room a half dozen women were sitting on canvas chairs. The guard shouted to me to sit with them. Some of the women held their heads in their hands, they were tense, none of them were talking to each other. As I picked my way across the room, careful not to step on the broken bodies of the men on the floor, and got closer to where the women sat, I saw one middle-aged woman with her hands pressed against her ears. Her eyes were drowned in tears and she was swaying from side to side. When I sat down on the one remaining chair, which happened to be next to hers, a piercing cry came tearing through the wall from the next room. The voice was that of a young boy. With each scream the swaying woman would groan from deep down in her body. There was another bloodcurdling cry and another, and then a gush of sobs, uncontrollable sobs accompanied by husky men's voices: 'Now will you tell us?'

"The boy being 'interrogated' in the next room, a woman sitting next to me whispered, was fourteen years old. He was the son of the weeping woman. The military were trying to force the boy to tell them the whereabouts of his father, an important Allende advisor who had gone underground. The torture had been going on for a long time. When I arrived it was almost over. Soon the limp, moaning body of the boy was dumped at his mother's feet. Blood gushed from his nose and mouth; some of his teeth were knocked out. The mother flung herself toward the boy. One of the guards at the door let her go to the lavatory nearby to wet her handkerchief to wipe off some of the blood. Some of us tried to help her, but there was an ugly shout from the other guard. 'Back where you belong. You'll get your turn.'

"I was now convinced that my future would be a lot more gruesome than I had anticipated. I was bathed in cold sweat as I imagined the horrors in store for me. At the same time I was worrying about Sergio, my husband. They might give me a very hard time, but I was a woman, I thought, so they probably would not hurt me physically. But the condition of the men in the room filled me with deepest anguish. Was Sergio also detained? Was he also being tortured? Suddenly the door to the room where the boy had been swung open and a soldier roared out my name and ordered me to follow him inside.

"I stood up but found walking almost impossible. There were only about ten steps to the door, but each step seemed like a mile. My feet, my legs seemed to be weighted down with heavy rocks. I was breathing hard, sweating, and my heart was beating like a runaway animal's. But somehow I made it. As I entered, someone from behind dropped a dark cloth bag over my head and immediately grabbed my arms to keep my hands from going up to my head to remove it. I was completely blindfolded. There was a slit at the mouth but no opening for the nose. I had to suck in the air at the mouth. Evidently I was about to faint, for I was being helped to a chair where I was told to sit up and not try to touch the blindfold.

"I was scarcely seated when a gravelly voice shouted, 'We know all about you. So you'd better cooperate. Who did you give the guns to?' Still struggling to get used to the darkness and to the bag over my head and face, I managed to reply in a skinny, muffled voice that I never had anything to do with the transfer of guns to anybody. I was suddenly jolted by a hard object in my back, I guess the barrel of a gun, and a loud command to 'speak up.' I tried hard to steady my voice and repeat that I knew nothing about gun traffic. The words were barely out of my mouth when a heavy blow on my back threw me right off the chair. The pain was sharp and quickly enveloped my body. I flailed about blindly, trying to steady myself. Again I was lifted and placed on the chair.

"'Look,' my inquisitor again demanded, this time in a milder tone, 'we've told you we know all about you. Are you going to deny your activities with the student organization?' I thought for a moment, remembered that my name was often on leaflets and letters as one of the officers of the association, and decided there

was no point in denying the obvious. So I said yes, I was in the
student organization. 'Fine,' my examiner growled with a hint of
friendliness. 'Now if you'll just get wise and cooperate, we'll let
you out of here in no time. So you also know Pedro Díaz and
Jaime Ocùña?' Their names also appeared on the student
association letterheads and often accompanied my signature on
various communications. Again I felt there was no sense in
making denials. 'So in addition to Díaz and Ocùña, who were
the others to whom you handed over the guns last week?' he
asked in a softer voice.

"Quickly I replied that I knew nothing of such activities. But
before I finished the sentence I was suddenly thrown out of the
chair and my captors' fists were pounding my back, chest, and
breasts to the accompaniment of curses and obscenities. Totally
blinded, unable to use my hands to ward off the attack, I
screamed and screamed. I don't know how long this assault
continued because I lost consciousness. I remember coming back
to life through a kind of blackened haze and then quickly back to
reality as my tormentors were at it once more, telling me that this
was only a foretaste of what was to come.

"This time I must have been on a different chair, with my
arms tied down to armrests, obviously to prevent my falling to the
floor if I fainted again. My body was all pain, the left side of my
head ached with needle-like jabs at the temple, probably from
the fall. But despite the throbbing physical distress and the
oppressive darkness of the blindfold, I do remember clearly that I
felt somehow I would survive. At the same time a deep state of
depression began to come over me. Would this torment kill my
unborn child? I was in my third month of pregnancy. Up to that
day, despite the shroud that the Junta had spread across Chile, I
must confess that I had continued to feel a certain euphoria. Was
it because of the nonspecific, biochemical changes that make a
woman with child become optimistic, anticipatory of good things
to come, expecting things to right themselves somehow? I never
probed the reasons for my attitude, but now I was seized with
despair, with fear that the other life within me would be snuffed
out.

"These waves of anxiety were woven into my thinking even as I braced myself to fend off the unending questions. 'What kind of guns did you deliver? Who were your contacts? Where are they hiding?' Again and again these questions, occasionally accompanied by a punch to the head or the chest. I have no idea how long this session went on. An hour? Three hours? When it finally ended I heard someone shout that unless I came across with the information I would be charged as an accomplice to an insurrectionary movement against the Junta; I would be tried before a war tribunal which might sentence me to the firing squad.

"My arms were unshackled from the chair and I was led away. I could scarcely keep up with my guards, as my blindfold made it impossible for me to have the slightest idea of direction. I was constantly tripping and bumping into furniture. With every misstep a stream of insults and curses came pouring out of the mouths of the torturers.

"Once outside the building, however, the crisp spring air revived me. I was pushed into a jeep, and after about an hour's drive over bumpy roads I was deposited at an old freighter, which, I learned later, was the infamous prison ship Lebu docked at the far end of the Valparaiso harbor. There I was held in a small cabin for five days, always blindfolded and fed bread and watery coffee from a tin cup.

"The days and nights merged into endless continuity. I didn't know until my blindfold was removed that my solitary confinement had lasted for five days. The only thing that sustained me, kept me from going mad," she said, "were my memories of the two-and-a-half years of the Allende regime, the wonderful things that happened to me in that time. I would relive my wedding with Sergio, an engineering student. It was a simple little party with only a few relatives and close friends, but there was gaiety and a warm glow of confidence in the future. The Allende years were hard, with the economic sabotage and all kinds of uncertainties, but there were also important changes for the better. We all felt a euphoria that most non-Chileans probably could not understand."

At the university Carmen worked on committees to help poor

and working-class students get textbooks and hot lunches.* The Allende regime took open admissions seriously, she said, so that universities and high schools had massive enrollments, requiring lots of remedial aid for those desperately trying to keep up with university standards.

"Notwithstanding my continuous darkness," Carmen said, "the images of my recent past were extremely vivid. Like broken records, playing themselves again and again, they shifted from my personal experiences to social activities. For instance, I thought over and over about our anti-illiteracy drive.

"We worked oftentimes well into the night. Some of our most rewarding experiences were connected with helping the illiterate in the shantytowns and the countryside. Every two weeks Sergio and I went with the Educational Brigades—nationally there were some 200,000 teachers, students, and professionals of all kinds—fanning out across the country to help the rural peasants and the men and women of the urban shantytowns learn the three R's, and to rouse them to improve their living standards." The Brigades' program, which called for a biweekly contribution of two hours by each volunteer, paid off handsomely, Carmen recalls, as Chile's illiteracy rate dropped from 20 to 12 percent in three years. "They grasped their newly discovered clues to the twentieth century with great enthusiasm.

"My friends, my husband, and I were heady with excitement." Her soft voice is elated. "It was no longer a matter of theory. We didn't sit around in the cafes, the way we used to before Allende's election, arguing what could or could not be accomplished once a people-oriented government came into power. We were actually doing it. We were directly involved in changing society and seeing the results of our effort. Those shantytown people, half-starved and demoralized, suddenly sprang to life. There was less despair, less drunkenness. They began to eat better, or more often, I should say. There is a statistic I always remember about the disparity in food consumption between the poor and the rich

* During the second year of the Allende administration (1972), 550,000 breakfasts and 700,000 lunches were served daily to students in various educational institutions.

in our country," Carmen said parenthetically. "In 1968, two years before Allende took office, 60 percent of the people—the low-income Chileans—ate an average of six chickens per family per year. Ten percent of the population—the high-income group—ate 96 chickens per family per year. With the Allende program the grinding poverty of the have-nots was eased very quickly. They began to earn regular wages because of government-supported job opportunities. But this didn't last very long. Rightist produce distributors, local manufacturers, and of course the foreign multinational corporations began to strangle the economy by creating an artificial scarcity of goods. So there developed what you North Americans call a 'Catch-22' situation. The urban workers and peasants had more money to spend, but there were fewer and fewer things they could spend it on.

"And while we young activists felt that we had a role in transforming society, we became aware that we too were undergoing a transition. We became less preoccupied with ourselves as individuals, with our personal hangups and frustrations. The notion of 'finding ourselves,' the 'do your own thing' concept, which we heard was of great concern to our contemporaries in the United States, didn't seem to fit into our thinking. Our emphasis was on the idea of being socially useful in the community you lived in, or the organization you belonged to." Carmen describes herself as from a "lower-middle-class background." She is one of five sisters and brothers. When the children were grown her mother worked as a secretary in a hospital; her father was a manager of a small business.

Carmen believes that it is this mixture of memories, Sergio's love, her work in law school, the anti-illiteracy campaigns in her beloved countryside, that made it possible for her to remain sane. But there were also flashbacks that brought melancholy and deep remorse. Why hadn't she and Sergio gone into hiding or tried to take refuge at some foreign legation? And where was he now, she asked herself inside the blackness of the blindfold.

Carmen first learned of the coup early in the morning of September 11th, before the Junta stormed La Moneda. The overthrow of the Popular Unity government actually began in Valparaiso. When Carmen and the rest of the city's 300,000 inhabitants awoke that morning, they discovered that naval detachments had cut off the roads leading to the downtown areas. And when they ran to turn on the radio they were greeted with a barrage of announcements that a coup was under way: everyone should stay indoors and await further orders from the Junta. While Valparaiso took on the image of a city at war, the TV from Santiago showed that the capital was still normal, except for a flurry of excitement around La Moneda where cabinet ministers and other government members were going into the building to talk to Allende.

"Is this really it? Is the dreaded coup really upon us?" Carmen and her husband asked each other anxiously. Was this a nationwide rebellion or was the mutiny confined to the navy and would it, therefore, blow over? After all, Chile had experienced a similar shock only six weeks earlier, in what was known as the June 29th Tancazo Incident when a tank battalion tried to storm the presidential palace and install a Rightist government. But the uprising was put down in a couple of hours. Was the Valparaiso rebellion equally doomed to fail?

With all phone connections cut, Carmen and her husband decided to try to find out what was happening in downtown Valparaiso. They took a circuitous route, walking along side paths and back roads. There was panic in the air. "Despite the road blocks, the streets were filled with people queuing up at bakeries and groceries, hoping against hope to stock up on bread and other foodstuffs before the supplies gave out. Marines and sailors, bayonets fixed to their rifles, displayed their machismo by threatening people, ordering them to return to their homes. The Junta military, drunk with power, would fire into the sky to scare those who weren't moving fast enough. And then loudspeakers on marine trucks began announcing a noon-hour curfew, warning that those still on the streets after twelve would be killed then and there." Carmen and her husband got back to their house just before the curfew. By then the news flashes from Santiago showed La Moneda in flames, and later in the afternoon came the announcement of Allende's death. As the day wore on, the radio and TV delivered a steady diet of Junta decrees, interrupted only by martial music.

For the next several days Carmen and her husband kept close to home. It was a dreadfully lonely period. Only occasionally were they able to make contact with a friend in a back alley or a secluded house. They grieved over Allende and over Chile, and became increasingly apprehensive as rumors multiplied about arrests and detention of prominent figures in the Popular Unity government, but it still did not occur to them that they too would be vulnerable.

These memories of the recent past gnawed away at her and at the same time kept her busy reliving them. On the sixth day of her stay on Lebu her hood was removed and she was led down to the hold of the ship, "into a sort of moldy storage area, where I joined about fifty other women prisoners. It was an airless hole. The stench from unwashed bodies, garbage all over the floor, and the doorless toilet was overpowering. The smells, combined with the motion of the ship at anchor, made a number of women seasick.

"As depressed as I was, aching all over, worried about my husband and the state of my pregnancy, the release from my blindfold gave me a momentary feeling of exhilaration. It took me a while to adjust to the world of the seeing, but it was a wonderful experience until I began to make out what I was seeing. All of us looked ghastly; hair uncombed, clothes rumpled, torn, some in shreds. As my eyes became more accustomed to the semidarkness I recognized a few who were well known for their leadership in the women's campaigns in support of the Allende program. As I looked more closely I began to realize how relatively light my ordeal had been compared to that of most of the women around me.

"There was an exceptionally attractive young woman, about nineteen or twenty years old, who sat in the corner, crying and moaning softly. From time to time she mumbled, 'I want to die, I want to die. I hope they'll kill me. I won't bear a Fascist child.' The woman had been picked up in a raid on a group of young Communists who were caught mimeographing leaflets attacking the Junta. For two days she was raped repeatedly, and then tortured with electric shocks to her vagina and breasts, as the

Junta tried to get her to reveal the names of her accomplices. She remained steadfastly silent. Some of the women, half-dead themselves, tried to comfort her, to convince her that if she was indeed pregnant her baby would be an extension of herself, not of any of those who had violated her. But she went on whispering, unable to respond to them.

"In the five days that I remained with these women I couldn't help being impressed with their courage. And so my morale improved considerably. Some of the prisoners were mere teenagers, others in their forties. Some were well-known political activists, Communists, Socialists or members of the ultra-Left MIR group, especially singled out for brutal treatment. Most of the women had black-and-blue marks across their arms, faces and bodies where they had been beaten. Some had livid cigarette burns on their breasts and abdomens. Many had infected wounds, untreated of course, and seeping pus. They tried to wash their wounds with the thin stream of tepid water from our one faucet in the lavatory.

"There was one woman who could scarcely move. Her hands had been tied to her legs and she had been left hanging from a bar for three days. Whether her blood circulation was permanently damaged or some of her bones were dislocated or broken none of us knew. The slightest touch to her body would send her off into whirlpools of excruciating pain. Another woman was obviously in a complete mental breakdown. She was a young MIR member who, after being raped in the presence of her husband, was thrown into a tank of human excrement and retrieved just as she was about to choke to death. She looked out with unseeing, haunted eyes, wells of pain. She never made a sound, never responded to our attempts at conversation, never ate. She just sat there dying.

"But most of the women somehow retained a kind of brooding defiance. And because we were guarded by a young marine corporal who seemed to be doing his job out of fear rather than pleasure, the atmosphere was somewhat relaxed. He stood at the door with gun in hand, asking us politely not to talk too loudly, more concerned about the threat of an officer bursting in to take us by surprise than by any dreams of escape we might have.*

"On the fourth or fifth day in these cramped surroundings, where we were forced to eat our prison fare sitting on the floor and sleep there as well, I began to bleed heavily. Hours went by before a doctor came down to look at me and, after a very cursory examination, decided upon the obvious—that I was having a hemorrhage. At what seemed like a slow-motion pace, I was taken to be processed for temporary release from the ship and then shoved into a jeep for an hour's ride over bumpy roads to the naval hospital. The bleeding was stopped and I didn't abort the child, principally because of a friendly nurse who whispered encouragement and tried her best to get me nourishing food.

"On the third day of my hospital stay, a prosecutor from the military adjutant general's office showed up and began to question me all over again about the charges that I had helped smuggle arms to resistance fighters around Valparaiso. The questioning this time was quite formal, with all my denials tape recorded. I was told that I would stand trial for high treason.

"The following day I was again taken to the ship Lebu, where I was alone in a cabin for nearly three weeks but blindfolded only occasionally, depending on the mood of the guard on duty. I was then told that I had been tried in absentia and given an indeterminate prison sentence. I was transferred to a women's prison north of Santiago. It was a complex of old, dilapidated structures. Masonry and other debris from the earthquake of 1970 still cluttered the grounds. Grime, litter, torn newspapers were everywhere. Most of the plumbing was out of order.

"But for me the removal of the blindfold was equivalent to

* Sometimes an enlisted man would reveal a deep sympathy and at great personal risk furtively extend a helping hand. When the coup took place, many in the military and in the *carabineros*—the national police—were as surprised as the victims. Although the overthrow of the Allende government was well organized, especially in plans for the liquidation of anyone even vaguely suspected of being a potential resister, most of the armed forces could not have been privy to these plans. Many of the junior officers and enlisted men were thrown into confusion when they were suddenly commanded to carry out punitive orders against individuals who in some cases turned out to be former schoolmates or even relatives. There were instances when soldiers who showed the slightest hesitation at making arrests or taking part in executions were shot on the spot by their commanding officers.

paradise. The compound I was assigned to was separate from the rest of the prison, reserved for the Junta's political opponents. There were fifty of us, ten women to each dormitory. We felt fortunate because it was a traditional Chilean women's prison, which meant that our jailers were nuns. They were hardbitten, and except for a few of the younger ones were severe and non-communicative. But because many of us were university students, and some came from upper-middle-class families, the nuns were grudgingly respectful. Most of these nuns came from rural Chile, with impoverished origins and only a smattering of primary education. Thanks to their inferiority complex we got better treatment than the other prisoners.

"I gave birth in the sixth month of my imprisonment. After three days in a city hospital under guard, I returned with my child to my dormitory. I remained with my baby behind bars for another six months. Needless to say, this was not an easy period for me. I don't know what the outcome would have been if not for the continued support of my prisoner friends. I named the baby Felice and she became a sort of lifeline to hope and to the future for all of us. She suddenly acquired ten mothers instead of only one. Even some of the frozen-faced nuns thawed when near the infant, and late at night there would be a little ritual. A few of the nuns, at considerable risk to themselves, would creep along the dimly lit corridors carrying bottles of hot water inside their black robes. With the aid of a flashlight or a candle, enough light was shed on a makeshift tub to enable us to bathe my baby. All the women shared in this ceremony.

"Fortunately the baby had no special health problems. I nursed her and did what I could to give her fresh air. But we were limited to only an hour a day to walk about in the prison yard. I'd bundle her up with pitiful rags and try to expose her face to the wan shafts of sunshine that filtered through the barbed wire on top of the brick walls that fenced us in. Perhaps it was the torrent of love from all of us—that girl not only survived but actually thrived.

"One day, without previous notice, the prison administrator summoned me to the office and told me to pack my belongings; I was to be released that very hour and returned to Valparaiso.

Perhaps some of the international organizations had pressured the Junta to let me go because of my baby. I could never find out. Altogether I was incarcerated for one year and two months."

Two weeks later Carmen applied for permission to leave the country. She was given a passport and received a visa from the Swedish consulate. She is now in France with her husband, who eluded the Junta police by hiding out in the hills and then making his way to the Swedish Embassy in Santiago, where he remained until he left for Europe.

Another graduate of the freighter Lebu has asked me to call her Clara, to protect the safety of her relatives still in Chile. She too is a native of Valparaiso. Clara was held in another part of the ship, away from the hold that Carmen lived in. For most of the forty-five days she was aboard, she remained blindfolded and endured a daily barrage of abuse and torture. The cloth-bag blindfold was inflicted on almost all prisoners, Clara says. It was designed to terrorize the captives and, at the same time, to shield the inquisitors from recognition. Its use was tantamount to "an admission of the shameful, sadistic atrocities that the Junta was involved in. Implicit also was the cowardice of the torturers—the fear that should they face a day of reckoning, that the survivors of the inquisition would turn against them and, as in the Nuremberg trials, demand retribution."

Clara's Gauleiters ordered her to lead them to the hideout of her husband, who had been a high-ranking Allende official. Clara wouldn't oblige for two reasons: because she couldn't conceive of herself being an accomplice against a man she loved and respected, "even if they tortured me to death"; and second, "I actually didn't know where he had gone to continue organizing the resistance." A handsome, firm-looking woman in her late thirties, with a mobile, expressive face, copper-colored skin, and deep-set black eyes, Clara was a high school teacher in Valparaiso. Perhaps because of that training she speaks very clearly and with a strong rising inflection when stressing a point. Her manner is not that of a teacher but that of a passionate arguer, with a very personal involvement in the outcome of a discussion.

Clara belonged to no party, but she was active in women's organizations that worked for better housing for shantytown dwellers and organized women to press for more jobs, which were basic goals of the Popular Unity program.

"When the Junta struck, Lucho, my husband, went underground with other pro-Allende activists to make plans to preserve what was left of the parties of the Left and to mount a resistance." This was no surprise to Clara. As the political situation began to deteriorate in the last months of the Allende administration, both Clara and her husband had agreed that if a coup occurred he would have to continue his political work, even if it meant separation from his family. Like many other Chileans, however, they had not foreseen that the Junta would be as brutal and far-reaching as it was in its reprisals. Clara was as shocked as the younger Carmen at the Junta's long arm.

When Lucho took cover on the day of the coup, Clara remained at home with their three children, but early in the afternoon Lucho sent a message that she too was in danger and that she and the children should take shelter in some friend's home. By coincidence, soon after the message came, a couple that lived down the block came to visit Clara. These were conservative people, critical of Allende, although they took no part in politics. But when they saw on TV the Junta's storming of La Moneda and the massacre of hundreds of people on the streets of Santiago, they were appalled. Quickly realizing that tragedy could overtake Clara's family, they had come to tell her that she and the children were welcome to stay with them for a few days.

Late that night—fortunately moonless—Clara and her family sneaked down the street to the neighbors' home. The next day word spread that the Junta dragnet was extending into the whole area, and Clara's hosts made contact with several similarly conservative friends who were also horrified by the reign of terror. And since they were least likely to be suspect, their homes became Clara's one-night havens. Clara was amazed at the generosity and courage of her protectors, since they too could have become victims if accused of harboring enemies of the state.

There was one especially close call for her and her benefactors in her third refuge, a big two-story house with many rooms. Clara and her children were lodged on the second floor, near what used to be the servants' quarters. They were having a snack and being very quiet when suddenly they heard loud knocking on the front door. Their host, an elderly man, was heading toward the door but he evidently wasn't fast enough. The door was smashed open and a gang of ten marines stormed in, shouting they were there to search the house. At that moment the owner's pet, a cocker spaniel, began barking fiercely and baring his teeth, but before the dog could even hope to leap to attack, a marine put a bullet through its head. Then the search began. Clara and her children huddled together in deathly stillness, paralyzed with fear. They heard the shooting and the loud stamping of the military in their hobnailed boots as they made their way up the stairs. Miraculously, Clara says, they missed opening the door of the room where she and the children were crouching in a closet. "The soldiers left and we remained in the house until dark. Then, on our way again, we whispered our thanks to our hosts

When the Junta took over, decades of Chilean democracy and liberty
went into eclipse. Even the words Viva Libertad *were flushed away.*
(United Press International Photo)

and apologized for being the cause of trouble for them, particularly the loss of their pet.

"This time we were picked up by a doctor whose MD insignia gave us a fairly safe passage to his home, whose basement was his laboratory. We spent the night surrounded by boxes and cages full of rabbits and guinea pigs.

"We hopped about from one friendly refuge to another for nearly a week. In the meantime things began to quiet down. The Junta snuffed out what remained of the pockets of resistance around Valparaiso. The house-to-house searches abated somewhat. Long lists of names of people wanted for hearings and questioning were posted on billboards and rolled out on TV. My husband's name was included but mine was not. Our transient existence was hard on the children—Gloria was eleven, Pedro was nine, and Jorge eight—and even though our immediate future was still murky, I felt that since I was not on the wanted list the Junta would probably let me be. So we went back home. A heavy-handed 'normalcy' descended on Valparaiso; it was a tranquility edged with dread, nevertheless stores began to reopen and commercial activity was encouraged. And about a week after we returned, the Junta issued a decree that all schools should reopen. I was faced with a momentous decision: Should I go back to teach or should I make myself scarce? A few friends whom I was able to see occasionally suggested that my absence from the job would probably call more attention to me. Also, I was now the sole breadwinner for the family; my job was going to make the difference whether we would eat or not eat.

"For the first few days back at work, all went well. But on the fifth morning the police came to the school looking for me. They walked right into my classroom, with the worried principal alongside, and told me I was under arrest. They then drove me to the Lebu and handed me over to the Junta's marines.

"I was astounded to see that one of the officers was a young lieutenant who had once been my student. Perplexed, embarrassed, he tried to get out of the situation by leaving the room. But his superior officer called him back, and so there he was, a crimson-faced, perspiring young man asking me about my profession and other questions, and politely addressing me as *maestra* (teacher). But that took only about ten minutes and then a curtain of darkness fell down to separate me from the rest of the world.

"I wasn't allowed to communicate with my children or anyone else. For the next forty-five days I was continuously blindfolded, beaten, abused—all to make me reveal my husband's hiding place. The torture was unbearable, but somehow it became more endurable as I began to challenge myself on how much pain I was able to tolerate."

Clara was flung to the ground and kicked every time she denied knowing where her husband was. She was stripped naked and burned with lighted cigarettes on her breasts and back. When pain overwhelmed her and she fainted, the Junta officers revived her by jolting her with electrodes applied to ears and temples. They would then force her to get up, and prod her with clubs to walk fast. "Not being able to see," she says, "I'd stumble against tables, chairs, trip and fall down, frequently hitting my head against the tile floor. And as soon as I was back standing again they would order me to sit down. Often, as I began to sit down they would pull the chair from under me. As I fell back with a heavy thud, pain engulfing my spine, they'd howl with laughter. It was all a joke. There were times when I sincerely wished I'd die. But for the most part there grew within me a hard sullenness, a defiance and a dedication to holding out, regardless of the humiliation and the torture. My very survival, I felt, was an act of reprisal against the Junta.

"Shortly before my release, my blindfold was removed. What it feels like to escape from continuous darkness is impossible to convey to anybody who has not had at least a temporary bout with blindness. But my exhilaration was tempered immediately when I saw my reflection in the cracked mirror in the ship's lavatory. Forty-five days of no air, sun, soap, or water had taken their toll. My skin was blotchy and coarse, quite unpleasant to behold. Probably motivated by a desire to mask their sadism, my captors sent a naval doctor to give me some creams and oils.

"I now shared a huge improvised dormitory with about a hundred women, all veterans of the Junta terror. Bruised and tormented, each of them wore that indelible look of people whose physical and psychological traumas will mark them for life. Because of their condition and because our lot improved somewhat, rumor spread that we were soon to be set free. As it turned out, except for a handful of us, the rest were shipped out to concentration camps for further torture. Several were released because of protests from abroad. For me and two or three others, I am sure it was the intervention of some highly placed relatives in the armed forces. Military careers were a tradition in my family, and one of my cousins was a naval commander. Some of them must have pulled the necessary strings to get me out."

Carmen, Clara, and many of the other women on the Lebu were typical of women who surfaced as activists and leaders in the Popular Unity Party campaigns. Clara believes that their competence as organizers is what made the Junta go after them with such ferocity. "In the eyes of the generals and the admirals who seized the government, these women represented a powerful reservoir of resistance that had to be stamped out."

In the three years of the Allende government, she explains, women became involved politically and organizationally as never before. They set up neighborhood watchdog committees to curb black marketeering, and they pressured deputies and senators to vote for legislation to improve housing, schools, and health services.

With Allende's specific encouragement, they drew up legislation to abolish the label of illegitimacy and to give women the right to divorce.* Allende tried to push through a bill to create a Ministry of the Family to be headed by a woman with cabinet rank. This was turned down by the Rightist majority in Congress, but a National Secretariat for Women, with less power, administered by a committee of six women, was established.

Women like Clara and Carmen have distinguished forebears

* In his campaign speeches Allende said: "For Chilean women we want equality under the law, equal opportunity; equality of rights under the law. We want equality for their children. No persecution of the unmarried mother. There should be no illegitimate or natural children; all children shall have the same rights. That the horizon of culture and education be opened up to women. That there be thousands upon thousands of day nurseries for the children of these women of the people. We want the working woman to know that we regard it as a right that she also have security as a housewife."

in Chilean history. Women's participation in Chile's political and social confrontations is not entirely a twentieth-century development. It is rooted in women's dissatisfaction with their status as "second-class citizens," very much as in other nations, though actions to redress these conditions along Chilean lines has been rare in the rest of Latin America. As early as 1886 Eloise Díaz was able to crack the walls of Chile's most aloof preserve, the medical profession. She was the first woman to be graduated from a Chilean medical school and given a license to practice. Six years later another closed establishment, the legal profession, was breached when Matilda Throup became the country's first woman lawyer. At about the same time women workers in the garment industry became openly restive because of unequal wage standards. At the turn of the century Chile was shocked when women joined their male co-workers in Valparaiso and marched in a May Day demonstration to demand better working conditions.

"Maybe it is only a romantic notion," Clara says with a smile, "but many Chilean women feel that their readiness to put up a fight against injustice, or for things they believe in, evolves from a long historical tradition." Three hundred years ago, when the Spanish Conquistadores invaded what is now Chile and tried to subdue the local Araucano Indians, the women fought side by side with their warrior husbands to defend their lands. In chronicling the events of that period the Spaniards recorded the names of at least two Araucano women, Fresia and Guacola, who distinguished themselves as fighters against the invaders.

In more modern times Chile's women became ever more assertive along social and political lines, increasingly active in battles to improve overall economic conditions.* As in other countries, some women complained that their husbands, though of the same political outlook, were insensitive to their need to get out of their kitchens and become involved in the world about

---

*Chile presented a lopsided picture as regards women's rights from the 1930s on. Women won the right to vote in municipal elections in 1934, but not in national elections until 1949, after ten other Latin American nations had already granted universal suffrage. At the same time, educational and professional opportunities were wide open, especially to middle-class women.

them. They quipped that their husbands "were full of Socialist consciousness the moment they got outside the door of the house, but had little of it left when they came back through the door on their return home." Other women, however, including Clara, thought that in view of the tensions during the Allende days, when the country was moving from crisis to crisis, "pinning the women's liberation flag onto an anti-male platform per se, as is frequently done in the United States, would have been inappropriate. Our approach is somewhat different from that of the women's movement in the United States," she says. "We certainly want to rid our country of the ugly, discriminatory practices associated with the traditional male chauvinism that has pervaded every sphere of our lives. But we don't see our emancipation in terms of a power struggle against the male sector of our society. In a semicolonial country such as Chile, with so many indignities heaped upon the working man, it may perhaps be more comprehensible that the attainment of a better life for men would also help raise the living standards of women. Only by understanding our plight in the context of the political and economic structure of our society, and the realization of the need for joint actions by men and women against those holding the reins of economic and political power, can true liberation of women take place."

By way of example Clara cited an incident dating back to 1910, when the wives of nitrate workers urged their husbands to demand pay increases to meet the soaring cost of living. "'Go on strike, or do something to get your employers to give you better wages for this killing work. Strike,' they warned, 'or we won't

---

By 1968, 46 percent of Chilean university students were women. With sexist bars down, entry into universities depended on secondary-school grades and aptitude tests, and women generally outscored men in both. Women entered the professions in large numbers. In the mid-sixties, women comprised 8.5 percent of Chile's physicians and 32 percent of its dentists. In the United States in this period, 6.7 percent of doctors and .08 percent of engineers were women.

In Chile's lower economic ranks, women traditionally found employment as dressmakers, retail sales clerks, and more recently as factory and clerical workers. But those coming to the city from the countryside or the shantytowns were doomed to only one occupation, that of housemaid.

cook your dinners.'" However simplistic the threat, it worked.
The men shut down the processing plants until they got their
wage increase and "the participation of women in that episode
heightened the men's respect for them."

As Clara told me this story I remembered that in interviews
with Chilean men now in exile, I had noticed that many referred
to their wives as *compañera* (comrade), rather than the con-
ventional *esposa* (wife).

The Allende regime's innovative programs attracted many
foreigners eager to participate in their implementation. Some
were economists, others public health specialists, still others were
agronomists and teachers. They came from Sweden, Denmark,
Spain, and other parts of Europe. Some were exiles escaping the
tyrannies of the military dictatorships of Uruguay, Bolivia,
Brazil, or Argentina. One foreigner turned out to be Señora
Joanna K., an Argentine by birth, of British parentage, who
came to live in Chile with her Chilean husband, a Protestant
minister. Their three children were born in Chile.

"About two or three weeks after Allende's inaugural," Señora
K. remembers, "I heard a radio announcement asking women to
attend a meeting in downtown Santiago to discuss ways of
solidifying support for the Allende administration. This was my
first introduction to any kind of political movement.

"Most of the discussion centered on ways to rebut the Rightist
attack against Allende. A hysterical campaign had been launched
charging that the Allende government would plunge Chile into
economic chaos and would turn the country into a Communist
state. And since about 75 percent of the press, radio, and TV was
controlled by the Right, a good deal of this propaganda had an
impact.

"The basic program of the Popular Unity Party called for
fundamental social and economic reforms that for the first time
in Chile's history would enable the disfranchised sector—a very
sizable part of the population—to eat decently; to provide better
care for their children, thus reducing one of the highest infant
mortality rates in the world; and to benefit from greater
educational opportunities. All this was not to be done by decree
but by parliamentary legislation." The challenge, therefore, to

those who supported these reforms was finding ways to reach the public with the facts; above all, how to get the information to those who would be the greatest beneficiaries, the impoverished.

"A variety of committees were set up to broaden media and other kinds of publicity. Some women volunteered to work with the women of the shantytowns, and I joined that group. Among other things, because of my training as a nurse I felt I could be useful in helping people improve their hygiene and nutrition, two areas which Allende, as a doctor, was emphasizing."

A serious, practical-minded woman in her late forties, Señora K. says, "It's hard to understand how anybody would have opposed the government's efforts to ease the plight of the shantytown dwellers. But the multinational corporations, their Chilean surrogates, as well as the landed gentry saw the proposed changes as a threat to the status quo.

"This polarization along class lines," she says, "was reflected sharply among Chilean women. Those who may have been moderately conservative now rallied around the extreme Right; women of progressive or liberal orientation moved to the general Left. The women who belonged to the aristocracy or to the upper-middle class saw their station in life infringed upon. Under the Allende program, for instance, they would have to surrender what they regarded as their privilege to hire or fire their domestic help at will. They were now to be constrained in such actions by legal requirements to show cause. These women could not countenance the idea that their children would sit side by side with those of their maids in the high schools or in the university. And they could scarcely conceive of the possibility that they would be sharing the fancy beaches around Valparaiso with the families of the shantytown poor whose vacations were to be paid for by the state."

What was "especially revolting," Señora K. says, "was the devious attempt by women of the aristocracy to terrorize their proletarian sisters who began to hope for a new day thanks to the Allende government. These stylishly dressed women appeared in the shantytowns pretending to be census officials. 'How many children do you have? How many are boys? What are their ages?' they asked the mothers standing at the doors of their rickety hovels with their undernourished, unkempt children tugging at their skirts. These impoverished women, most of them illiterate, looked with mistrust and fear at the fake census takers. And when some of them summoned enough courage to ask about the purpose of the census, they were told that the incoming regime wanted a head count of all children; many of them, they said, would be sent to Cuba and other Socialist countries for indoctrination."

This rumor swept Santiago's slum areas like wildfire. Mothers began hiding their children at the mere sight of suspicious-looking strangers on the block. The census hoax came to light with the disclosure that two children had died of suffocation when their panicked mother pushed them under pillows and bedclothes to hide them from two smartly dressed women who knocked at her door.

This was the political climate, Señora K. says, that enveloped Chile at the start of the Allende administration. She was happy to see, however, that although the Rightists' acts of sabotage intensified with each day, in some ways they began to backfire. For once some of the government's social reform programs were set into motion, pro-Allende sentiment mushroomed, particularly in the shantytowns.

The variety of legislative bills proposed by the new government was a Magna Carta for Chile's women. Some were pushed through in quick succession, others were held up in endless debate or rejected outright by the conservatives in Congress. Some had already been approved by previous administrations but never put into effect. But if not all the bills were implemented right away, the blueprint for the future was there.

In a speech early in 1972, President Allende declared: "The woman fighting against the discriminatory practices of her boss should not stand alone, certainly so far as pay is concerned. It shall also be the obligation of all workers not to permit, not to tolerate, and not to accept the greater exploitation of the woman."

One law declared that men and women must get equal pay for equal work. Another ruled that pregnancy was no longer to be a threat to job security. Whenever a woman factory or domestic worker was ready to return to work after giving birth, a job similar to the one she had held before confinement was to be made available to her. Moreover, if she decided to nurse her baby, the new work regulations allowed her to stay at home with full pay for as long as a year. And in cases when a child was not sick enough to be hospitalized, but required special home care, the mother was permitted to stay away from the factory at full pay until the child was two years old. Although some of these regulations, especially those concerning servants, could not yet be fully enforced, the handwriting was on the wall.

Government-funded nurseries and kindergarten programs got started even before Allende became President. But they were few in number and poorly staffed. With the Popular Unity administration, Señora K. says, there was a big push to help mothers with the care of their children whether they were at work in the city or in the agricultural regions. The law entitled all working mothers to have their children attend these nurseries to the age of three. All factories, offices, and business enterprises with twenty or more employees were obliged to set up nurseries where mothers could visit with their children during lunch or coffee breaks.*

In a matter of months, Señora K. recalls, many women responded enthusiastically. They shed their timidity and emerged "as a grass-roots auxiliary of the government." This was reflected in congressional elections of 1973 when despite the tottering economy the pro-Allende vote rose significantly.

When Señora K. began working in the shantytowns she was "positively shocked" to see the misery in which the inhabitants lived. She thought it outrageous that Chile's previous governments had been so neglectful of these people. Their knowledge of hygiene and of basic nutrition was virtually nonexistent. "When the Allende government launched the daily free milk

---

*In the year 1972 alone, 133 kindergartens were opened to care for about 8,000 children. The following year the government planned to add another 240 kindergartens and the Rightist majority in Congress turned it down. The Allende regime's goal was a plan for the care of 1,200,000 children. The mothers were to receive free breakfasts supplied by the employers whether on the factory or on the farm.

distribution for children under fifteen, mothers had to be taught how to prepare the milk, which came in powdered form. Volunteer health workers told them how to keep utensils clean and why the milk should not be left exposed to the sun or dust and insects."

The women of the shantytowns required little prodding to accept these aids to better health, according to Señora K. They hungered for this enlightenment. Lack of health care and scarcity of food made death a constant companion in their midst. As late as 1968, only two years before Allende's election, Chile's infant mortality rate was 86.6 per thousand compared to 16 per thousand in the United States, which itself does not have an enviable rating in this regard. Chile also had a 30 percent maternal death due to induced labor. And because of malnutrition many thousands of children suffered from physical and mental retardation. By early 1971, the new health measures produced dramatic results. Infant mortality dropped by 10.5 percent and maternity death went down to 17.6.

In the first several months of the Allende government, Señora K. says, salary increases and more jobs led to a surge in the consumption of meats, potatoes, sugar, milk, and eggs. But this development was short-lived because many Rightist meat ranchers and other large-scale farmers cut back on production to embarrass the administration. To offset the scarcity, the government undertook to popularize meat substitutes, such as fish and vegetables. "Ironically, despite the long Chilean coast and the availability of a rich fish supply most Chileans never cultivated a taste for fish. And apart from greens used in salads, the Chileans were also unaccustomed to such vegetables as spinach. So we volunteers started classes on how to cook fish and vegetables so they would be accepted at the family table."

As the price of staple foods skyrocketed, another women's meeting was held in Santiago. After a frank presentation of the facts, Pedro Vuscovic, Allende's Minister of Economy, said: "We would like to have your ideas on what should be done to cope with this deteriorating situation. After all, it is the women who are bearing the brunt when trying to get food to the table. It is you who are directly responsible for feeding the family." After a lengthy discussion there emerged the idea of organizing what soon became known as JAP, Juntas de Abastecimiento y Control de Precios—in rough translation, a committee to oversee price control and fair distribution of food and other products.

"The JAP was to operate in the neighborhoods. Women volunteers took an informal community census and set up a basis for rationing such items as sugar, rice, and bread. It was an unofficial operation, a kind of populist pressure action, to try to substitute for the anti-black market law that Allende tried and failed to push through Congress. The legislation would have imposed stiff fines on store owners hoarding food and confiscated the seized merchandise." Blocking this regulation was exactly the same thing as formally legitimizing black marketeering, as Señora K. saw it.

"The JAP was quite successful in the shantytowns," she says. "As soon as a truck was spotted unloading at a grocery or a butcher shop, the JAP committee alerted the neighborhood. Men, and especially women, queued up and bought whatever goods were delivered, to make sure the store owners didn't stash them away for under-the-counter shenanigans.

"By the beginning of 1973, there were 1,500 JAP committees across the country, including 900 in Santiago. More than two-thirds of JAP members were women. But the JAP idea did not catch on as much in the middle-class areas as in the poorer ones because many of the women there associated themselves ideologically with their economic betters and wouldn't do anything that might help the Allende government. In a way they were cutting off their noses to spite their faces. For the fact is that the very rich were able to stuff their larders at whatever price, while the others spent more and more time on longer and longer food lines with very little to show for it. All too often when their turn came the shelves were already swept clean. Their frustration was directed at the Allende government, however, not at those responsible for the crisis."

Seizing upon this rising disquiet, the Right intensified its anti-Allende campaign in terms of "consumerism," that is, that the economic hardships, which it had helped to create, was Allende's doing. The media campaign was quite successful in blurring the distinction between upper-class women, who were stockpiling their pantries from the black market, and the empty-handed lower-middle class and the poor. The Rightists' propaganda proclaimed that it was an "all women's problem," since it was the housewife who bore the brunt. It was not an issue between classes: rich and poor women suffered alike.

More and more Chile appeared to be headed toward a collision course with itself. On the one hand there was a mounting demand for the expansion of programs that had a touch of the rosy future, something which until then seemed beyond the rainbow. On the other hand, those in opposition did everything in their power to hold the country back. But the Allende people continued to press forward with their reforms.

For instance, a pilot project was started in Santiago to free working mothers from the chore of preparing the family dinner after a day in an industrial plant. Meals were cooked and attractively packaged in a central kitchen and then distributed by a fleet of trucks to the various factories participating in this experiment. Each of the women was given as many dinners as there were members in her family, all at minimal prices. At the outset some 8,000 women were involved. For the year 1973, the plan was to provide 40,000 women with this service.

But perhaps the most dramatic achievement designed to brighten the lives of women, especially poor women, was the regulation to give them and their children annual vacations free of charge. As Señora K. describes it, "The very idea of so many factory workers as well as domestic servants getting time off with pay strained one's credulity. But in addition, to have these women avail themselves of a two-week vacation, with all expenses paid, was simply an echo of paradise." The Allende government began putting up large hostels, with dormitories and dining rooms, at seaside resort areas. "It is a sad commentary," Señora K. observes, "that many of these people saw the splendor of the Pacific for the first time in their lives, despite its proximity to most of Chile's cities." Chile's coast is nearly 2,500 miles long, from the Peruvian border in the north to the Strait of Magellan at the Antarctic. Nowhere is the country more than 125 miles wide. Though the beaches are easily accessible by rail or bus, few poor people could afford the fare. And even if they could have made the trip, where would they have stayed?

The vacation program won instant acclaim from Chile's shantytown dwellers. The well-born and well-to-do did not share their elation. Some of these people were outraged at the sight of hordes of children running by the sea, shouting gleefully at the sight of the rolling waves. The quiet elegance of Viña del Mar and other choice spots on the Pacific was besieged by the ebullience of the underprivileged. The aristocracy had never expected to have to share their private playgrounds by the sea with the children of their parlor and scullery maids.

Enthusiasm for the government's programs was on the rise in early 1972 and was reflected in the March congressional elections, when more than 40 percent of the votes went to pro-Allende deputies. In return the Right worked hard at fanning anticommunist hysteria. The specter of communism was portrayed through images of horror in posters plastered on billboards, in newspaper and magazine articles, and in soap operas that pursued the housewife via the transistor radio while she did her chores from room to room.

As the political crisis deepened, the women's magazines *Eva*, *Paula*, and *Vanidades*—the latter produced in Miami and printed in Chile—became more militant. While the Allende people were calling on women to participate politically to safeguard the legislation that fortified their basic rights, the Right was agitating for women to become activists in bringing down the Allende regime. Society women began to show their muscle. They abandoned their Wednesday and Thursday afternoon tea parties and threw themselves full force into spreading discontent, and dramatizing their opposition by mobilizing street demonstrations.

One of their much-publicized actions was "The March of the Empty Pots and Pans," which they began organizing at the very beginning of the Allende administration. "It was ironic," Señora K. says, "that these well-fed ladies belonging to the extreme Rightist parties were the ones who launched the food shortage protest. It was ridiculous to see society women, with their carefully coiffured hair, their made-up faces, and dressed in smartly tailored jeans, arrive in chauffeur-driven cars which were discreetly parked several blocks away from where the demonstrations were scheduled to take place. They would strut down to the meeting place, take out their pots and pans, and begin banging away as they shouted accusations at Allende for having brought Chile to the brink of starvation."

These demonstrations made front-page news in the local press and received a good deal of publicity abroad. The Allende supporters responded with countermarches. "What was striking," Señora K. says, "was that pro-Allende women brought along their children, unlike those of the Right who left their children behind with the maids. The poor had to take their children with them because there was no one to leave them with, not even a neighbor. The neighbors wanted to participate too."

The "Pots and Pans" marches evoked a variety of satiric commentaries. One of these was a song made popular by the famous *Quilapayun* folk singers:

> *The Right Has Two Pots*
> *One Very Small*
> *And One Very Large.*
> *The First is Beaten in the Streets.*
> *The Second is to Hoard and Accumulate.*

Women of the nation's social elite were also called upon to do their bit at whittling away the morale of the military. It was important to the reactionary forces of Chile to provoke officers in the armed forces to turn against the government which they had sworn to defend. A favorite tactic for the women was to humiliate military officers in public. At parade formations or other public functions, as the officers stood at attention in their resplendent uniforms, women would break through the police cordons and spray the men with chicken feed, symbol of their being "chicken," gutless in their hesitation to topple the government. In a country traditionally machismo-minded, these assaults on the male ego found their mark.

One of the most savage attacks along these lines took place a few months before the coup. Wives of many of the high-ranking officers completely broke with protocol to picket the residence of the army chief of staff, General Carlos Prats, shouted insults at him, and called him a coward for his support of Allende. Prats resigned within a day, believing he no longer had the confidence of the officer corps.

Once the coup took place the pro-Junta press proclaimed the return of "the good old days." Señora Pinochet, wife of General Augusto Pinochet, went on the air to hail the Chilean women "whose suffering, humiliation, and heroism saved the hope of freedom for Chile." Señora Pinochet heralded "the rebirth of Chile" a few hours after the murder of Allende, and at about the time the Pinochet forces began rounding up men and women in shantytowns and universities alike.

In a matter of days the Junta swept away almost all legislation for the protection of women's rights. Once again pregnancy can be cause for dismissal from work. Most kindergartens and crêches in factories and out on the ranches are shut down. The daily distribution of a pint of milk to every Chilean child, Allende's special weapon against infant malnutrition, has been discontinued. Hospital care is no longer free to those unable to pay; not even emergency first aid is given unless the patient has a minimum of 100 pesos in hand. Child labor laws are ignored: youngsters of twelve can be seen working in plants and factories all over Chile. And though they work full shifts they get half the pay of their adult co-workers. Prostitution has made a big comeback and those forced into plying this trade because of mass unemployment are mere juveniles, some as young as fourteen years of age.

"With the overthrow of the Allende regime," Señora K. says, "not only were our wonderful social programs destroyed but women had all doors slammed in their faces. We were told to get back to our houses or to our hovels and to stay there. The women are now shut out completely, except for those who continue to resist the Pinochet dictatorship. But that's another story."

Señora K.'s husband was imprisoned in April 1974. Because of pressure from international church organizations he was released soon afterward. He left Chile in May of that year, and Señora K. and her three children followed him to the United States two months later.

8

The Agony of Pablo Neruda
and the Murder of Victor Jara

> *I see the sobbing in the coal at Lota*
> *and the wrinkled shadow of the beaten-down Chilean*
> *pick away at the bitter vein in the core, die,*
> *live, be born in the petrified cinder*
> *bent over, fallen as if the world*
> *could arrive like that or leave like that*
> *among black dust, among flames,*
> *and all that would come out of it would be*
> *the cough in winter, the step*
> *of a horse in the black water, where*
> *a eucalyptus leaf has fallen like a dead knife.*
>
> PABLO NERUDA
> *from "Hunger in the South"*
> (TRANSLATED BY ROBERT BLY)

> *He died without knowing why*
> *they riddled his chest with bullets*
> *struggling for the right*
> *to a place to exist on earth. . . .*
> — Victor Jara's commemoration
> of a police massacre in the
> town of Puerto Montt

PABLO NERUDA was Chile's most illustrious man of letters. Victor Jara was Chile's most popular folk singer. Each held the other in high esteem.

Neruda's father was a railroad worker. His mother died of tuberculosis early in his childhood, "before I could have a memory of her." His father remarried and took the family from the town of Parral, where Neruda was born in 1904, to Temuco, a kind of frontier city in the southernmost part of Chile. There, in a hostile climate, where a cold, needle-sharp rain swept down from the frigid Antarctic for weeks at a time, Neruda received his high school education. There too he found encouragement for his writing, which he began at about age twelve, from Gabriela Mistral, then a schoolmistress and later, like Neruda, a Nobel Prize winner for poetry. Neruda went on to the university in Santiago, where he launched his career as a poet.

Neruda's name was Neftalí Ricardo Reyes Basualto. But when he published his first poem at the age of fifteen he signed it Pablo Neruda, a pseudonym which remained with him for life. For some unexplained reason he picked up the new surname from the Czech writer Jan Neruda.

Neruda's prolific outpouring of poetry (he wrote 2,000 pages of verse) and the singularity of his creativity established him as one of the world's great literary figures. Even in translation his work moved critics to describe it as "volcanic . . . overwhelming . . . dazzlingly original." Some have called him "a surrealist who is never out of touch with reality . . . the major poet of today . . ." Certainly in the Spanish language he is considered the most important poet of the century.

In Latin America writers and poets were sometimes appointed to diplomatic posts once they have achieved recognition, on the theory that these assignments gave them the financial means to continue their creative work. From 1927 to 1932 Neruda lived in Rangoon, Colombo, Singapore, Batavia, and other parts of Asia and Oceania. He was then shifted to Buenos Aires and in 1934 was assigned as consul in Madrid. It was here, when the Franco legions, with the help of Hitler and Mussolini, assaulted the legitimate government of the Spanish Republic, that Neruda became politicized. Neruda did everything possible to help the Loyalist forces in his official capacity as consul. But the Chilean government frowned on his activities and he was recalled. However, instead of returning to Santiago, Neruda went to France, where he helped organize a series of fund-raising campaigns in support of the anti-Franco forces.

Despite these frenetic activities, Neruda was able to continue writing at his regular pace. However, his approach to poetry changed. He never abandoned his awe of nature and his involvement with verbal imagery, but he did move away from some of the romanticism and surrealism which characterized his famous earlier works, such as *Twenty Poems of Love and a Song of Despair*. As the poet Luis Monguió has written, Neruda "now . . . sought above all things to communicate—to abandon whatever might tax the understanding of his reader . . . Neruda's wish is to understand and to be understood by all."

In "The Grapes and the Wind," Neruda openly committed himself to this purpose:

> *I don't write to be imprisoned by other books*
> *or the lily's incarnate apprentices*
> *but for simple sojourners whose need*
> *is the moon and the water, the immutable bases of order,*
> *bread, wine, and schoolhouses, guitars and the tools of*
> *their trade. . . .*
> *when all's known*
> *and each is made equal,*
> *I write*
> *I write with your life and my own.*
>
> (TRANSLATED BY BEN BELITT)

There were those who predicted that once a poet takes a political stand, his work will deteriorate, become "hard-bitten" and lose its lyricism. Others, however, such as the American poet Robert Bly, felt that this did not apply to Neruda. In his view, "Neruda has written great poetry at all times of his life."

One of Neruda's greatest epics, *Canto General*, a sort of poetic, geopolitical celebration of Latin America, consisting of 250 separate poems in fifteen cycles, was written as he escaped from his native land in 1948 following his denunciation of the reactionary regime of President González Videla. Referring to this work when citing Neruda for the Nobel Prize, the Congress of Swedish Academicians said it was "poetry that, with the action of elemental force, brings alive a continent's destiny and dreams."

Jara's beginnings were even more humble than Neruda's. Jara,

Pablo Neruda (right) receiving the Nobel Prize for Literature from the King of Sweden (December 1971). (Wide World Photos)

born in 1938, was a survivor of crushing poverty. What meager earnings his father was able to eke out, first as a plowman in the countryside and then as a day laborer in Santiago, he spent on alcoholic sprees to drown his despair. It was his mother, an unusually vital person, who kept the family afloat. And when she died as Jara turned thirteen, the family quickly fell apart. Despite the succession of harrowing experiences throughout his adolescence he not only managed to stay alive but to develop a warm sensitivity and empathy for people in despair. He could have become embittered and brutalized in reaction to the destitution forced upon the "have-not" sector of Chile's population.

His meteoric rise from the lowest rungs of Chilean society represented an affront to Chile's aristocratic elite. In Jara's triumph Chile's Establishment saw a challenge to its claims of superiority and, therefore, to its legitimacy to power. Here was this upstart who began life with a family that shared a one-room hovel with a few pigs, some chickens and river rats in one of the miserable *poblaciónes* that ring Santiago, and who later put to ridicule with his sardonic, infectious wit some of the most powerful representatives of Chile's landed gentry and its industrial complex. He wrote his own lyrics and music, and, accompanying himself on his guitar, took his strong, brilliant one-man performances to country towns as well as to city concert halls.

What is perhaps even more miraculous is that from the time he first savored the romance of the theater, when he was about twenty, to the time of his murder, when he was in his middle thirties, Jara had become one of the most successful stage directors, an actor, and above all the rage of Chile and many other Latin American countries as a folk singer and composer.

Neither Jara nor Neruda ever forgot his origins. Both had the deepest concern for the plight of Chile's down-and-out sector of the population. Jara's songs again and again bewail the lot of the shantytown dwellers, a lot he shared in his childhood, or that of the copper miners, trapped for life in the barren highlands of the Andes. And Neruda's majestic verses, so frequently focused on the same themes, cascaded down upon the conscience of the nation with the force of landslides unleashed by the ever-present tremors in Chile's mountainous terrain.

As he grew older Neruda became even more conscious of the social and political inequities, whether in Chile or other parts of the world. He perceived his role as that of a partisan in the struggle against reaction. In his poem "I Come From the South," he declared:

> I was born to sing these sorrows
> to expose destructive beasts . . .
> I stir up the grief of my people,
> I incite the root of their swords,
> I caress the memory of their heroes,
> I water their subterranean hopes,
> for to what purpose my songs,
> the natural gift of beauty and words,
> if it does not serve my people
> to struggle and walk with me?

> (TRANSLATED BY MIGUEL ALGARÍN)

Their concern for Chile's poor, and for the whole nation's well-being, endeared Jara and Neruda to millions of Chileans across the board, whether intellectuals, students, peasants or laborers. In 1972, when Neruda returned to Chile from France, where he had been Allende's Ambassador, an ecstatic crowd of 10,000 admirers showed up at the Santiago sports stadium to listen to him read his latest poems.

Both Jara and Neruda rallied to Allende's Popular Unity program. In the election campaign of 1969 and during the tumultuous years of Allende's presidency, the two were tireless in promoting hopes for a better future. Both traveled extensively, making personal appearances in cities, towns, and hamlets to explain in song and poem the significance of Allende's "New Deal."

In many ways Jara and Neruda were more of a threat to the anti-Allende forces than the oratory of its political opponents or even armed resisters. A speech can rouse hundreds and thousands—it can become central in the national political debate. But with time it becomes an echo. When published, it becomes a document. A machine gun is as good as its supply of bullets. Without ammunition it is useless, dead. But a song that catches fire or a poem that takes wing can stir people indefinitely. Music and verse can become a part of a continuing present. They can be hummed or recited in the privacy of one's home or among friends. And the images they bring to life each time can inspire and reinforce personal dedication. In effect, even posthumously Jara and Neruda were able to reach over the heads of the Junta generals and catapult their message of defiance to those chafing under the repression of the Pinochet regime.

Naturally, the Junta went after Chile's two greatest artists with special ferocity. Jara was seized the second day of the coup and taken to the detention center at the Santiago sports stadium. He was immediately singled out by the Junta tormentors, who beat him, applied electric shocks, and then broke his hands. "Victor's hands were unusual not only because of what they were able to bring out of the guitar," his widow Joan recalls. "His hands were unique because of their sensitivity, their expressiveness. The palms were square and wide but his fingers were long and agile, like those of a Hindu dancer. His hands were soothing and caressing. Our daughters would run to Victor to have his hands 'make good' whatever little injuries they suffered while at play."

It is interesting, Joan says, that Jara himself was fascinated by hands—working hands, friendly hands, hands that brought in the harvest, hands that fashioned art objects, hands which laid brick. He devoted several poems to the subject of hands.

The same week the Junta soldiers assaulted Jara, they also laid siege to the Isla Negra home of Pablo Neruda, near Valparaiso, where the poet did most of his writing. Four busloads pulled up to the door, and the captain in charge shouted that a search for weapons was under way. Bristling with machine guns and bazookas some of the men took up positions around the house, while the rest burst inside and ransacked everything in sight. They broke open the wardrobes, they rifled Neruda's desk and writing table; they even suspected a heavy, leather-bound volume of Rimbaud's poems, lifting it off its special stand to see whether it was hiding a secret weapon. And they ordered Neruda out of bed, where he lay gravely ill with cancer of the prostate, so that they could pick through the bedding.

For the next day or two every window of the house framed the head of a Junta trooper, who, with gun in hand, peered menacingly into the house, including Neruda's bedroom. The poet was fully conscious, and his close friends say that the shock of the coup, the murder of Allende, and the invasion of his house hastened his death. He began to fail rapidly, and three days after his house was searched he was taken by ambulance to a Santiago clinic, over 120 miles of mountain roads. Neruda needed medication to ease the pain of the journey, but his doctor was no longer available to give him a prescription; he had been arrested as a pro-Allende suspect. The trip seemed endless. The ambulance was stopped and searched at every Junta command post.

In the few days that remained of Neruda's life, the Chilean poet drifted between semiconsciousness and spurts of energy during which he tried to read and even to dictate the last paragraphs of his autobiography. Close friends who visited him speak of his indomitable will to survive. He was determined to tell the story of Chile's tragedy to the world. Neruda's spirits brightened when he was told that the Mexican Embassy had a plane ready to fly him to Mexico City any time he felt able to make the trip. But his condition deteriorated rapidly and he died on September 23rd, twelve days after the coup.

Neruda was spared the humiliation and brutality visited upon Jara and thousands of others, but he too was made to suffer more just before he died. On September 20th, his home in Santiago was attacked. Junta police and members of Patria y Libertad smashed to bits everything dear to him and to millions of Chileans. The vandals tore to shreds the books in his fine library and the manuscripts of his yet unpublished works. They broke the water pipes on the second floor, flooding the rooms below, and tried to set the house afire.

When the coffin containing Neruda's body was brought home, it stood in the water-logged living room. Torn pages from his books and manuscripts littered the damp floor and blew about in the desolate courtyard below. Rubbish and little heaps of ashes were everywhere. The windows of the house were broken, the jagged glass protruding like crazed abstractions. The venerable grandfather clock that Neruda had brought home from Switzerland no longer ticked away in its imperious fashion. The looters had eviscerated it and smashed its face. It stood there in the living room empty of life, a mute testimonial that time in Chile had come to a halt. The great room was now barren of everything that had made it "an oasis of geniality," as Professor Armando Cassigoli, a close friend of Neruda's, remembers it. "It was difficult to imagine that this room had once been decorated with the myriad art objects that were so dear to Neruda's heart." The striking portrait of his wife, Matilde, painted by Diego Rivera, was gone. Vanished were the wonderful collections of folk art, stuffed animals, and dolls, which Neruda had lovingly assembled on his numerous visits to Guatemala, Spain, Sweden, the Soviet Union, Indonesia, and so many countries of Africa and Asia.

This was the room, Cassigoli says, which in happier times resounded with laughter, with animated discussions on everything from poetry, literature, and art to the politics of every part of the world. In addition to his dedication to poetry and his keen political awareness, Neruda was intensely interested in a variety of subjects, including the natural sciences and botany. He was blessed with a great sense of humor and enjoyed practical jokes. He loved to talk, but he would not play the prima donna. He listened readily to other people's views and opinions.

On the morning of the funeral, this devastated room was the reception area for those who were still free and had the courage to risk their freedom by paying last respects to Neruda. At the far end of the room sat Neruda's wife, Matilde, ashen gray, her eyes filled with tears. She stared silently at the coffin. At her side was Neruda's sister, Laura Reyes, quiet and stunned.

Dozens of people made their way inside through the broken door. Ambassadors, students, workers, and a few peasants, who had walked many miles from the country, shuffled past the bier, mumbling words of grief to Señora Neruda and her sister-in-law. All the Chileans in the room had braved the scrutiny of the Junta police and photographers outside.

Meanwhile the streets near the house had begun to fill with men and women waiting for the funeral procession to start. They shuffled about in a kind of a macabre charade. Resolved to show their love and admiration for their beloved poet, they were at the same time haunted by fear of the police, who were everywhere. Some were stationed in large army trucks, others were patrolling with submachine guns slung from their shoulders. And of course everybody knew that the DINA plainclothesmen, the Chilean Gestapo, were everywhere.

In their attempt to achieve anonymity, some of the mourners stood staring at store window displays as though contemplating a purchase. Others queued up at a bus stop, seemingly awaiting transportation. Many were dressed in their Sunday best, not only to honor Neruda but hoping to look middle-class and "respectable." The coup had already brought the conservative look into fashion. Long hair was out, crewcuts were in. Casual clothes, especially jeans, made one a Leftist suspect.

As more and more people crowded the street, military and

police cars prowled with greater energy. Occasionally they stopped someone and demanded an identity card. Tension thickened but few people left.

Then the coffin was carried out and the procession got under way. Neruda's home is in the foothills of Cerro de San Cristobal, only about fifteen blocks from the Santiago cemetery. Immediately behind the hearse walked Neruda's wife and his sister, escorted by several close friends. Alongside were Joan Jara; Fernando Castillo Velasco, dean of the Catholic University; Radomiro Tomic, a leader of the Christian Democratic Party; Martinez Corbalá, the Mexican Ambassador; Harald Edelstam; and several well-known writers and poets.

And then, behind them, people in the street began falling in, at first hesitantly, looking over their shoulders to see whether the police would lunge at them. Then more and more people dropped their pretense at window shopping and other disguises. Suddenly, as Cassigoli describes it, "there was a huge, packed mass of mourners like an enormous dark stain spreading across the entire width of the street. There were thousands in the line of the procession."

At first this ever-growing multitude marched silently, heads bowed in mourning. Low-hanging, leaden clouds swept overhead as a biting wind buffeted the marchers. Men and women wept openly, grieving for Neruda, for their murdered friends and families, grieving for Chile. Then somebody shouted, "Neruda, we salute you!" The cry was picked up by others. This outburst sent shock waves through the crowd. It began shedding its paralysis of fear, despite the sullen glances of the military. Fortified by the Neruda salute, a few people shouted pro-Allende slogans, and these too were picked up by the marchers. By the time the river of humanity reached the cemetery gates, the procession had become a political demonstration against the Junta. Ignoring police orders to disperse, some of the marchers began singing "The Internationale" while others called out vows to remain true to the memory of Allende and Neruda. As the coffin was lowered into the grave, a young man was lifted on the shoulders of another. He made a brief farewell speech and read a few verses from Neruda's poem *Canto General*. The police began pushing the mourners out of the cemetery. Once again the awareness of the deadly peril confronting them returned, and so the crowd melted away quickly.

When news of Neruda's death was flashed to the world, every major country responded with condolences from its most prominent citizens. Cables to his widow came from Georges Pompidou, then the President of France; from Vargas Llosa, the famous Peruvian writer; from Yevgenye Yevtushenko, the Russian poet, and other literary figures in the Soviet Union; from Gabriel García Márquez, author of the internationally best-selling novel *One Hundred Years of Solitude*; from Rene Naheu, the Director General of UNESCO; and from many other world notables. But in Chile the news of Neruda's death was at first unreported, presumably because of the fear that it might spark violent political reactions. On the day of the funeral, however, the newspapers carried an oddly worded one-paragraph notice: "Today marks the end of the third day of mourning for Neftalí Ricardo Reyes Basualto, the poet Neruda."

The Junta was eager to blot out the Neruda legend, especially because of the poet's identification with Allende, and because he was a member of the Communist Party. But how could it disown a man who had brought this little nation of ten million people into the world's limelight, if only because of the Nobel Prize? Domestically the Junta tried to have the Chileans ignore Neruda's death, but, to the rest of the world, it bowed its head in sorrow, as it were. And when news began to leak out about the assaults on Neruda's homes, the Junta charged that they were the work of Leftist-provocateurs hoping to smear the good name of the Junta.

Such professions of innocence were very much at variance with what foreign correspondents were witnessing. Á la Nazi Germany, Junta mobs, aided by the military, broke into bookshops and libraries, seized thousands of books which they decided were Leftist in character and fed them to the flames. Up in smoke went copies of the works of Neruda, as well as those of such giants as García Lorca, Pio Baroja, Unamuno, Walt Whitman, and John Steinbeck, to mention just a few. Not even

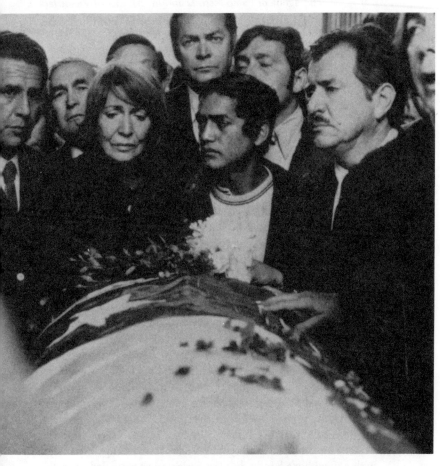

*Matilde Urrutia, widow of Pablo Neruda, at his funeral
with thousands of the poet's admirers. Defying the threat of mass arrests
by the Junta police, the mourners burst into the singing of
"The Internationale" as they reached the cemetery. (Wide World Photos)*

the writings of such liberal Catholic educators as Ivan Illich were spared.

With Jara it was different. There was no need for the Junta to shed crocodile tears over Victor Jara for the benefit of world opinion. Some thirty years younger than Neruda, Jara was still unknown to Europe or to the United States. But he was decidedly a thorn in the side of the Chilean establishment. His repertoire was made up of songs to which Chile's shantytown dwellers responded heartily. Jara's songs breathed fire and protest against political and economic injustice because he knew the misery of the poor only too well. Alcoholism, disease, gang warfare, and violent death were the ingredients of his early life.

Jara probably escaped delinquency because of his mother—a strong and vivacious woman who saw to it that Victor continued at the parish school even though, long before she died, he was working as a parcel carrier at the public market, where she ran a vegetable stall. He may have owed her his musical talent as well as the will to persevere. Completely self-taught, his mother played the guitar and sang in what her son remembered as a sturdy, appealing voice. She augmented her meager income from the market stall by entertaining at weddings, wakes, and whatever festivities the shantytowns could organize.

Victor did not remember singing in his childhood, although he responded to music with warm interest. His mother apparently had no time to teach him any music. It was a neighbor who taught him to play the guitar.

After his mother's death young Victor found temporary shelter with a neighbor's family, but the parish priest prevailed upon the local church authorities to have Victor enrolled in the seminary. He felt that the boy's alertness and interest in studies made him promising material for the clergy. Victor remained in the seminary for most of his high school career, but the strict, confining routines were not in keeping with his temperament. He missed the freedom, such as it was, that he had had as a delivery boy in the vegetable market; he would not bend to the discipline of the seminary. And even though he enjoyed singing liturgical music in the seminary choir, it didn't satisfy his need for the strong, direct folk songs he had heard from his mother.

When he was about sixteen, Victor ran away from the seminary, and after floundering at various jobs he signed up for two years in the army. It was one of the bleakest periods of his life. His army years were filled with suffocating constraints and with demands for blind obedience to senseless orders. But he gritted his teeth and tried to make the most of it by taking whatever educational courses the army offered. Despite his visceral resistance to army life, his commanding officers gave him high grades for his military performance and urged him to enter officers' training school. Victor, however, breathed a deep sigh of relief when his two years were up and he was again "free" to search for the elusive job that would feed him and at the same time give him a purpose in life.

He slept in shantytown rooming houses and ate irregularly, but somehow he still looked at life with optimistic curiosity. One day he happened to walk by a theater which was advertising a mime performance. Although he had never been to the theater before, the advertisement intrigued him. He had just enough money to buy a top balcony seat.

This first exposure to mime opened up a totally new world for Victor Jara. Soon afterward he found himself at the University of Santiago applying for admission to its drama school. He lacked a year of high school to graduate, but he was persuasive enough to be allowed to audition for several roles, and acting talent was one of the requisites for acceptance. The examiners were so impressed with his auditions that they waived the high school diploma requirement and accepted him as a fully matriculated drama student. From then on Jara threw himself into the study of theater technique, and he soon overwhelmed everyone with his innovative, imaginative approach to problems of directing and acting.

The drama school provided another turning point in Jara's life. Soon after he enrolled, he met his future wife, Joan Turner, an Englishwoman who had lived in Chile since the middle fifties. Joan was a ballerina who had trained as a dancer since childhood. After a brief encounter with academia at the University of London, where she considered majoring in history, Joan turned to dance as her profession. She became a member of the Ballet Joos and other ballet companies.

On a visit to Chile she was invited to join the Chilean National Ballet as a prima ballerina, and decided to stay. She also became a member of the faculty of the drama department of the University of Santiago where she taught body movement. Jara was one of her students.

Joan recalls the early days of her acquaintance with Victor with a warmth and enthusiasm that breaks through her usual reserved manner. A handsome woman, with searching brown eyes and a friendly, animated expression, Joan depicts Victor as "a very industrious student . . . a very talented person." He was intensely interested in every aspect of theater—acting, producing, staging, and directing. But it was as a director that Jara first made his mark. In his first year of drama school he and a few other students formed a theater group that began producing plays from both the traditional, classical repertoire and the moderns such as Brecht, as well as some plays by a member of the group, Alejandro Sieveking, who later became an important playwright and is now living in exile in Costa Rica.

Their presentations, with Jara as director, were much above the expected level of a student amateur group. By the time Jara was completing his third year at the University the group had made an impact on professional theatrical circles in Santiago and was sent on a very successful tour to other Latin American countries. Victor took his final examinations in December 1962. A month after graduation he was working at two jobs, as director of a professional theatrical company and as a faculty member at the Technical University, the second largest in Chile, where he was to teach for the rest of his life.

At this point, Joan Jara says, Victor considered himself strictly a theater person. It was not until several years later that he began to emerge as a composer and a folk singer, the talents which brought him fame and affection all over Chile. But his interest in folklore had always been with him. His roots, after all, were in the peasantry.

One of the things that surprised people when he suddenly catapulted to stardom as a folk singer was the fact that he had never studied music formally. To the very end of his life, according to Joan, Jara was unable to read or write music. When he began composing he would render the melodies by singing and accompanying himself on the guitar. Then he would write the lyrics and have his music scored by a professional arranger. Nevertheless, in only a few years Jara's songs filled some sixty record releases, and at the age of thirty-five he was the most popular folk singer in Chile.

From the start his songs had a captivating melodic richness and a consistent theme—the despair of the poor, the anguish of the hopeless copper miners, the life of Chilean peasants ignored by the absentee landowners busy with their frivolous lives in Paris, Rome, or Buenos Aires.

It is almost a miracle, Joan says, that Jara's songs became so popular just at the time the Beatles brought rock music to Chile as to most of the world. She thinks that both of these musical forms had a symbiotic relationship as "people's music." Certainly the Chileans found a new pleasure in their heritage of folk music as Jara revitalized it. In a nationwide folk music festival and competition at the Catholic University in Santiago, Jara won first prize, and with that impetus he began to devote more and more time to his compositions and recitals. He spent long hours writing and rewriting his lyrics and polishing the tunes. The songs themselves had great appeal, and people loved to sing them, but he also had what Joan calls a "magical" touch when he sang them himself. He had the unique gift of communicating with every kind of audience in a very personal, warm manner. "In the middle of the song Victor would talk a bit or perhaps tell a joke. Then he would lead the audience back into the song with a specific reference to the particular political issue of the moment." He had "extraordinary sensitivity" when performing for children. He would involve them in a kind of dialogue that they responded to with surprise and ringing laughter. When he sang before groups of working mothers he would talk and sing about their particular problems. "Life with him was fun," Joan says. "He enjoyed living and he made people around him enjoy life."

Before the elections of 1969, Jara was one of the many artists in Chile who began traveling around the country to give performances for the Allende campaign. In 1970, when Allende took office, Jara became deeply involved in setting up music and theater groups among trade unions in Santiago and in the countryside. He still taught at the university, but he found time for many new compositions. His music now reflected the optimism of a new era. There was an upbeat rhythm in his lyrics. His records were increasingly popular on radio and he was often seen on TV.

But this happy interlude in Chilean political life did not last very long. Within months Allende's opponents began to shatter early hopes for the country's future, and reform projects were hamstrung in parliament and by the judiciary. There was also a nagging suspicion that the military could not be fully depended upon to defend the Popular Unity government should a crisis take place. Toward the end of the second year of Allende's presidency, it became increasingly obvious that the dynamics for the coup were in the making. The political atmosphere became tinged with the fatalism of a Greek tragedy. Victor Jara kept on composing his songs and singing them, but he and Joan as well as thousands of other Chileans sensed that Chile was heading for a tragedy.

"Early on the morning of September 11th," Joan remembers, "I got up before Victor did and drove the girls to school. Coming back home I switched on the car radio and realized with horror that the coup we had talked about so often was actually upon us. The radio said something about troop movements, and that Valparaiso had been cut off by the navy. I turned the car around and went back for my children. When we came into the house it must have been about eight o'clock. I met Victor as he was coming down the stairs.

"'Well, it looks like this is it,' he said in a somber tone, so atypical of his cheerful manner. Both of us went to the living room and rushed to the radio and TV. At first there was no hard news, just a series of bulletins followed by repeated pleas to the citizenry to keep calm, with assurances that Allende was still in La Moneda. This was followed by a news flash in which the

Victor Jara, Chile's popular folk singer,
serenading his wife and their two daughters
a few weeks before the coup and his murder. (Sing Out! Magazine)

government asked everybody to report immediately to their places of work and await further instructions there. Victor phoned the university and was told that many of the students were already there and most members of the faculty were expected to arrive shortly.

"Then Allende began speaking but I really didn't hear all of the speech. I could scarcely concentrate. You must understand the sort of state we were in. My mind was spinning. A torrent of questions assailed me, but there were no answers. What do we do with the children? My youngest daughter is a diabetic. I knew my place was with the girls, but where were we to go? I also knew that Victor would have to go to the university and take his stand there. I understood that because we had both accepted a program of total commitment and this was a call-up, a mobilization to defend Chile against its enemies. No one was obligated to respond; it was a voluntary dedication in support of a government whose program was to free Chile's people from chronic want and disease. Thus Victor had to take his stand like anyone else. He couldn't just say 'I'm going to save my own skin and my family.' He wasn't the kind of artist who agitated and got people involved, then took off to a safe hiding place.

"We had tried to prepare ourselves psychologically for the possibility of a coup. But I don't think anyone would have predicted the ferocity and the horror the Junta used against the Chilean people. It was a war with modern technological weaponry against a defenseless people.

"Victor left the house at about 11 or 11:15 that morning. To avoid the center of the city he took a circuitous route to get to the university, which is at the other side of Santiago. Once there he phoned me (the telephones were still functioning) and said that so far everything seemed to be all right. He told me he was going to stay there and would phone me later. At about 12:30 or 1:00 we heard a tremendous explosion from the direction of Allende's residence, some eight blocks away from where we lived. This was the first attack by the dive bombers, but apparently they were off target. I learned later that they hit a wing of the hospital in a shantytown near us. In a few minutes they came back and began attacking around Allende's house at Tomás Moro Street. Rocket after rocket came plummeting down with heavy explosions in the wake. I ran to the balcony and saw bombers and helicopters hovering around that part of the city. My youngest daughter, Mandy, who was then eight years old, was playing with a friend outside the house. I rushed out, brought them upstairs, and shoved them under the table, just as my parents did with me during the blitz over London. I tried not to panic. I guess there *is* something British about me. I was trying to preserve an aspect of normality about the whole thing; calm and collected. But it was difficult. Very difficult. With each rocket explosion I felt as if a massive weight had hit me in the stomach."

Joan smiled wryly. "In spite of all that happened later, I still remember how shocked I was at the revelation of local hostility I got that morning. We lived in a rather well-to-do area, where most of the people were against Allende's reforms. So that when the radio began announcing the mutiny of the generals and admirals who headed the Junta, many of our neighbors came out into the streets, shouting anti-Allende slogans and celebrating.

"When I ran downstairs to fetch Mandy and her friend, a woman who lived in a very handsome house two doors away suddenly darted out onto the sidewalk, shouted an insult at me, and at the same time made a vulgar gesture with both arms. In Chile this is considered completely foul and obscene. The act was unbelievably shocking because her usual appearance was so ladylike and genteel. She was always well groomed, hair stylishly dressed, fingernails neatly painted. She had a lot of servants and drove about in an expensive car with a chauffeur. This outburst of hatred was chilling, to say the least. When I got back to our apartment with the girls I couldn't stop thinking about it. Fear began to envelop me, I felt as if I were smothering. The explosions and the sudden realization that our neighbors were really our enemies sent me into the depths of depression.

"My apprehensions were soon reinforced when I saw lorries filled with armed men and women who were not in uniform. They were members of the Patria y Libertad organization, breaking into homes of pro-Allende suspects and looting whatever they could lay their hands on. I saw them carrying out a TV set, kitchen appliances, even a child's tricycle, and throwing the things into the van while they jeered and laughed at the owners.

"Were we to be next?, I asked myself. Victor's activities were certainly well known. The fear kept mounting. Our TV set suddenly took on the appearance of a milestone on the road to doom, as it kept blurting out the latest bulletins. There was a steady stream of announcements. Allende was dead . . . The Junta claimed full control . . . A curfew was declared with the warning that until further notice anyone out on the streets after 3 P.M. faced execution on the spot . . . And where was Victor?

"At 4:30 that afternoon I breathed a sigh of relief. Victor called. He tried to sound his optimistic self. The conversation was brief. He said it was impossible for anybody to get out of the university because of the curfew. However, he said he hoped to be with us the following morning, when the curfew was due to be lifted. I didn't know that by then the university was surrounded. Those who tried to leave were machine-gunned as they went out the gates. One of the first victims was a news cameraman.

"I wasn't able to sleep at all that night. Next morning the curfew was relaxed for a few hours, so I started waiting for Victor to come home; and I waited and waited and waited. I had no way of reaching him since the university switchboard no longer responded; it had been smashed to pieces by the Junta soldiers. There was nothing on TV or radio about the university.

"Is he still there?, I asked myself. Has he managed to get out? Has he gone into hiding? I kept telephoning friends and acquaintances hoping to get a clue, a suggestion as to what might have happened to Victor and his colleagues. But no one had any information. As the day wore on we became more circumspect in our conversations; word got around that our phones were being tapped.

"I went outside for a little while to get a feel of the climate around us. There were groups of people talking, laughing, greeting each other with a sense of jubilation. Although I knew very few people in our immediate area, I had always exchanged a 'good morning' with many of them simply because we met at the bakery or the grocery. These people were now avoiding me, turning their backs, or just not taking notice of me. Fortunately I met a friend who lived close by. She too was a member of the

Popular Unity Party. She was scared too, especially because she lived alone. So she came over to our house and stayed with us for several days.

"In the hope of getting some news about Victor we kept the television going all that afternoon. Pinochet and others in the Junta clique were on the tube all the time. Warnings against resistance were becoming harsher and ever more threatening. Then about 6 P.M. there was an announcement that the Technical University had been occupied by the military and that a number of 'extremists' had been rounded up.

"All that day I'd been haunted by the specter of Victor being taken prisoner. But when I heard the 6 o'clock report, the grim reality was staggering. It may sound illogical but all at once it seemed to take me by surprise, as though I hadn't expected it after all. Once again I was at the phone probing the chances of discovering Victor's whereabouts, with the same unrewarding results.

"The next day, however, I got a call from someone who had just been released from the stadium where he had seen Victor briefly. He said that Victor wanted me to be calm and stay in the house with our children as much as possible. Further, Victor wanted me 'to be brave and courageous.' The caller added that Victor didn't think he'd be able to get out of the stadium, and then hung up.

"I was completely confused. I honestly didn't know how to interpret the message. Maybe it was denial of reality or wishful thinking that distorted my understanding of the message. When the person said Victor didn't think he'd be coming out, was it only for the next few days? The fact that he asked me to stay in the house, did it mean that I should be on hand to expect him?

"I must admit to a certain feeling of guilt that has remained with me through the years. Perhaps I could have saved his life had I been less British in my reserve. Perhaps the moment I heard about Victor I should have rushed down to the British Embassy, created a rumpus, and demanded help to save my husband. After all I am British. But the idea never occurred to me at that time. Victor was a Chilean national and I scarcely thought of myself in terms of being British. So I flung myself anew at the phone seeking advice from Chileans who themselves were under the gun, as it were, and looking for a place to hide.

"The next two days were sheer agony. Then on Saturday, in the middle of the night, the idea struck me that my being British might indeed be significant. As soon as it was a reasonable time of day, I dressed in my best clothes and drove off. I knew that the embassy and consulate would be closed, this being Sunday. I went directly to the Ambassador's residence. The building was surrounded by police, but when I told them I was British they let me through into a driveway which led to enormous gates at the main entrance. But the gates were closed. I rang the bell and knocked; somebody moved and came near the gates. I told him through the grille that I was British and that I needed help and advice. 'Please, may I come in?' I asked. The person said 'No, you can't come in, but show me your passport.' This I did and he told me to wait as he disappeared through the door into the building. There was a long pause as I stood like a mendicant waiting for a pittance. Then the man reappeared (I believe he was the second secretary or someone on that level), and we began our conversation, all the time through the grille of the gate. To begin with he said an audience with the Ambassador was out of the question. So I gave him all the facts and asked what the embassy would do about Victor. 'Well,' he said, 'there is nothing much we can do since he is a Chilean. But perhaps we can make some inquiries through our naval attaché; I think it would be more suitable than doing it via diplomatic channels.' I tried to press him for something more definite than making inquiries, but he just held back and maintained that Her Majesty's government could not become embroiled in a Chilean domestic affair.

"He then apologized for having held our discussion through the bars of a gate. 'Our orders are not to open the gates to anybody,' he said. 'Not even to a British subject?' I asked. 'That is correct,' he replied, 'not even to a British subject.' [In 1973 the British government in office was Conservative and therefore unsympathetic to the Allende programs or to Chilean refugees. The United Kingdom was the only Western European country that would not provide asylum to those fleeing the Junta terror.

Not one Chilean refugee was allowed to find shelter at the embassy.]

"I really didn't care whether I was inside or outside those gates. There was a feeling of abandonment; not even a hand of friendship from my own government. 'What's the use of arguing?' I said to myself. There was nothing more I could do for the moment. On my way home anxiety about Victor simply overwhelmed me. Part of my mind was filled with what now seem unbearably trivial worries: Was he getting nourishing food? Was his jacket warm enough to shield him from the unseasonable cold weather? (September is usually a warm, pleasant month, but that year, the night chill would not go away.) And then my mind would suddenly come to a halt, overcome by the awesomeness of the big question: Is Victor going to come out alive?

"Victor was a special case. I knew that. Years before the Junta took over, some of the people who were right now rounding up and torturing pro-Allende people had a special grudge against Victor because his songs satirized those who were smug, rich, unconcerned with the plight of the disfranchised. Many of them were indignant when Victor adapted the American song "Little Boxes" and made a Chileanized version of it, mocking the establishment for its conformism, for its insensitivity and intellectual vapidness. They attacked him in the reactionary press, and they incited people to throw rocks at him even during a church-sponsored concert. But he always shot back with an even more biting array of songs. Now, however, Victor was at the stadium entirely at their mercy and not likely to become repentant regardless of the pressure they would put upon him.

"I scarcely could have known as I left the Ambassador's mansion, that creature comforts were no longer of importance to Victor.

"As I learned later, the very moment he was seized at the university they battered him over the head; he was hauled to the stadium with blood all over his face. Those who were with him said that he somehow held himself together. That night he lent his jacket to someone who was in even greater distress and agony than he was. And in the two days he was at the stadium he managed to scribble a song of resistance that somehow got around and helped prisoners' morale. Some of his fellow inmates memorized the lyrics and smuggled them out by word of mouth.

Joan had a copy of Jara's song, "Chile Stadium," in English translation:

CHILE STADIUM

*There are five thousand of us here
in this little part of the city.
We are five thousand.
I wonder how many we are in all
in the cities and in the whole country?
Here alone
are ten thousand hands which plant seeds
and make the factories run.
How much humanity
exposed to hunger, cold, panic, pain,
moral pressures, terror and insanity?
What horror the face of fascism creates!*

*How hard it is to sing
when I must sing of horror.
Horror which I am living.
Horror which I am dying.
To see myself among so much horror
and so many moments of infinity
in which silence and screams
are the end of my song.
What I see I have never seen.
What I have felt and what I feel
will give birth to the moment. . . .*

"When I got home from the Ambassador's house, the sight of my children calmed me somewhat, but not for long. I, too, had to be calm for their sake, but I was ever more aware that danger was on our doorstep, too. There was a Junta military patrol circulating all over the neighborhood. They would descend on a house suspected of harboring a pro-Allende resident, smash open the doors, loot the place, and take the people away for 'interrogation.' So suddenly I and my thirteen-year-old Manuela got busy burning all the books and posters that had anything to do with Victor's music or Allende's programs. We went through all our personal papers. Some we fed to the fire and some we tried to hide. Luckily, because of the sudden drop in temperature, no one took notice of the smoke billowing out of the fireplace chimney, where so much that was dear to us was turned to ashes. Manuela began to show signs of great concern. She became jittery and apprehensive; she grasped the seriousness of our situation all too well.

"Two more days of leaden agony. Then on Tuesday, early in the morning, shortly after the curfew was lifted to allow Santiago people a few hours to purchase groceries and other essentials, there was a knock at the door. I opened it hardly a crack and saw a young man outside. He whispered, 'Please trust me. You don't know me, but please trust me because I am a *compañero*; could I please come in?' When he said *compañero*, that meant he was a supporter of Allende's Popular Unity Party. I let him in, and he told me he worked as a clerical employee at the city morgue. I stared at him. He hesitated a moment and said, 'I'm terribly sorry to tell you this, but I believe Victor Jara is dead.' He said that his job for the past three days had been establishing the identity of the bodies brought in from the concentration camps. He asked me questions about Victor's appearance and finally wanted to know whether the trousers that Victor wore the day he left the house were blue and carried a foreign label. I said yes. 'Well,' he said, 'I'm afraid those details check with the description we got. You have to come with me to identify his body. We must go very quickly because the body has been there almost three days, and if it is not claimed right away the authorities will order us to bury it with the others in a common grave. We must not lose any time.'

"The finality of his remarks removed all thought. The man had said hurry and I did precisely that. There was something grotesquely ridiculous in the way I began to race to get ready to get to the morgue, as though I was on my way to save Victor rather than to bury him. I didn't even say goodbye to Mandy and Manuela. But I told the friend who was staying with us not to say anything to them. 'Just tell them I had to go out. Just say I've gone out to buy something.'

"When we got to the morgue, people were milling around at the entrance. Inside the little lobby there were lists of names posted on the walls, marked male and female, and there was a list of unidentified bodies with brief descriptions. My young *compañero* showed his pass and we were allowed to go through a side door and then on to a foyer which led into an enormous room. And there I saw something that defies description. It was like a painting by Hieronymus Bosch, a scene from *Marat/Sade*. There were mounds of bodies all over the floor—young people and old people; men with their helmets still strapped on, the kind workers use on construction jobs. Some still had their hands tied behind their backs. Some looked as though they had been

For many weeks Chileans congregated at the Santiago morgue searching for the bodies of relatives who had been executed by Junta torturers. It is here where Joan identified her husband, Victor Jara. (Marcelo Montecino)

dragged by their feet over cobblestones. There were a few corpses of young women. And most of the bodies had terrible wounds. Dried blood was everywhere. I wasn't thinking such literary thoughts at the time, but it may have been the closest thing to what Dante conceived of as an inferno.

"I stood there in the middle of the room unable to move, but I must have uttered a loud gasp. My young companion turned toward me with terror in his eyes. 'Shh . . . Shh . . . we must be careful; you must control yourself; if they find us here they'll throw us out. I know exactly how you feel but you must not make any sort of demonstration whatsoever.' We began sidestepping the corpses as we searched for my husband's body. It was an unbelievably gruesome task as we stopped at each body and examined it closely to make sure. Then, on the second floor, we found Victor. His beautiful hands were broken and swollen. I stood before his body just staring, unbelieving. His face was so discolored and torn up that I could hardly recognize him. The young *compañero* at my side was warning me again that time was running out, that the bureaucratic arrangements had yet to be made. But I continued to stand there, unable to move, unable to say anything. My friend began to push me on and he whispered to some of the morgue employees who were extremely sympathetic. We went back downstairs and he filled out the forms and made arrangements for the removal of the body. This man was taking enormous chances, and he was very brave, but there was one thing he couldn't do for me, and that was to produce our marriage certificate as proof of my right to Victor's body. So while he stayed at the morgue to order a coffin, I had to drive all the way home to get the marriage certificate, and then all the way back.

"I can't understand how I managed to drive without crashing into things. I was dazed, just doing things like a wind-up doll. As I was going through my papers to find the certificate I received a phone call from an old friend, probably on the Junta's wanted list himself. I whispered to him about Victor and he said he would meet me at the morgue. And sure enough when I got back, both the friend and the young *compañero* were waiting for me. They helped take Victor downstairs and out the side door. The main entrance was jammed with ambulances as more corpses were being brought in and unloaded.

"About three o'clock that afternoon Victor was buried at the far end of the Santiago cemetery. There were only the three of us at the grave. And now I had to go back home and try to tell my children what had happened. It was a bleak day, a fit setting for the tragedy that settled on our little family and on Chile.

"Only one newspaper reported Victor's death. It carried a one-paragraph item at the bottom of an inside page: 'Victor Jara, the theater director and folk singer, died the other day.' One would have thought Victor had died of a cold, or pneumonia, something like that. The report went on to say that Victor was buried privately, in the presence of his relatives. Very private indeed.

"The moment the news got around about Victor's death there was a flood of telephone calls. The British ambassador, the man who couldn't give me an audience when I needed it so badly three days before, sent me a note of condolence.

"All I wanted then was to get my children and myself out of Santiago as soon as possible, but some of our friends persuaded me that the horror should not go unreported. It was important that the story of the putsch should be publicized. Maybe it would help save the many lives that were still in jeopardy. In the next few days a Swedish television group interviewed me in a private home outside Santiago. Then I was interviewed by a correspondent of the *London Times*, who wrote a detailed account of what happened to Victor. The Swedish TV report and the *Times* story were given great prominence in Europe, and protests from all over the world poured into Santiago. I suddenly understood that that was what Victor would have wanted me to do. And that is what I have been doing ever since. I am trying to give Mandy and Manuela some stability here in England, as much as Victor and I gave them in Chile. But I spend every moment I can, telling the story of what happened in Chile at rallies and meetings in Europe, Australia, Africa, Canada and the United States. The girls like England but they feel decidedly Chilean and I expect they'll be going back to Chile when the Junta nightmare is over."

9

The Junta Under Siege

"**Y**VA A CAER!
La Dictadura Va a Caer! Pinochet Va a Caer!" (And it will fall!
The dictatorship will fall! Pinochet will fall!)

The cry for the downfall of the Junta and its caudillo, Dictator-
President General Augusto Pinochet, was heard throughout the
land, from Arica in the north to Punta Arenas in the south—a
distance of some 2,300 miles.

As Isabel Letelier described it (one of the first exiles allowed to
visit the homeland), the cry *"Pinochet Va a Caer"* usually began
as a hushed, eerie buzz which grew ever louder in a surging
crescendo until it became a roar. This happened at theaters, at
soccer games, at union meetings, as well as at outdoor political
demonstrations.

Since May 1983, hundreds of thousands of Chileans—men
and women, workers, students, professionals, and shantytown
dwellers—took to the streets demanding that Pinochet resign, that
a constituent assembly be called to write a new constitution, and
that elections follow soon afterward: in short, that democracy
return to Chile. These protests took place against the backdrop of
banging pots and pans and the din of blaring automobile horns.
Barricades of burning auto tires were set up at principal intersections of the shantytowns to obstruct police vehicles.

Considering the awesome reign of terror which the Fascist
military dictatorship had imposed on the Chileans, this sudden
defiance of the regime staggered the imagination. As if on signal
the people decided that neither death nor torture would stop them
from reasserting their rights. Barehanded they confronted the
gunfire, water cannon, tear gas, and clubbing of the police and
militia. Thousands were arrested, many subjected to beatings,

237

torture by electrodes wired to breasts, genital organs, mouth, temples. At least 100 were shot to death in the first nine months of these demonstrations. But the protests continued.

No longer was hatred of the regime confined to the Left, labor, and the desperately impoverished shantytown dwellers, three groups especially targeted for brutal repression by the Junta. Anger, a sense of having been deceived, and profound disillusion also pervaded ever larger sectors of the middle and even upper classes, which had been the most ardent supporters of the Pinochet dictatorship.

And with every new anti-Junta demonstration the chorus of those demanding that Pinochet step down was bigger and louder. Not even the most optimistic of those who believed the Junta would eventually collapse anticipated the suddenness of the political ferment that gripped Chile. It was as if all at once the Junta had been caught in a pincer movement in which economic collapse and mounting demands for political liberation came together on signal.

Chile's so-called "economic miracle," which was heralded domestically and abroad as proof of the wisdom of the "monetarist," "supply-side" economic theories of the University of Chicago's Milton Friedman and those of the Reagan Administration, began to come apart in 1982, and come apart it did with explosive force by January 1983, when the most important banks closed their doors and the country found itself nearly bankrupt. Unemployment soared, hundreds of business enterprises went into eclipse, agricultural stagnation deepened, and malnutrition, no longer the monopoly of the poor, sidled up close to the middle class.

Chile was then considered an economic basket case. As one top American bank official, who did not want to be identified, declared, "Chile is in ruins; its industrial base is virtually blitzed out, physically obliterated."

Pressed by panicky creditors, manufacturers tried to meet their debts by selling off capital equipment and machinery to purchasers abroad. In the countryside, medium-sized farmers, caught in the same squeeze and finding few buyers for their agricultural machinery, smashed farm implements into scrap metal and sold it as such, mostly to Japan.

Police tear-gas Chileans celebrating the rejection of Pinochet's bid to continue as dictator in the plebiscite of October 5, 1988. (Bustamente)

A Chilean economist, who also refused to be identified, viewed these developments as "shattering . . . body blows" to the well-being of the country. Even "under optimum conditions, with generous availability of foreign financing, and a takeover by a government dedicated to reversing the nation's plight, it would take years to restore Chile's production levels to what they had been in 1969."

And to top it all, the country was saddled with a foreign debt of nearly $21 billion, the highest per capita repayment obligation in the world, much of it resulting from shady speculative ventures by several powerful conglomerates which also controlled Chile's principal banks.

Even among Rightist sectors, confidence in Pinochet, the self-appointed standard bearer of national morality, was plummeting because of disclosures about corruption at the highest levels of government.

Most observers agreed that the Junta was tottering and Pinochet was on the ropes. Just how the demise would be brought about was the most debated question. Would the continuing protest, the work stoppages, the seething agitation be sufficient to bring the Junta to its knees? Or would the impatience and desperation of the shantytown dwellers move the forces that made up the opposition to take militant action? And what of the Rightists who also felt that Pinochet should go, if only to salvage what remained of their industrial holdings? Would they work with the Left to accomplish this objective?

And finally, what of the role of the United States, the country that did so much to pave the way for the Allende government's downfall? Would Washington be content to sit by and do nothing if even a slightly left-of-center government took over from Pinochet?

Pinochet was to hang on because of several factors. With Washington's help via the International Monetary Fund, credits from the Export-Import Bank, and loans from American private lending institutions—what Chileans call "oxygen relief"—he tried to patch things together on the economic scene. Also in his favor was the wrangling among the various factions and parties within the opposition of that period. This made it easier for him to crack down on the Junta resisters with ever increasing savagery. However, both in Chile and abroad the bets were not on whether his rudderless, floundering ship of state would eventually go to the bottom, but rather on how soon this would happen.

From the very day of the putsch, Pinochet justified the Junta's Draconian methods of destroying its opposition on the grounds that no obstacles should stand in the way of the country's recovery from the Allende "chaos" (a chaos created by Chilean Fascists' sabotage and by the CIA). While this rationale scarcely blinded politically-aware Chileans, much of the middle class and the landed gentry were only too willing to go along.

But, as the cracks in the Junta façade widened, more and more of the true character of the regime came to light. It was no longer possible to hide the fact that chicanery, deceit, and self-aggrandizement were the modus operandi of those who took control of Chile in 1973. Scandal after scandal revealed how the pro-Pinochet elite, referred to as "piranhas," looted the Chilean people and deprived them of their historical heritage of democracy. This was done under the guise of a program to push the country to prosperity free of the "socialistic constraints" designed to protect the public interest against rapacious entrepreneurs.

The Pinochet program was based on the "free-market," "supply-side" economic theory which the Junta proclaimed would lead to a "capitalist revolution." Ostensibly there was much to commend it. It had the stamp of intellectual integrity: after all, its author, Professor Friedman, was a Nobel laureate. And it received plaudits from American financiers and industrialists some of whom may have been involved in grooming Reagan for the presidency. The Chilean technocrats assigned to implement the program were bright young scions of the country's well-to-do, many of them trained at the University of Chicago and soon known as "los Chicago boys." As an American investment consultant with an extensive clientele in Latin America put it, "Chile became a vast experimental laboratory for the testing of monetarism developed by the Chicago School as never before anywhere."

The scenario called for the following: that entrepreneurs aim their products at a world market, where the profits were likely to be much higher than from sales in the domestic Chilean market; that Chilean industrialists, with foreign capital assistance, concentrate on producing and exporting raw and processed materials native to Chile and not generally available or as efficiently produced in other parts of the world. For their part, foreign exporters were to be free to unload their goods in Chile with minimal or no tariffs to protect Chile's domestic industry. It was to be a "two-way street," with open competition deciding which industries should live and which should die.

To remove encumbrances to this free-market paradise, the Junta killed price controls; withdrew subsidies to fledgling industries; froze wages; and in effect eliminated strikes. This marked a fundamental departure from the economic policies pursued over decades in Chile. Whatever the political coloration of past Administrations, the goal was to create industries responsive to domestic consumer needs, not only for profits; and to free Chile from dependence on foreign markets.

The scenario also required reducing the inflation rate from 280 percent (the figure at the end of the Allende period, when U.S. financial blockades and domestic sabotage strangled Chile's economy) to 35 percent. Here the Junta took a meat cleaver to government expenditures on social security, pensions, and the comprehensive health system. The immediate result was idleness for thousands of civil service employees—who were assured, however, that with the new monetarist program they would eventually get better jobs and enjoy greater benefits as prosperity "trickled down" from the fortunes of those at the economic helm. This annihilation of social programs affecting the public sector was yet another departure from a long tradition. As a recent UNICEF study pointed out, in Chile "social problems since the beginning of the century ceased to be regarded as problems of individual responsibility and became community programs calling for public action. The State was given the responsibility of organizing, on a social basis, the coverage of elementary needs in respect to education, health, nutrition, housing and social security."

As it turned out, the free-market Chilean experience became a one-way street. When foreign exporters began to dump their goods freely, many Chilean enterprises, unable to hold their own, were quickly wiped out. As mass-produced clothing flooded into the country from South Korea, Hong Kong, Taiwan, and other cheap labor areas, even the well-established Chilean textile industry went into oblivion, and many thousands of workers were out of work as factories shut down.

Despite ominous signs that the upbeat prophecies of "los Chicago boys" were not squaring with reality, the experiment continued to be hailed as an "economic miracle" and a model for other countries to follow. As late as September 1981, while on a visit to Chile, Jeane J. Kirkpatrick, the U.S. Ambassador to the U.N. declared that the Reagan Administration "shares the same convictions of the architects of Chile's economic policies—that the free market approach will prove more effective in restoring fully the economic strength in the U.S." Later that year *Forbes* reported that Administration boosters were "pointing to Chile as proof that the Reagan economic program is sound and will really work."

But scarcely a half year later, in January 1982, the *Wall Street Journal* reported that Chilean "firms in structural steel, tools, canned goods, refractory bricks, agribusiness, forest products, and fruit exports have closed." By way of example the *Journal* cited the many failures in the wheat-growing area around the city of Talca. Growers had gone deep into debt trying to rebuild farms, but were so "squeezed by import competition, high interest rates, rising costs, and falling land values that they are forced to sell their land to cover their debts." A Talca banker told the *Journal* reporter there were some 15,000 cases of bounced checks and that "some landowners are just turning their keys into the banks instead of making payments on their loans."

Similar conditions were to be found in other parts of Chile. For example, Maria B. recounted her experience returning to the town of her birth after five years of exile in Europe. Before the coup, she told this writer, its industrial plants had kept most of the work force employed, so that many of the inhabitants lived in relatively comfortable economic circumstances. "I was startled, therefore," Maria B. said, "on seeing the destitution all about me. When I went to the central plaza where the town was celebrating its four-hundredth anniversary I burst into tears. But I did not cry because of nostalgia. I wept because I saw young people, some only eight or nine years old, who were emaciated, gaunt and worn out. Malnutrition was written all over their faces. Most of them were barefoot and their clothes were threadbare.

"But what made it all especially grotesque was the sight of youngsters trying to keep in step to the blare of rock music amplified by ten enormous speakers. They didn't seem to be dancing, they were shuffling along in a zombie-like state. From time to time, a boy would dart out to pick up a half-dead cigarette butt."

Maria subsequently learned more about how the children of

the Chilean poor were being deprived of what were long considered basic rights. Though some of the elementary schools were still tuition-free, "the very poor children are barred from entry simply because they have no shoes, a school requirement for neat appearance. Other children may be denied admission because their dresses or suits have too many patches. Yet others, whose parents cannot afford to provide competent medical care, may not go to school because of untreated scalp infections."

In the late 1970s such cities as Santiago and Valparaiso had a heady air of prosperity, certainly in the downtown areas and the well-to-do residential neighborhoods. Money was still flowing in from American and European lenders to Chilean bankers and financial organizations. New buildings, mostly luxury apartments, were being built, and old buildings were being renovated and freshly painted. The streets were swept clean and the boutiques rivalled those of Paris or Rome.

Salaries were high for money management executives, computer programmers, industrialists, tradespeople, professionals, and real estate developers. Consumerism was the leitmotif. With no import duties, everything that entered the country was sold at bargain prices. The well-heeled were on a buying binge, spending their money on color television sets and hi-fi equipment, refrigerators, whiskey, perfumes, and whatever new fangled household appliances.

The elegant restaurants were jammed. Dinner was served at about 10 p.m., as is usual in Latin America, although the diners didn't linger in the relaxed manner to which they had been accustomed before the coup because of the unpredictable behavior of the Junta patrols after midnight. Dinner for two at these restaurants cost $100 and up.

The impression of affluence in Santiago would have been reinforced by a visit to such residential areas as Vitacura and Las Condes with their handsome tree-lined streets and manicured gardens. Until the summer of 1981, apartments were still being grabbed up at an average price of $200,000, some still under construction. Typical rentals were $3,000 a month.

But on the other side of Santiago, in the shantytown of Lo Hermida, ragged children and beggars deluged the visitor. Scores of fourteen-year-old girls offered their bodies for a fee that would not have bought an entrée in a Las Condes restaurant. Mothers with tots in their arms twisted and turned in a halfhearted dance as they stretched out their hand for a coin. These *poblaciones*, always an eyesore, turned into wastelands jammed with a steadily increasing army of homeless families. Downtown Santiago and Valparaiso seldom saw these starving people because the police made sure they were kept out of sight.

In 1983 it was virtually impossible to draw the shades on those begging in Santiago, whether in the center of town or in the suburbs. Those looking for a handout were not only the slum-dwellers but growing numbers of the erstwhile well-to-do. Most of the elegant restaurants were closed, their torn, faded canopies flapping in the wind. A good dinner could be had at some of the best restaurants still open for $15 to $25. But there were very few diners, and restaurants continued to close. Prices of many luxury condominiums and apartments dropped from $200,000 to $30,000, with a car thrown in to sweeten the deal.

Those who controlled the country's finances and banking contributed much to the malaise of Chile's economy. Their speculative manipulations, which put Chile in hock for many years to come, took on momentum in the late 1970s when the Junta began auctioning off several hundred companies that the Allende government had nationalized. This was to be yet another demonstration of the Junta's determination to remove the government from involvement in the economy. Even more important was the hope that multinationals would rush to outbid each other, thus adding a desperately-needed flow of hard currency to a half-empty national treasury. But there were few bidders from abroad. Not many foreign companies were eager to purchase their previous holdings or acquire new ones.

But Chilean conglomerates, soon known as "crocodiles," "sharks," and "piranhas," began snapping up many of the plants and banks that the Junta put up for sale at a bargain prices. And to accomplish this they looked to foreign banks and financial institutions for loans. American banks such as Morgan Guaranty Trust Company, the Bank of America, Manufacturers Hanover Trust Company, Chemical Bank, and consortiums of smaller organizations readily obliged, especially since "supply-side economics" was the wave of the future and the Chilean industrialists were willing to pay unheard-of interest rates—2 to 4 per cent monthly, for an average rate of 30 percent annually. (Over the past decade, former Economics Minister Pablo Baraona said Chilean companies "increased their capital by 40 percent and their indebtedness by more than 1,000 percent.")

Between 1976 and 1979, the so-called boom period of Chile's monetarist phase, most of the economy became concentrated within a handful of powerful conglomerates, or *grupos*. Chilean economist Fernando Dahse, of the Catholic University, in 1979 published *Mapa de la Extramea Riqueza* ("Map of Extreme Wealth") in which he named 36 "grupos" that commanded the country's economic fortunes. Of these the most important were the Grupo Vial and Grupo Cruzat, which controlled two-thirds of Chile's largest companies.

Javier Vial and his former associate Manuel Cruzat, bankrolled by loans from abroad, took only a few years to spread their tentacles into every facet of Chilean business. As *Institutional Investor*, an American financial publication, reported, the Vial-Cruzat combine "had interests in assembly-line manufacturing, oil distribution, mines, farms, supermarkets, commercial fishing, vineyards, real estate, beverage companies, paper mills, lumber, food processing, metallurgy," and other areas. In addition, they controlled much of the nation's finance through the two largest private banks. They also had a 90 percent share of mutual funds, and a 60 percent share of the life insurance market.

A charismatic individual, never at a loss for words in praising "los Chicago boys," Vial, according to *Institutional Investor*, became "the darling of international bankers ranging from the bin Mahfouz family of Saudi Arabia to top management at Morgan Guaranty Trust Company." Vial-Cruzat used loans from abroad to purchase its acquisitions and to set up their own lending operations to Chilean business entrepreneurs who did not have privileged contacts via top Junta channels to the banks abroad. The Vial and Cruzat banks, as well as other Chilean banks, lent their money at the unprecedented rates of 50 to 150 percent interest.

Moneylending at these usurious rates was not only quite in keeping with the monetarist "free enterprise" philosophy; it was also expedited, as in the case of Vial and Cruzat, by the participation of Junta cabinet ministers. Rolf Luders and Boris Blanco, at different times, were either directors of the Vial-Cruzat enterprises, or held the posts of Finance Minister and Superintendent of Banks, respectively. Having these individuals oversee the integrity of the Chilean banking system was "the same as appointing a reformed Mafioso as the Chief of Police," quipped the *Institutional Investor.*

Perhaps the most spectacular piece of Vial-Cruzat skulduggery was the creation of the Banco Andino in Panama. Vial's Banco de Chile deposited in it some $350 million, ostensibly to provide capital for doing business with other Latin American companies. Actually, however, Vial used this money for two purposes: to extend substantial loans to his own business enterprises in excess of the legal limit—5 percent of the bank's capital; and, according to mounting accusations, to stash a substantial amount of the bank's capital in his private accounts in Switzerland.

Finally, in 1981–82, when the bubble began to burst, and the Chilean supply-side economic miracle went into limbo, what began to emerge was that 60 percent of Chile's massive foreign debt was of private origin. The flow of dollars from the United States and other places to cover the speculative ventures of Vial, Cruzat, and other piranhas of the Chilean banking establishment became part of the $21 billion national debt. The Chilean citizenry was saddled with the burden of paying for what the speculators either squandered or salted away in personal accounts in Swiss banks. Most of the money from the loans negotiated with the International Monetary Fund and private foreign banks went to pay off interest; scarecely anything was left to expand the industrial or agricultural development of the country.

When the Junta took over some of the banks that were on the verge of bankruptcy in January 1981, Pinochet, always a shrewd maneuverer, began pointing the accusatory finger at some of the financial malpractitioners. Regardless of how close their association with him had been in the past, he intended to make sure he was unblemished. By 1982, when the Vial-Cruzat banks collapsed, Pinochet was making even greater efforts to distance himself from his former cabinet ministers and former financial angels. As public clamor intensified, with bank depositors demanding restitution, Pinochet ordered not only an investigation into the overall banking situation but also the arrest of Vial, Luders, and Blanco.

There is considerable irony in the fact that the government intervened in the administration of these banks, an action which drew a storm of protest from the Right when Allende tried to do the same thing to protect the financial integrity of his government.

While Chile's "miracle" held the headlines of the world's newspapers, reportage of the Junta's continued repression was treated as much less newsworthy. The continuing and growing resistance against the Junta was, to say the least, underreported.

In fact, there were public confrontations as early as 1975, when women demonstrated in downtown Santiago demanding that the government disclose the whereabouts of their "disappeared" sons, daughters, and husbands. This was followed by other protests, and by 1980 homeless shantytown families occupied unused municipal land, where they tried to set up a tent city, despite police clubs, tear gas, and arrests. That same year, in defiance of labor restrictions, textile workers went on strike and marched through downtown Santiago demanding better working conditions.

There were also acts of sabotage: a hundred Renault cars went up in flames at the International Trade Fair in Santiago to warn foreign investors not to do business with the Junta; Santiago and other cities were plunged into three hours of darkness as bombs knocked out power stations; University of Chile students held rallies to protest detentions, explusions, and banishment of dissidents.

Terror, Repression Legitimized

To blunt this upsurge of disquiet, the Junta orchestrated a plebiscite in which the Chilean people were to affirm their confidence in Pinochet. It was a maneuver to institutionalize terror and give it legitimacy through a constitution.

Chileans called the plebiscite *una farsa,* and it was a farce, since every citizen of voting age was obliged to vote or face imprisonment. And to make sure there was compliance, each voter was ordered to sign an assigned ballot and put his or her fingerprint beside it, according to Father Stephen De Mott, a Maryknoll priest who witnessed the act while on a five-year assignment in Chile, where he worked with shantytown people in Santiago. The voting areas bristled with military, "as though Chile was about to go to war; police and soldiers, armed with machine guns, stood guard inside and outside the polling booths, eyeing each voter as if he or she were about to commit a crime." The votes were counted behind closed doors by Junta officials, and to no one's surprise the results overwhelmingly favored Pinochet. He could now reign with the seeming approval of the Chilean people.

Revulsion spilled far beyond the frontiers of Chile. In the United States forty members of both houses of Congress signed a statement deploring the plebiscite as a "transparently fraudulent" affront to the Chilean people. The Junta, however, claimed that the plebiscite gave it authority to revoke the pre-coup constitution and replace it with another. The new document struck down a vast number of social and political advances. It gagged political expression and, in effect, legitimized a perpetual reign of terror against those who challenge the Junta. What was especially cynical, Father De Mott pointed out, was that the Chilean people were forced to approve a so-called constitution that made them renounce their right to a voice in government for years. It empowered Pinochet to do with their freedom as he chose, and "It is one of the most immoral documents ever foisted on a people."

The 1980 constitution authorized Pinochet to rule by fiat during the presumed "transitional" phase. It permitted his Minister of Interior to arrest anyone and hold a person without charges in any place for up to twenty days, which were usually twenty days of torture. It also allowed him to banish political opponents to remote parts of the country or to exile abroad. During the "transitional" period, which was to continue until 1989, all political parties were banned and Congress remained closed. Furthermore, Father De Mott said, an individual who by word or action tended toward philosophies construed to be of "a Marxist character" would be regarded as a threat to the security of the state. The authoritative Chilean Jesuit publication *Mensaje* charged that this constitution was "entirely foreign to Chilean historic tradition" and "institutionalizes a permanent state of violence."

The fraudulent enactment of the plebiscite constitution enraged large sections of the population and eventually moved many to join the opposition, especially as the economic situation deteriorated. To hold down the growing dissent, Pinochet reacted by intensifying terror, but with a more subtle strategy aimed at deluding the world into thinking that a new day had dawned in Chile, that anti-Junta suspects were no longer killed, or at least not on as massive a scale as during the coup.

The new terror strategy was designed largely to accommodate potential business partners abroad. Kidnapping, torture, and murder, with bodies floating down a river or prominently displayed on roadsides or in city parks to intimidate the public, were difficult to explain as methods to enforce law and order. Some foreign governments and multinational companies eager to do business with Chile simply looked the other way, but other countries—Holland, Italy, and England—whose citizens were especially outraged by the Junta's excesses, had been slow to resume trade. Hence the new method.

When a person was carried off by the CNI (the Chilean secret police) for "interrogation" there was first a thorough physical examination as though in preparation for surgery. It included blood and urine tests for such diseases as diabetes, hypertension, and heart irregularities. "It is also very scientific," a Chilean Human Rights Commission representative explained. "The physician in charge decided the maximum of shock or other torment that the victim's body would tolerate. A young prisoner in good physical condition would, of course, receive much stronger electrical charges than a man or woman who was older or had heart trouble. Rubber truncheons rather than wooden clubs were used for beatings, so there would be no visible bruises, such as black-and-blue marks. When a person was finally released there was no physical evidence of abuse. Later, of course, a number of these individuals would die or be disabled from irreversible kidney damage or heart injuries. By then, however, he or she would have been at 'liberty' for some time."

Survivors said that questioning under torture generally began with a demand for information about the individual's family, such as the name of the wife or husband, names and ages of the children, of parents, and brothers and sisters, and where all of these work or go to school. The inquisitors then demanded that the prisoner name all friends, with short biographical sketches. This information was collected in the Junta's data bank. Those named might not be Junta opponents, but by association with the arrested person they became suspect and were added to the master list of those to be watched or immediately detained for questioning. Information gathered by the Vicariate of Solidarity (a Catholic Church unit aiding families of repression victims) from victims who were released because of public outcry revealed that most of those detained held up astonishingly well under physical assault when resisting pressure to become informers. Psychological terror, it was said, is what eventually breaks people down. And once a person's resistance falters the next step is a "most barbaric attempt at mind and behavior modification." The prisoner is bullied into humiliating "revelations" about his or her life and is forced to undergo such degrading experiences as eating excrement. There were reports that psychotropic drugs were used on prisoners. It appeared that sodium pentothal was especially favored by the torturers.

From May 1983, when the protest demonstrations began, to May 1984, upward of 50,000 people were held in custody by the police, some forced to stand for hours in the open stadiums and other collection points while pelted by heavy winter rain. Of this number more than 15,000 Chileans were put under arrest and subjected to beatings and electrode torture. Among those jailed were youngsters, some only eleven years of age, who were held incommunicado for as long as a week. *Mensaje* charged that a number of children "disappeared," that is, were kidnapped, and their whereabouts were unknown.

Police terror was most conspicuous in the slum districts. In May 1983, during a protest demonstration in La Victoria, a shantytown in the southern part of Santiago, the police seized the entire district, arrested hundreds of the inhabitants, and began interrogating them in front of the crowds of onlookers. Those suspected of being activists were thrown to the ground and tortured with electric cattle prods, all in public view. Many were then taken away for more punishment and imprisonment in police vans.

In addition to the wholesale arrests at protest meetings, people suspected of leadership in the various opposition organizations were arrested singly, usually at their homes. Frequently it was done at night when CNI secret police would rip down the door and take the suspects away. There was no advance notice and there were no arrest warrants. Those taken prisoner included reporters, teachers, editors, feminist leaders, labor leaders and even Catholic priests who worked in the poor areas. Between April and July 1984 alone, approximately 400 such arrests were made.

Chileans were profoundly upset because the Reagan Administration was eager to accept the Junta's assurances that human rights were no longer being violated, even as most of the world community continued to view the Junta as a pariah. *

*After a visit to Chile in mid-September 1981, Jeane Kirkpatrick, U.S. Ambassador to the United Nations, was reported by the *Washington Post* to have publicly praised the policies of General Pinochet. The United States intended to "normalize completely its relations with Chile in order to work together in a pleasant way," and she declined to comment when asked about Chile's human rights record. But within forty-eight hours after Mrs. Kirkpatrick's departure, the *New York Times* reported, "plainclothes agents stormed into the home of Jaime Castillo, a sixty-seven-year-old Christian Democrat and former Minister of Justice. He was beaten, dragged into a car and, along with three other opposition leaders, dumped on the Argentine frontier." Among other things, Castillo is President of the Chile Human Rights Commission. The Pinochet government accused the four of supporting a "Marxist" labor union movement by signing a petition protesting the imprisonment of two officers of an outlawed labor organization. Castillo also represented the family of Orlando Letelier in a legal appeal for redress. Letelier and an American aide, Ronni Moffitt, were assassinated in September 1976, in Washington, D.C., by Junta secret police agents. Castillo was allowed to reenter Chile in the wake of the mass protest demonstrations in 1983. He is still president of the Human Rights Commission.

With low-income housing programs halted for ten years, the plight of families seeking basic shelter became critical.

With no space, with a continuous din from infants, children, and young people, the poor suffered from what they call *enfermedades de los nervios* (bad nerves). At times the situation became so desperate that the *pobladores* threw caution to the wind and organized a squatter move to seize vacant land. In the summer of 1980, about 1,200 people—families with children—made such an attempt near La Bandera shantytown. When the police ordered them to disperse, they took shelter on the grounds of an adjacent church, which protected them from the police attack while an enormous police force, heavily armed, surrounded the entire area. Church groups and human rights organizations supplied them with what food, clothes, and medicine they could, in spite of police obstacles. The families remained in this tent city throughout the long, bitter-cold winter, and their self-discipline astonished everybody.

Most of this encampment finally broke up because of disease and malnutrition, but before long the squatters were organizing again. Comites Sin Casa (Committee for the Homeless) emerged and soon became integrated into a central body, La Coordinadora Metropolitana de Pobladores (The Metropolitan Coordinating Body of Shantytown Dwellers). In the increasingly anti-Junta atmosphere that developed with the protest demonstrations of 1983, the Coordinadora Metropolitana seized the moment and on September 22 mounted a spectacular land seizure in the Santiago outskirts. Operating in secrecy, the various shantytown committees launched their occupation at dawn. Their initial plans called for the participation of about 5,000 people, but word of their action spread quickly and some 8,000 families, a total of 32,000 people, laden with the few belongings they possessed, began their massive march into the area.

They had scarcely arrived when the carabineros, armed with machine guns, clubs, and teargas bombs, rushed to the scene. There were at least four police assaults resulting in many injuries to men, women, and children. But the people regrouped. Knowing the police would be especially savage toward the men in yet another foray, the women insisted on making up the rear guard, hoping that the police would waver when deciding to shoot at the women. And indeed this tactic worked; although the police wounded scores of people with clubs and rifle butts, they did not shoot. And they were unable to dislodge the oncoming waves of squatters.

Under a temporary truce, an official of the adjacent La Granja municipality ordered the squatters to leave. But the people stood their ground: there was nowhere else for them to go. Yet another high government official was summoned and he finally acceded to their remaining where they were. When news of the march was broadcast, dozens of volunteers—doctors, nurses, social workers—arrived to provide assistance. The squatters divided their settlement into two areas, one called the Fresno Encampment, in honor of Juan Francisco Fresno, the new archbishop of Santiago, and the other in honor of his predecessor, Cardinal Raul Silva Henriquez, who had been closely allied with those in need of protection from the Junta.

In a matter of days the squatters set up a highly efficient system of self-government to administer such essential services as policing, sanitation, soup kitchens, and a makeshift infirmary. They even had a press and information committee that informed the outside world of what they were doing and what specific help they needed. With the assistance of sympathizers in neighboring communities, the encampments replaced their tents with wooden shacks. Even kindergartens sprang up, staffed by enthusiastic volunteer teachers.

But the going was rough, particularly during June and July, Chile's winter months. An unusual bitter series of storms swept down from the Andes bringing record rainfall and flooding. Many of the squatters, still living in tents, suffered intense hardship. Several infants died of pneumonia. Yet when officials offered them shelter and vague promises of land providing they left the encampments, the overwhelming majority turned down the offer. They would leave only to go to permanent living quarters, or to land on which they could build homes. As Manuel Maturana, president of the encampments, declared: "We arrived here with the rains when we took this land, we have suffered cold, hunger and the death of our children. We shall depart from here directly to the land we have been promised, but not to any shelter."

Political observers felt that this seizure of land was one of the most significant challenges to the Junta. For it demonstrated that civil disobedience on a mass scale could work. When thousands of people stood up against the armed constabulary, they were able to prevail. And this was not lost on those in the opposition who saw that such body blows to the regime would steadily sap its strength and create doubts about Pinochet's invulnerability, even within the governing elite.

Anger, bitterness, and humiliation were not confined to the destitute squatters. Similar discontent was rising among those still holding on to jobs and keeping a roof over their heads. As inflation edged up, salaries remained frozen. And because the State no longer assumed responsibility with respect to health services and pensions, in keeping with the Junta's market-oriented policy, large sectors of the population found themselves excluded from the "privatized" health care programs because of the cost.

Attempts by labor to raise salary levels to keep up with rising costs were out of the question since low-cost industrial output was essential in maintaining "free market" policies. The Junta's labor code nominally permitted strikes, but in fact it guaranteed that the employer would win. The law limited the strike to continue for no longer than 60 days. If there was no settlement in that period, the strikers had to return to work or face a lockout.

Labor, Students, Defiant

These and other strikes began with the traditional demands for salary increases, but soon took on a political dimension. The newly-organized labor alliance, Coordinadora Nacional Sindical (CNS), representing one million workers in 267 unions, presented a petition to the government in which it called for reinstatement of full trade union rights, large increases in minimum wages, freedom for political prisoners, abandonment of "free market" policies, and an end to the violation of human rights.

Even though the Junta rejected the petition and arrested ten of the Coordinadora leaders, the petition gave impetus to more militant trade union activity, leading directly to labor's present assertiveness against the regime.

The 1980–81 period also witnessed intensified anti-Junta activity on university campuses. As one Catholic University professor put it, "What we are seeing in the universities is a polarization of pro- and anti-government positions. It is simply a smaller-scale version of what is happening throughout Chile now."

The professor made this observation for the *Chronicle of Higher Education*, an American publication which reported on the situation in Chilean universities. According to the *Chronicle*, "the movement among labor-union leaders and opposition politicians for a return to electoral government in Chile has spread to the campuses. Students with little or no political experience have begun to choose sides and to stir up new issues of their own."

For the first time since the Junta took power, students openly displayed posters of Allende and banners bearing the insignias of outlawed Leftist groups. But this upsurge against the Junta was not without sacrifice. Government-inspired "goon squads," professors told the *Chronicle*, attacked critics of Pinochet with sticks, rocks, and clubs to intimidate them from holding protest rallies.

Interior Minister Jarpa in a speech in September 1983, urged citizens to "organize themselves to defend the home, workplace, and the campus from subversive protests." This was a call to set up vigilante groups to assault government critics. And indeed, the *Chronicle* said, "there were many reports of unidentified civilian groups attacking peaceful demonstrators with stones and weapons." The casualties were high. A number of students were shot to death. The widespread agitation on the campuses for Chile's return to democracy was a dramatic testimonial to the Junta's failure to bring the universities to heel, "to end their role as a source of social criticism and political opposition."

Since much of the intellectual and academic world had been generally supportive of the Allende regime, professors and students in many cases were targeted for arrest, torture, and execution. Successive waves of dismissals of professors were carried out at the University of Chile, the Catholic University, the National Technical University, the University of Concepción, and a number of others. Interestingly enough, among the first to be ousted from his post was the rector of the Catholic University, Fernando Castillo Velasco. As his successor Pinochet appointed Jorge Swett, a retired admiral. This became the pattern: higher educational guidance was entrusted to admirals, colonels, and generals.

Political surveillance offices were set up in all schools. Security agents of the CNI continued to sit in classrooms, spying on students and faculty. Tuition was raised to unprecedented levels, thus excluding not only children of the working class but also many of the middle class.

Enrollment dropped substantially. By 1984, upward of 18,000 students and faculty had been expelled from Chile's eight universities, whose total enrollment until the coup was about 135,000, according to estimates in *Science* (March 27, 1981), a publication of the American Association for the Advancement of Science. On matriculation, students were forced to sign pledges not to engage in political or ideological activities at the university.

As anticipated by *Science*, the universities began to eliminate a variety of subjects from their curriculum, retaining only those which would be related to business management, computer programming, engineering, medicine, and dentistry. A Chilean educator commented that Pinochet was converting the universities into "vocational training institutions" designed to conform with the country's free-market politics. Since the late '70s, university graduates had been expected to dedicate themselves to streamlining Chilean business operation to the exclusion of other concerns. And the effects of this policy were profound. By 1981, *Science* pointed out, "virtually no organized studies in the social sciences" were available in Chile. Research in the natural sciences also suffered severely because of funding restrictions and the departure abroad of some of Chile's best-known scientists.

Opponents of the Junta, who firmly clung to the hope that Chile would rid itself of the dictatorship, made every effort to have their children continue in school regardless of the sacrifices. They rejected the possibility that it was the privileged who would hold the key to education and culture. Their sons and daughters were made to feel that it was a matter of Chilean honor and political resolve to continue with schooling and to stand out scholastically. Many youths, frequently with no money for carfare or lunch, walked miles to get to their classes. One teacher observed, "It is not at all unusual to see students from workers' families go without food all day, and yet carry on with their studies." Paradoxically enough, however, he added, many of these same students joined anti-Junta activities on their campuses that could lead to their suspension or explusion from school.

Unlike the Brazilian military dictatorship, which tried to project an image of having broad support via government-sponsored trade unions and business associations, the Pinochet-led Junta remained dependent, for the most part, on the armed forces. Thus with every new assault on labor, students, or the homeless, Pinochet became more and more alienated from the mainstream of Chilean life. When the first massive protest against the Junta was called on May 11, 1983 by Rodolfo Seguel, the twenty-nine-year-old president of the Confederation of Copper Workers of Chile (a 22,000-member union), there was a ready response from a broad range of Chilean society. Except for the top officialdom— the "piranhas," "los Chicago boys," and the military—everybody seemed to have been nursing bitter complaints against the Junta for economic and political reasons.

The Junta was taken aback. In its decade of rule, there had been no such massive defiance. Unprepared to deal with recalcitrance except through terror, Pinochet lashed out at the protesters with unrestrained violence. Two young people were shot to death, hundreds were arrested, and two shantytowns were raided by security police.

But massive reprisals designed to intimidate the Chilean people produced the reverse effect. Anger and bitterness swept the nation. And so the opposition began mounting one protest after another. The Seguel-led copper workers entered into a broad alliance with other labor unions, forming the National Workers Command which called a protest rally for June 14, 1983. This time, four people were killed and the number of arrests more than quadrupled—some 1,350 throughout the country. Early in July, Seguel was arrested and 10,000 workers struck three major copper mines in protest. The government promptly fired 830 workers.

The third national protest came on July 12, and again the government responded by killing a number of protesters and arresting hundreds of others. Three weeks later, five political parties—though still illegal under the Junta constitution—organized the Alianza Democratica, which included the Christian Democrats, sections of the Socialist Party, the Radical Party, and even a Rightist group. The Communist Party, considered the best organized despite ten years of Junta terror, and representing approximately 20 percent of the population, was not included.

In August the Alianza called yet another mass demonstration against the government. This time Pinochet ordered 18,000 troops into the streets of Santiago. Most of them were trucked in from distant garrisons—there was to be no camaraderie between soldiers stationed in Santiago and family or friends among the marchers. The behavior of the military lived up to Pinochet's expectations—it was vicious and savage. At least 2,600 people were arrested and many killed. Doctors, nurses, and other health professionals from human rights organizations issued a report which declared that the Junta violence "created a medical emergency comparable to that of a major natural catastrophe, or that of war." Whatever the official count of dead and wounded, the report charged, the real fatality totals could not be known because hundreds of those seriously injured were not taken to hospitals for fear of arrest.

Especially "barbaric and sadistic" were the attacks by the military and police in the shantytowns where the inhabitants built bonfires in observance of the protest. Many of those killed, the report charged, were passers-by and non-participants in the demonstrations. It said that "there are proven cases of attacks on very old people, the handicapped, and even infants. There was evidence that many of the military and police who participated in these atrocities were drunk and/or under the influence of drugs."

Mensaje referred to the behavior of the military and the police as "the most brutal since the tragic days of 1973." In describing the police violence in the shantytowns, *Mensaje* said "there were young people who were stripped of their clothes and forced to put out the flames of the bonfires with their naked bodies, their bare hands and feet, others were forced to run naked through the streets while the soldiers and the police took delight in firing bullets over their heads." But it was not only the slum areas that suffered this abuse: some of the middle class sections were also under attack with teargas bombs and shotguns.

But this violence, according to *Mensaje*, did not succeed in quieting the protest din created by the banging of pots and pans throughout the city to the rhythmic shouts of "assassins." *Mensaje* noted that the government blamed the protesters for the dead and injured. There was no explanation, however, it added, "of how the banging of pots and pans discharged the bullets that did the killing . . . but with 18,000 troops in Santiago with orders to 'act with force' there was no doubt as to who was responsible for the deaths. . . . The armed forces, because of this conduct, found themselves more and more isolated from the people and regarded as an occupation force in enemy territory."

After this Junta assault, the will of those committed to the ouster of Pinochet hardened. Prey to constant police harassment, they no longer had anything to lose by striking back. And the indiscriminate bloodletting of August was counterproductive in another way. It brought Chile back to the front pages of the international press and alarmed many of Pinochet's foreign backers.

Under pressure by the Church and even some of his closest advisors to do something before the country was plunged into civil war, Pinochet made a gesture at willingness to listen to what the opposition complaints were all about. It turned out to be an empty gesture, but the very fact that for the first time since the coup Pinochet had made such a move, showed the growing importance of the opposition.

Pinochet appointed Sergio Onofre Jarpa to be Minister of the Interior and assigned him to begin talks. Jarpa, a long-time reactionary politican, who had been a leader of the conservative Nationalist party, held two dialogues with the Alianza Democratica, whose agenda called for the resignation of Pinochet, the convening of a constitutional assembly to write a new constitution, and the holding of elections.

Jarpa agreed in late August to hold the talks, but there was a September protest all the same. People came out in the tens of thousands all over Chile. Police violence this time was relatively restrained but, even so, a number of people were killed, hundreds injured, and 2,300 arrested.

For a short interval there developed a kind of thaw. Political parties declared illegal by the Junta Constitution of 1980 suddenly surfaced with their original identities—the Christian Democrats, Socialists, Communists, Christian Left, and other left-of-center groups. Also, a number of magazines began to publish without first getting permission from the Junta. Among these were *Cauce, Analisis, Critica, APSI,* and *Fortin Mapocho.* Some of these poured out anti-Junta material that could not have been printed for a decade. As a consequence, the continuance of these publications was under constant threat. The crackdown from the censors was frequent, resulting in the confiscation of complete editions as they came off the press.

It was even more risky for the editors, who seemed to be shuttling to and from jail for having violated press regulations that were not in the statutes and were usually dictated at the whim of the police. For instance, in the case of Jorge Lavandero, publisher of *Fortin Mapocho,* punishment for his attempt to expose Pinochet's shady real estate deals took the form of murderous attacks by thugs in the employ of the CNI. Lavandero was left lying near death in his wrecked car. After weeks of intensive care in the hospital, he was said to be recovering but with at least one permanent injury, deafness. The documents he carried with him were stolen.

In September, still another major opposition force came into being—the Movimiento Democrático Popular (MDP)—the Popular Democratic Movement, consisting of the Communist Party, a sizable section of the Socialist Party that differs with the Socialists in the Alianza, and MIR—Movimiento de Izquierda Revolucionario, the Left Revolutionary Movement. And soon after there emerged yet another opposition group, Bloque Socialista— the Socialist Bloc—made up of yet another faction of the splintered Socialist Party, and various Christian Left parties.

On the occasion of the sixth national protest, in October, this time called by the MDP, the Alianza demurred: such action should be postponed in the hope that the talks with Jarpa would be productive. The MDP, however, pressed on, questioning the value of the negotiations with Jarpa. Many critics of the Alianza maintained that the initiative was with the protesters, and that continuation of the dialogues without the accompaniment of public protest would buy time for Pinochet and drain the strength of the opposition. The Alianza gave in and joined the MDP as co-sponsor of the protest.

In terms of numbers, the October demonstration was among the most successful. At least 100,000 people participated. And the casualties were fewer than in September. About ten people were killed and hundreds arrested over a period of three days as the protests continued in the shantytowns.

Junta Breaks Democracy Promise

In mid-October, the Alianza-Jarpa dialogue was broken off because the government refused to accept the Alianza's principal demand that Pinochet resign. One commentator called it "a dialogue of the deaf." Scarcely a week later, students and workers organized a protest march to the presidential palace. Two of them were killed, forty injured, and at least sixty-three arrested.

By far the largest anti-government demonstration took place on November 18, when the Alianza and the MDP joined forces, together with 150 other opposition groups, and issued a call for the abdication of Pinochet. The demonstration, held at Bernardo O'Higgins Park, was attended by a crowd estimated at 500,000 to a million people.

In March 1984, after a hiatus of some three months—the Chilean summer—the opposition once again called on the Chilean people to come out and insist on a changeover in government. Because the Junta refused a permit for an outdoor demonstration, the protest took on a passive, but perhaps more ominous character; it resembled a rehearsal for a general strike. Most public transportation came to a standstill. In Santiago and other major cities, fewer than 15 percent of students attended school. What was especially significant was that store-owners, merchants, lawyers, doctors, engineers, and other professionals throughout the country also took part. By two o'clock in the afternoon, nearly all stores had drawn their shutters and the streets of Santiago, Concepcion, and Valparaiso were empty.

In a frantic attempt to bolster its damaged economy, the Junta made a complete turnabout from its free-market policies without ever admitting it. It quietly jettisoned "los Chicago boys" and reintroduced protective tariffs. There was even talk about reinstating subsidies for developing industries. One of those most likely to get assistance was a munitions manufacturing and bomber aircraft construction company headed by Carlos Cardoen, a prominent landowner and industrialist, which began exporting its wares to the Middle East. The company specialized in cluster bombs which were reportedly of American origin, a development that should have raised questions in Washington, since all weaponry for Chile was banned by an act of Congress because of the Letelier-Moffitt assassination in 1976. The aircraft construction was licensed by Spain.

In addition to the squalor, wretchedness, and hunger that typified the shantytowns of Chile, emotional crises afflicted many a family. As a physician who headed a shantytown clinic told Señora Letelier, "Sure, we can use more medicine, but that isn't our top priority. What we need is food and jobs . . . because unemployment is causing tragedies, especially among young couples, and hunger is killing them."

It was not surprising that these shantytown dwellers comprised the front ranks of those ready to do battle, somehow, with the government. This was especially true of the youth, whose patience with the Junta had reached zero level.

The Junta's *carabineros* were actually intensifying hostility toward the poor. There was considerable evidence that the Junta deliberately tried to provoke the slum dwellers into violent defensive action, giving it an opportunity to raise the cry that rebellion is threatening the pace of the country. The specter of violence was anathema to much of the population which, after ten years of dictatorship, hungered for a return to civil normalcy.

The Junta charged that Left extremists were responsible for a number of bombings throughout the country. With this excuse, on May 16, 1984, the government put into force the dreaded Anti-Terrorist Law. The principal aim was to intensify the intimidation of the citizenry. Of course, Chile was ruled for a decade under repressive laws, but the Anti-Terrorist Law gave the Junta even greater power over individuals accused of anti-government conspiracy.

Among other things, anybody could be charged with terrorism and held incommunicado for thirty-two days by the dreaded CNI secret police for "investigation," the euphemistic term for torture. During this period the person had no access to a legal defender and could be denied the right to learn the accuser's identity. Following the "investigation," the case was turned over to a court in which there was no jury and where the proceedings could go on for years, depending on the whim of the judge. Throughout this period, the accused remained in prison. Once sentence was pronounced, and this could include capital punishment, there could be no pardon or amnesty.

This law was widely criticized. José Aldunate, a Jesuit priest, writing in *Mensaje,* declared that if anyone was involved in terrorist activities, it was the Junta. He traced a variety of assaults by the Junta on political parties, trade unions, and individuals over the past ten years. He was especially outraged that the CNI was permitted to hold detainees in its own headquarters for questioning before they were transferred to the Justice Department. As he put it, "What the CNI did outside and against the law with the tolerance of the government, now it will be able to do according to 'law.'"

Ironically, the first case before the courts under the new terrorism law was brought against the government by the Vicariate of Solidarity of the Catholic Church. It centered on a case involving two people who were kidnapped and tortured, allegedly by the CNI. One of them, a young woman, was killed by a bomb placed on her body as she was dumped from an unmarked car on the outskirts of Santiago. The case received nationwide press coverage and the government found it difficult to ignore.

In spite of the Junta's massive efforts to hold down the opposition, it was the dictatorship that was increasingly under siege by the Chilean people, and not the other way around. The cry for change could be heard not only in the capital, not only in the larger cities, such as Valparaiso and Concepción, but in the most remote areas of rural Chile as well.

Nevertheless, General Pinochet still swaggered pompously be-

Women of the Association of Relatives of Disappeared and Detained
Persons protest in front of the Moneda Palace. (Deborah Shaffer)

fore the TV cameras with the arrogance of an emperor. To all
appearances, he remained confident of his own special role as the
answer to Chile's prayer. During her interview, *Newsweek* correspondent Patricia Sethi observed that the dictator "has a crusader's
zeal about him; he genuinely believes he is Chile's savior, leading
the fight for Christianity and spiritualism on the one hand, and
against Marxism and materialism on the other." Pinochet told her
that he "has God on his side."

Sallow-complexioned, his eyes always behind dark glasses,

Pinochet projectes a kind of metallic hardness. His charisma, in the opinion of one wag, "has the thud of a sawed-off howitzer barrel." But he does not look like a man who had spent most of his life in the Spartan environment of a garrison community. He favors affluent surroundings, whether at his residence or at La Moneda, the presidential palace. His home on fashionable President Errazuriz Street, at the corner of Asturias, is guarded by soldiers armed with machine guns. They stand outside as well as inside the entrance with guns drawn, and helmeted militia guard the rear of the house. The array of weaponry is in stark contrast to the beauty of the building itself, with its elegant doors decorated with figurines sculpted by some of Chile's outstanding artists.

Pinochet made even more ambitious plans for his future presidential residence, referred to as the "Bunker Palace." According to such Chilean publications as *Cauce* and *Analisis*, Pinochet's mansion had been built at the cost of many millions of dollars, estimated at 5 percent of the nation's public works budget, at a time when Chile had a catastrophic housing shortage, especially in the slum areas. Chileans were further incensed when they learned that costly marble, imported from Italy to cover the walls of the cavernous lobby, was returned to Rome because its color was not to the liking of Señora Pinochet. A new shipment was ordered, more to the taste of the First Lady.

Built in the shape of a bunker, presumably to withstand a possible assault from fellow Chileans, this stronghold contained dozens of dormitories and a dining room with a capacity for several hundred people.* Because the information about the exorbitant construction costs of this edifice were made public, Pinochet's plans for resettlement appeared to have been stalled. It now stands empty.

Pinochet was now beset with personal embarrassments that called into question his self-proclaimed virtues as a leader. It

---

Cauce began running a contest for recommendations on what to do with the "Bunker Palace" once Pinochet resigns. Among readers' suggestions:
- That it be made into a psychiatric hospital for "los Chicago Boys."
- That it remain as a historic testimonial to the arrogance and bestiality of fascism.

appeared that Pinochet's daughter Lucia and her husband had been involved in transactions between a state-owned insurance agency and several other state agencies, thereby earning a commission of nearly one million dollars. This broke all precedents, since no such service charges had ever before entered into intragovernmental agency arrangements.

The disclosures of his daughter's shenanigans were followed by exposes of Pinochet's real estate deals related to purchases of land in the Melocoton suburbs of Santiago from the army at bargain prices in noncompetitive bidding. This venture was likely to have deeply hurt Pinochet's prestige within the armed forces. Chilean tradition requires the military to remain free of any taint on the honesty and dedication of those committed to safeguarding the country. It was rumored that some of the younger officers were taking the Pinochet family scandals very much to heart.

Pinochet, however, continues to insist on pomp and circumstance. For instance, when he travels between his residence and the Presidential Palace, he and his entourage move against traffic. Every street intersection en route is taken over by soldiers, and all other movement comes to a halt for some four or five kilometers. This takes place several times a day. But notwithstanding his bombast and his claims of omnipotence, his erratic and edgy behavior has pointed to a shaky grip on himself in times of crisis.

Soon after the protest demonstrations began, Pinochet was said to have become so emotionally disturbed as to require a two-month rest at the seaside with continuous psychiatric attention. He was especially upset when he visited the city of Punta Arenas, in southern Chile, when the local church officials were said to have joined with the people to denounce him in public. There were reports by a number of journalists who accompanied Pinochet on a helicopter tour of Santiago during one of the days of national protest that the general was visibly shaken when he saw Santiago encircled by the bonfires of the shantytowns. It was like an augury of fiery events to come.

Perhaps the most astounding demonstration of Pinochet losing his cool occurred during the interview with Patricia Sethi, when her photographer attempted to pose Pinochet under the portrait of Bernardo O'Higgins, who led Chile to liberation from Spain.

The photographer tried to replicate the scene in which O'Higgins is shown standing with his arm resting on a chair. He posed Pinochet in the same position under the portrait. "Hardly had Diego (the photographer) set the scene," Sethi reports, "when the president shouted: 'Nunca, nunca' [never, never]. He picked up the chair with both hands and flung it across the room with such force that it hit the wall and toppled over." Shock permeated the room. No one moved. Soon Pinochet recovered, but made no explanation.

When Chileans heard of this episode, they understood it at once. Though the hero of Chilean independence, O'Higgins soon ran into opposition when he took over as head of state. Rather than insist on holding on to power with the risk of plunging the country into civil strife, O'Higgins decided to abdicate and leave Chile. Quite obviously, the idea of emulating O'Higgins selfless act of 1823 was not on Pinochet's agenda.

Pinochet still has the support of the armed forces, especially the army. It is not only because of his tight reign, administered through some sixty generals, more generals than Hitler had in his entire Wehrmacht. More important, perhaps, is that Chile's men in uniform, especially the enlisted men, have been virtually sealed off from the Chilean people. Little had spilled out from the closely restricted barracks to indicate whether the ongoing disquiet had penetrated the thinking of the military.

Recruits entering basic training undergo continuous indoctrination to accept the Junta dogma: that anyone questioning Pinochet or the Junta was unpatriotic, subversive, and Marxist. The ideological orientation is conducted with Prussian discipline. For the first several months of training, home leaves are suspended and contact with civilians is prohibited. By the time the brainwashing is completed, the new soldiers follow commanders with no second thoughts.

Enlisted men, and particularly the officers, are cared for considerably better than Chileans. They get the best medical care, their food allotments are generous, they are well clothed, and living quarters are adequate. And their pay is good by comparative standards, particularly for the officer corps. It becomes especially appealing because of an extra bonus equivalent to up to 50 percent of the base salary when the Junta decrees the country to be in a state of continuing emergency (*pertubación de la paz interna*).

Yet another reason why the armed forces continue to band together is the fear of reprisal should Chile follow the example of neighboring Argentina once democracy returns. The indictments of Argentina's military chiefs produced a chilling effect on their Chilean counterparts. The Army's role remains most puzzling in the constellation of problems facing the opposition.

There were attempts both by the Alianza and the MDP to reach individual high-ranking officers as well as enlisted men who were known to be free of any repressive taint. The prime objective was to bargain for the army's neutrality once the final showdown with the Junta got underway. On the one hand, to loosen Pinochet's hold on the military, there was need to assure them that it was in their interest to change allegiance. On the other hand, the roles of executioner and torturer that so many in the officer corps had assumed since the overthrow of Allende made it virtually impossible to promise forgiveness after the democratic forces took over.

The U.S. and the Junta's Deepening Crisis

The role of the United States was critically important as the Junta's crisis deepened. According to a Santiago opposition leader, in the eyes of many Chileans "Washington is maneuvering with duplicity. It is claiming to be uninvolved and is talking a lot about encouraging the Junta to go democratic. But at the same time it is doing its best to bolster Pinochet with financial bailouts and pro-Junta public policy declarations in the United Nations."

Indeed, the record of the Reagan Administration speaks clearly. A month after his inauguration, President Reagan revoked a ban on the United States government's financing of exports to Chile through the Export-Import Bank. President Carter had imposed the ban when Chile refused to extradite three of its secret service agents indicted by a Washington grand jury as the murderers of Orlando Letelier and Ronni Moffitt.

This act of international terrorism shocked the world and infuriated much of Congress. There was no question about Pinochet's complicity in the crime and in the refusal to extradite the assassins. In the words of E. Lawrence Barcella, the U.S. prosecutor in charge of the case, the Chilean authorities "haven't done spit since the day this thing happened. In fact, they have been dilatory and obstructionist."

But the Reagan Administration spokesperson announced that, although the United States still hoped the Junta would prosecute the assassins, Washington was "no longer an active party to the investigation of the case in Chile." And so yet another sanction would be lifted—the United States Navy would once again hold joint exercises, known as the UNITAS maneuvers, with the Chileans in the South Pacific.

Members of Congress who had influenced the Carter Administration's human rights policies were dismayed. Senator Edward Kennedy said: "I strongly object to the Administration's decision today to make Eximbank credits available to Chile, and to permit the Chilean Navy to participate in the Inter-American naval exercise. The new Administration has made the fight against international terrorism one of its highest priorities, yet it is now associated with a military regime which has not only engaged in repression of its own citizens, but which is responsible for the terrorist assassination of former Foreign Minister Orlando Letelier and his American associate, Ronni Moffitt, in the streets of Washington . . . the United States must not condone acts of terrorism anywhere in the world—but the Administration has failed its first test in the case of Chile."

Senator Claiborne Pell of Rhode Island charged that the ban had been lifted without consultation with the Senate Foreign Relations Committee. The Reagan Administration was "condoning government-sponsored terrorism by Chilean agents in the streets of Washington." Senator Thomas R. Harkin of Iowa (then still a congressman), declared that "the decision to drop sanctions against Chile . . . makes a mockery of the Reagan Administration campaign against international terrorism."

In July 1981, the Reagan Administration ordered its delegates at the Inter-American Development Bank to vote in favor of a $161 million dollar loan package to the Junta, the largest loan the bank had ever made to Chile. A Treasury Department statement explained that the human rights situation in Chile "does not require opposition to such loans."

But that was only the beginning of a policy aimed at having the world know that Chile had been returned to the fold, that it was to enjoy the warmth and friendship of a trusted ally. At hearings held in October 1983 by the Congressional Subcommittee on Western Hemisphere Affairs, a number of human rights advocates protested this policy.

Jo Marie Griesgraber, Deputy Director of the Washington Office on Latin America, deplored the fact that in May, 1983, just as the Chilean anti-Junta protests erupted, the Administration extended more credit to Chile. She cited the following:

- The Reagan Administration notified Chile's creditor banks that $144.5 million in Commodities Credit Corporation guarantees and $150 million through the U.S. Export-Import Bank had been approved by the U.S. government.
- The Overseas Private Investment Corporation, in deadpan timing, announced to Congress on the anniversary of the Letelier-Moffitt murders, an agreement with the government of Chile to extend guarantees to U.S. investors.
- The Bank for International Settlements granted Chile a $350 million bridge loan.
- The International Monetary Fund and the Inter-American Development Fund lent Chile over a billion dollars.

There were also a number of symbolic acts by Washington to point up the rapprochement between the U.S. and Chile. Aryeh Neier, Vice Chairman of the American Watch Committee, told the Subcommittee that, since taking office, the Reagan Administration had:

- dispatched U.N. Ambassador Jeane Kirkpatrick to Chile to give gifts to President Pinochet and to proclaim the desire of the U.S. "to fully normalize" relations with Chile.
- dispatched State Department official Everett Briggs to Chile to proclaim the restoration of a "normal bilateral relationship" and the end of a "confrontational diplomacy."
- opposed every U.N. vote critical of Chile's human rights practices.

- sought to end the work of the U.N.'s Special Rapporteur on Chile.
- received Mrs. Pinochet for tea at the White House while barring Hortensia de Allende, widow of the last democratically elected President of Chile, from visiting the United States.

Despite these developments, Washington insisted that it supported the return of democracy in Chile and favored neither Pinochet nor the opposition. In a speech at the University of Arkansas on April 12, 1984, James H. Michel, Senior Deputy Assistant Secretary of State for Latin American Affairs, declared that although "the United States has firmly avoided taking sides in the internal Chilean debate . . . the Reagan Administration has endeavored to carry out our stated policy of support for democracy in Chile by encouraging dialogue and accommodation. We have stated clearly and unequivocally that we support a return to a democratically elected civilian government in Chile. But in supporting a democratic transition process," he continued, "the United States has taken several steps to restore constructive relations with the current government, including altering several sanctions imposed by the Carter Administration."

He referred to the Administration's lifting of sanctions, to the "renewed high level visits in both directions," and to Washington's opposition to having a special rapporteur monitor human rights violations in Chile as mandated by the United Nations Human Rights Commission and the General Assembly. He made no effort to reconcile Washington's professed dedication to human rights with its objection to the U.N.'s plan to monitor them in Chile. Instead, he criticized Congress for standing in the way of the President's certification of Chile as eligible to receive military assistance.

A close reading of Mr. Michel's speech indicates that Washington, when viewing the possible transitions within Chile, was not that interested in whether the Junta would be chastened and become democratic. It appeared more concerned with the possibility that a new government might tilt leftward. As Michel put it, "Let me just say that in the choice between totally isolating ourselves from such regimes [the Junta] and thus making them fair game for the left or other reactionary forces, versus promoting change through diplomacy, this Administration has opted for the latter approach."

This was quite consistent with the views Ambassador Kirkpatrick expressed during the U.N. General Assembly debate, in December 1983, on whether Chile should be condemned for its human rights violations. Ambassador Kirkpatrick put forward the United States position within the context of East-West antagonisms. The resolution calling for condemnation, she charged, "has nothing to do with promoting greater respect for human rights, but would instead encourage an outcome that would move Chile in the direction of absorption into the bloc of Marxist-Leninist states tied to the Soviet Union." She insisted that Chile "is involved in a serious and, we believe, hopeful process of liberalization moving toward democratization."

Kirkpatrick's remarks ran counter to those of the resolution's supporters, such as A.D.M. Hamer of the Netherlands, who contended that "the habitual practice of torture and inhuman treatment . . . countenanced by the [Chilean] government must be condemned." The anti-Junta resolution was approved by a vote of eighty-nine nations in favor, seventeen against, and thirty-eight abstentions. The United States voted against the resolution—the only big power in the Western bloc to do so. Kirkpatrick's "no" vote distanced the United States from some of its closest European allies.

The Kirkpatrick-Michel position made many Chileans suspect that the Administration was giving lip service to even-handedness while in fact bolstering the Junta and Pinochet. According to the publication *Mensaje*, because of President Reagan's Rightist world outlook, concern for human rights was not among his highest priorities. For Washington, *Mensaje's* commentator said, it was more important to evaluate a nation within the framework of an East-West polarization. With this as the premise, "a government such as that headed by Pinochet satisfies these criteria: it is a friendly government; it is anti-communist; and it is a supporter of the free-market philosophy." The *Mensaje* writer said that because of protests in Chile, Washington had been somewhat critical of the Junta's human rights violations. "This serves to support a political opening with Pinochet, and to leave the road open for a quick realignment in the event that there is indeed a change in government."

The Reagan Administration, he wrote, "will not come up with a formula that calls for *democracy now, elections now,* a formula which the United States applies to Nicaragua. At best, it would have the United States appear as not having supported Pinochet to the end, nor being a supporter of the opposition. The United States position is not based on principle but on cautious pragmatism. . . . It must not be forgotten that the North American forces of the Right which influence foreign policy are more inclined to be friendly to the interests of the multi-national corporations and banks."

Certain that the Reagan Administration will stand behind the Junta, and convinced that the opposition remained so divided on tactics and strategy that it no longer constituted the threat he perceived it to be when the protests began in May 1983, Pinochet reasserted his claim to rule via dictatorship. In August 1984 he told the *New York Times*, and thus the Chilean people and the world, that he was backing away from his previous promises to return democracy to Chile.

According to an interview with the *Times*, August 8, 1984, "the Chilean President said he would not speed up the transition to democracy, despite clamorous demands to do so by the opposition and even members of his own government." Pinochet will "not call Congressional or municipal elections or even appoint a Congress," as his own supporters have been urging. The Chilean dictator said he would continue as President until 1989, in keeping with the 1980 constitution, of which he was the principal author. In fact, the *Times* added, "he has even hinted strongly that he might try to succeed himself," which would enable him to remain in office until 1995.

A strong admirer of Spain's Fascist dictator, the late Francisco Franco, Pinochet was frank about his feelings on democracy. "I don't have confidence in orthodox democracy," he told the *Times*. And he warned that he would enforce tranquility in Chile by strong-arm tactics against those suspected of being Marxist.

Denunciation of Pinochet's broken promises came quickly from all quarters.

The Alianza Democratica called for a protest demonstration on September 4 and 5, one week before the eleventh anniversary of the Junta coup. Pinochet wasted no time in letting the country know what lay in store for those who questioned his authority. Soon after the Alianza's announcement, the police launched nationwide raids on so-called "armed Marxists" allegedly plotting violence against the government. Eight people, purportedly left-wing guerrillas, were killed when government agents broke into private residences and opened fire. There were no warrants; there were no arrests. The Junta described it as a "security" operation. The Chileans called it an "assassination" operation.

Contemptuous of this act of intimidation, and despite the ban on street protests, Chileans heeded the Alianza call. For two days and two nights the cities reverberated with the sounds of gunfire, ambulance sirens, and the shouts of "assassins," as the police tried to disperse the crowds. Once again international television provided the world with the spectacle of helmeted police assaulting unarmed men and women with clubs, water cannons, tear gas, and bullets. Torn, bloodied faces, cracked skulls, broken arms and broken legs filled the screens. At least ten people lost their lives and many hundreds were injured. One of the casualties was a French priest, Reverend Andre Jurlan. He was shot by police while in the study of his house in La Victoria shantytown, where he was well known as a dedicated community worker. Among the wounded was Rodolfo Seguel, one of the originators of the protest marches and leader of the copper workers union. And many prominent political figures were dragged by their hair and then thrown into a police wagon.

In addition to the thousands of Chileans who braved police terror in the city streets to demonstrate their hostility to the Junta regime, many more thousands expressed their anti-Pinochet sentiments through various forms of civil disobedience. Shopkeepers closed their stores. Professionals did the same with their offices. Even truckers, known as the most conservative of the entrepreneurial sector, took part in the stoppages. And schools and universities not only showed a dramatic drop in attendance during the two-day protest period, but in many instances became battle-grounds for opposing factions.

Pro-Junta supporters who nurtured the hope that the opposi-tion was running out of steam and was coming to a halt (June, July and August having been relatively quiet) were taken aback. But it is not only the spectacular street confrontations that reflect the willingness of the Chilean people to challenge the regime. More significant, an opposition leader pointed out, is the ongoing work to raise the anti-Junta consciousness of the people who are searching for tactics that eventually will lead to a final showdown.

"These quiet happenings," he explained, "don't make head-lines. But their impact is enormous and far-reaching." It appears that people, especially at the grassroots level in the working class and slum areas, are being made aware that they can generate considerable pressure on various government agencies by de-manding assistance, whether food for malnourished children, housing, potable water, or more public works jobs for the unem-ployed. There is little likelihood that many of their demands will be satisfied. But the continuous pressure on government officials has a "wear and tear" effect on those governing the country.

Much of this activity stems from the *Comunidades Christianas de Base*, community groups initially sponsored by the Church. Many of these include socially-dedicated priests, some of whom live in the shantytowns to which they have been assigned, as well as political activists and, of course, the neighborhood leaders.

Through a variety of committees, the shantytown dwellers try to control petty crime, monitor sanitation (always a threatening health hazard, since the Junta bureaucracies ignore such respon-sibilities), and promote mutual aid efforts. They even have com-mittees to guard against harassment for the city police. As a Chilean Human Rights activist observes, "It is indeed a paradox. The police, supported by citizen taxes, is actually the enemy to those it is supposed to protect. Anyone poor is automatically a likely subversive in the eyes of the Junta."

Since there is much discussion associated with these activities, the committees become forums for the analysis of the social and political insufficiencies of the Pinochet dictatorship.

In addition to the neighborhood committees, there are also national organizations which keep badgering the government for redress. Among these: Associations for the Disappeared, ceaselessly demanding that the Junta provide information on the fate of their sons, daughters, husbands, and brothers believed to have been executed; women's groups demanding welfare assistance; student associations vociferously clamoring for the recall of military deans and rectors, and the reinstatement of professors and educators expelled by the Junta.

One of the most important national organizations that keeps Chile and the world apprised of the Junta's violations of human rights is the Chilean Human Rights Commission. Aided by 1,000 volunteers across the country, many of whom are lawyers, editors, and parish priests, the Commission documents charges of torture and detention by the Junta police. Although its officers are always under threat of arrest and worse, the Commission appears to be tolerated because of its affiliation with the International Commission of Jurists in Geneva, the International League for Human Rights in New York, the Federation of the Rights of Man in Paris, and the International Movement of Catholic Jurists (Pax Romana) in Paris.

Agitation for revival of democracy in Chile and the abdication of Pinochet is continuous. Increasingly the city streets provide setting for what amount to public forums. And this is not only during protest marches or when mothers of the disappeared chain themselves to government buildings to draw attention to their plight. Writers, poets, and actors add a special dimension to these protests. In 1984, with Chile's book publishing industry moribund since the coup because of heavy-handed censorship, writers and poets began putting out their work in limited photocopied editions of a few hundred copies, which they themselves tried to sell at busy interesections.

Occasionally some of the authors began reading their stories or poems aloud at street corners. Since much of the material centers on the Chilean condition, a sympathetic audience of passersby would gather quickly and that, of course, brought on the police. A shoving and pushing match ensued to the accompaniment of epithets directed at the police as they tried to put the author under arrest. There are also street theater groups who are expert at putting on a five or ten minute improvisation on the latest Junta misdeed. These "act-and-run" artists deliver satiric blows at the government, and then quickly melt into the crowds.

Despite the thickening clouds of near-insurgency that were enveloping Chile, Pinochet continued to cling to his swashbuckling claims of invincibility, that he is on a par with "the best Roman Emperors," as he put it to the *New York Times* (May 8, 1984).

On September 11, 1984, when marking the eleventh anniversary of the Junta's seizure of power from the Allende Government, the dictator heaped scorn on the opposition, and blamed Chile's troubles on the "Marxists." There was the usual flourish and glitter at the ceremony, but a few notable absences put a pall over the proceedings. Archbishop Juan Francisco Fresno of Santiago was not there. Instead he sent a substitute whose noncommittal comments left the impression that the Archbishop stayed away to signal a protest. Also refusing to be present—for the second year in a row—were representatives of the member nations in the European Economic Community, and that of Spain. Many Chileans were pained to learn that the American Ambassador did attend.

For yet another four years Pinochet continued to hang on to power by torture and murder of his opponents. And then, in the plebiscite of October 1989, ironically enough his own creation, he found himself on the road to his own Waterloo.

10

The Plebiscite and the Future

On the historic evening of October 5, 1988, the impossible had the potential of becoming possible. The Chilean people, glued to their radios and televisions, heard that General Augusto Pinochet, the dictator of Chile, was rebuffed in his bid to continue at the helm of state for yet another eight years.

After fifteen years of bloody rule, Pinochet was told by the people of Chile, via a nationwide plebiscite, that they had had enough. And that their choice for the nation's next chief magistrate would be made through a democratic election on December 14, 1989. It was a humiliating blow to this would-be Goliath, who struts about in his impeccable uniforms, projecting an image of invincibility and power that is not to be tampered with.

The following morning the cities throbbed with the most jubilant celebrations ever witnessed in Chile. People danced in the streets, they hugged one another, they kissed. Some even extended a friendly hand to members of the police, who found it awkward to reject such amity, despite the years of brainwashing to regard any critic of Pinochet as an enemy of the state.

Victory was especially heart-warming for the campaign managers of the Opposition (*Concertación opositora*), considering the disadvantages they had to overcome when countering pro-Pinochet propaganda. They were allotted only fifteen minutes a day on TV for two weeks prior to the plebiscite. Despite this severe restriction, the Opposition successfully imparted an upbeat tone to its campaign. Some of the most talented artists and directors were involved in the production of the fifteen minute segments, which included humor and satiric barbs aimed at the Junta regime. Much of the material was designed to appeal to the younger sector of the population. There was an avoidance of

279

ideological confrontation or expression of hostility toward the armed forces.

The Pinochet forces, on the other hand, campaigned many hours a day, for a more than a year, on government-controlled radio and TV, as well as in the press. Basically the pro-Pinochet message was the same, a litany of warnings that a "no" vote against the dictator would return Chile to the chaos and economic disaster experienced in the last days of the Allende regime. Needless to say there was no mention that the crisis in 1973 was caused by an embargo by the Nixon Administration that shut off Chile's imports as well as exports. And nothing was said, of course, about the sabotage carried on at that time by Chilean Fascist and Rightist forces within the country.

In addition to its virtual monopoly of propaganda outlets, the Pinochet camp also employed a two-pronged campaign for the "yes" vote among the most defenseless members of society—the poor of the shantytowns. One approach was to bribe these people with promises of better things to come. The government even went so far as to build some 45,000 dwellings across the nation, some with running water and toilets. Painted in a yellowish, bilge water color, they stand in formation, like barracks in a prison camp, against a treeless background.

How ironic it was that Pinochet, after having ravaged these people with physical abuse for fifteen years, should have turned to them for help in the voting booths because they now represented strength through their ballots. His seemingly compassionate approach made grist for effective public relations. Assuming the role of the great benefactor, with a grandfatherly smile on his lips, Pinochet took center stage to hail the opening of the housing projects. But considering the critical housing shortage throughout Chile, estimated at one million units since Pinochet seized power, these few additions scarcely made a ripple in the overall housing crisis.

The regime also employed a variety of unconscionable arm-twisting tactics and threats to bring the slum dwellers into line. Junta-appointed mayors of the various *poblaciones* (shantytowns that surround the cities) threatened to shut off what meager social services are available to the desperate, indigent inhabitants, if they failed to come across on voting day. This openly expressed policy was enunciated by the Interior Ministry's Civic Action Plan, which declared: "Mayors should let 'political' enemies feel the full weight of the Government."

Fear of bodily harm also intimidated those planning to vote against Pinochet. Opposition activists, frenetically campaigning in economically depressed areas, received death threats from such Fascist gangs as *Acción Chilena Anticomunista* and *Patria y Libertad*, which are convenient unofficial auxiliaries of the government. Civil service employees, such as teachers, many factory workers, and public works employees (the $25-a-month street cleaners), were threatened with job loss if they voted "no." There is little question that to some degree these scare tactics did effect the "no" vote.

"In this atmosphere of tension and threatened reprisals," a Chilean voter explained, "the people went to the polling stations with a vigor and determination expected of soldiers going to battle. For us, a "no" vote was the nearest thing to open defiance of a despised despot. This was the first time Chileans had the privilege to fulfill a deep yearning, to tell Pinochet how they really felt about him, regardless of the risks."

People began queuing up to cast their ballots as early as 5 a.m., though in some areas the *mesas*, the voting tables, did not open until 9:30 in the morning. Even invalids and very old people, tended to by relatives and friends, were well represented among the throngs of voters. Women with babies in their arms patiently stood in line for hours to await their turn. (Despite the Latin American tradition of women tending to be more conservative in outlook than men, the plebiscite results showed that this is no longer the case in Chile. In Santiago, Valparaiso, and other large cities, the women outnumbered the men in the "no" vote.)

Finally, when the tabulations were officially announced, it was dramatically evident that the majority of Chileans had refused to be swayed by Pinochet's promises or by his bullying. Nearly 55 percent of the electorate cast votes against Pinochet; 43 percent voted in favor of the dictator.

Just as soon as the voting results were made public, employers and shantytown mayors made good on their earlier threats. Across the land, hundreds of teachers and many thousands of other workers, whether in private industries or in government-administered services, were fired. The brunt of the vendetta was borne by the shantytowns, where the "no" vote, despite the threats and blandishments, remained very strong. Many of the basic services there, such as schools and clinics for children, were closed temporarily and in some instances permanently. Junta Commander Hernan Nuñez, the Director of Non-Government Organization, described the slum dwellers who receive occasional food subsidies as "malagradecidos," the ungrateful ones, because of their anti-Pinochet vote.

The day after the election, Pinochet, sullen and angry, agreed to accept the verdict, while at the same time reaffirming his decision to stay on as commander-in-chief of the army even after the elections in December 1989.

This was the first personal defeat Chile's dictator had experienced since the Junta seized power on September 11, 1973. Ironically the plebiscite was to be the crowning triumph of Pinochet's dictatorial career. So confident was he of winning that he consented to strict voting rules in order to satisfy the hundreds of foreign observers who went to Chile to make sure that there would be no fraud in the plebiscite. He felt that a substantial vote in his favor would establish once and for all before the entire world that he—Pinochet—enjoyed the confidence and approval of his people. As some political figures pointed out to me, the taint of illegitimacy that shadowed his claims to the presidency has troubled Pinochet throughout his "reign." And for good reason.

He declared himself President of the Republic late in 1974, even though no one elected him. Three years later he conducted his first plebiscite which, in effect, was designed to confirm both his presidency and his policies. And sure enough the government announced that 75 percent of the electorate had voted "yes" in support of both objectives. Since this was a period in which repression was at its worst, the world gave little credence to the claim that these votes were cast voluntarily.

In 1980, Pinochet called a second plebiscite, this time to demand acceptance of Chile's new constitution, which he authored and which institutionalized his sweeping dictatorial edicts. And again he claimed victory, this time with the support of 67 percent of the voters. The third and latest referendum, designed to extend and legitimize Pinochet's tenure, was called for by his own 1980 constitution. Some felt it was also aimed at defusing a steadily growing restiveness and impatience with the Junta among ever-larger segments of the population. Discontent was no longer confined to the Left and the slum dwellers. It had infiltrated even the bastions of the pro-Junta establishment. Some of Pinochet's advisors hoped that the plebiscite would present an opportunity for the opposition to speak out, blow off some steam as it were. They remained confident that Pinochet would prevail in any event.

Others in the Junta camp, however, were not as certain of the outcome. As a matter of fact, two of the four-member directorate of the Junta, General Fernando Matthei, Commander of the Air Force, and General Rodolfo Stange, the Director General of the National Police, were quite unhappy with Pinochet's insistence on being the candidate. They would have been much happier with a civilian Right-winger in the plebiscite.

Irascibility, if not actual discord, within the Junta became evident when General Matthei, while on the way to meet with Pinochet on the night of the plebiscite, made an off-the-cuff remark to the press that the "no" votes appeared to be in the majority, even as government radio and television continued to claim victory for Pinochet. And later that night the Junta meeting reportedly became rancorous when Generals Matthei and Stange refused to sign a decree giving Pinochet broad emergency powers. There was speculation that when the outlook looked grim for Pinochet the proposed decree could have been used to disrupt the vote counting, thus nullifying the entire plebiscite.

The plebiscite campaign against Pinochet was directed by *Commando NO*, the top leadership of the sixteen parties that make up the Opposition alliance, plus a seventeenth party, with the acronym PAIS, which did not receive full status as a party until after the plebiscite. The political spectrum ranges from the Rightist Christian Democrats and Centrist parties to PAIS, which includes the Socialist party headed by Clodomiro Almeyda, Allende's Foreign Minister, other left-of-center groups, and individuals of Communist persuasion. The outlawed Communist Party was not included.

The seventeen-party alliance was scarcely an overnight phenomenon. It was the result of a series of grueling attempts in the 1980s by a variety of Pinochet opponents to find agreement on how to unseat the dictator. But apart from this objective, there was much diversity on what the future of Chile should be once Pinochet and the Junta were out of the way. The years of barbaric repression since the Junta seized power, coupled with the collapse of the economy in 1980, following Pinochet's rigid application of the free market theories set out by Chicago University's Milton Friedman (as profiled in Chapter 9), set off mammoth protest demonstrations throughout Chile that the police and armed forces broke up with water cannons, tear gas, and bullets. It became increasingly obvious that Chile's polarization and bankrupt economy were menacing the very lives of its unemployed and poverty-stricken citizens, as well as raising the specter of the profound decline, or complete wipe-out, of sectors of the upper middle class.

The need for the immediate return of democracy to Chile became compellingly urgent; there was mounting anxiety about an impending slaughter by the military to repress the uprisings of the poor, as has happened in 1989 in Venezuela. The augury of a civil war enveloped the political climate. For a time the awareness of the gravity of the situation united the Christian Democrats and the parties of the Center-Right with those of the Left, including the Communists. At that point it was indeed possible that the Pinochet regime could have been toppled.

But Washington, according to well-informed Chileans, became concerned that a left-of-center government in Chile might emerge from the ashes of the dictatorship. And so it prevailed on the Christian Democrats to withdraw from the coalition. This, coupled with intensified police harassment, brought the anti-Pinochet effort to a halt (see Chapter 9).

It was not until the plebiscite emerged as a possibility for moving toward democracy that several of the parties once again considered the matter of a united effort to oust Pinochet, but this time in the context of his own constitution, which specified 1988 as the year for transition through a plebiscite. Others, however, felt that such a hope was illusory, that it would prove to be a cynical scheme to entrap the people into legitimizing the military dictatorship.

As the debate on this issue broadened it became evident that the more conservative elements within the potential anti-Pinochet alliance felt that participation in the plebiscite was worth a try. Though chafing under the high-handed ways of the dictatorship, and feeling isolated from much of the world because of its revulsion to the Pinochet tyranny, they still were part of the establishment. And so, if they failed in their effort and Pinochet continued to rule for yet another eight years, as outlined by the constitution, they could still survive, some quite comfortably.

It was another matter, however, for the disenfranchised sectors of the people, 50 percent of whom are holding on to life at a poverty level. The prospect of having Pinochet continue in power, should the opposition fail to get the necessary majority of the votes, was totally unacceptable. Especially critical of the plebiscite proposal was the Communist Party, which has an estimated 20 percent following among the electorate.

As the fine print of the constitution came under closer scrutiny, more and more people were taken aback. Among other things the document would have Pinochet continue as head of the army for six years even if defeated in the plebiscite. Also, he would become senator for life and have the authority to appoint 25 percent of the senate. Yet another provision would have him head a National Security Council consisting of four military and three civilians with the authority to veto whatever congressional legislation or presidential executive order it deemed threatening to national security. Also, under Article 8 of the constitution, the Communist Party, or any other Marxist political party, would be permanently banned.

The pro and con debate over whether Chileans should take part in the plebiscite seized all of Chile. However slender the hope that anything positive could come of the plebiscite, people felt increasingly drawn to taking a chance. So once again political parties began negotiating to take a united stand in the plebiscite.

Though still contending that the plebiscite was yet another Pinochet stratagem, the Communists finally went along. And once having adopted this course, they made an all-out effort to recruit the pro-"no" vote, especially in the slums where they have a very loyal following.

As Juan Pablo Cardenas, an editor of *Analisis*, a prominent opposition magazine, put it in an interview with the *World Policy Journal*: "It is clear that the decision of the Communist Party . . . to commit itself to the "no" campaign definitely secured the opposition's triumph. If the Communists had not taken that step, the vote would have probably been close, or the government simply could have won." Cardenas is a former member of the Christian Democratic Party.

The plebiscite has indeed opened a new era in the life of Chile. As I witnessed during a visit to Chile soon after the plebiscite, people in the big cities, such as Santiago, are openly speaking out against the regime, something which would have landed them in torture chambers only a few years ago. (In 1985, according to police records, about 800,000 people, 8 percent of the population, underwent arrest. The U.S. equivalent in that stretch of time would have totalled close to 20 million people.)

The newsstands, which seem to be everywhere in the central areas of Santiago, now prominently display the newspapers *La Epoca* and *Fortin Mapoche*, both critical of the Pinochet regime. Also on display are four magazines of a similar hue, thirty of whose editors and reporters are awaiting trial in civil and military courts for having written articles deemed by the regime to have been disrespectful of the armed forces.* Even the Communist cultural magazine, *Pluma y Pincel* (Pen and Artists' Brush), is available at some newsstands, though hidden from public view. And various Opposition party leaders air their views at press conferences and while traveling the country to help create grass-root support organizations.

But side by side this seeming tolerance of freer expression by

---

*Juan Pablo Cardenas has been behind bars on several occasions because of his investigative reporting. Recently he completed a jail sentence that forced him to spend 531 nights in a prison cell, though during the day he was allowed to work at the offices of his magazine.

the regime, the repression continues, especially in the provinces. A talk with Luis Toro, one of the lawyers of the Vicariate of Solidarity, the human rights agency of the Catholic Church, whose offices are adjacent to the Santiago Cathedral, reveals a picture of ongoing atrocities which, as usual, are especially directed at leftists, labor activists, and the poor. Within days after the plebiscite there was an encounter in a small town in southern Chile in which a policeman was killed. Subsequently three youths, allegedly involved in his death, were forced into the nearby river and drowned. Needless to say, there was no trial.

In various small towns, Toro explained, "individuals known to have been active for the "no" vote were assaulted with impunity the very next day after the plebiscite." Frequently, masked hoodlums, members of the Fascist *Patria y Libertad* (Fatherland and Liberty), which dates back to the anti-Allende days when it was financed by the CIA, break into homes late at night and indiscriminately beat up the occupants. Some of the victims are maimed both physically and emotionally, especially when they are threatened with the kidnapping and death of their family members.

Toro cited one of several such incidents as described to him by one of the victims. This took place in a town in close proximity to Santiago. The assailants, all masked, broke down a door at about 2:30 in the morning, grabbed a man out of bed and demanded to know where he hid ammunition. The man was known in the neighborhood as a pro-union sympathizer, but he was in no way associated with any armed or illegal activities.

When he denied having any weapons, he told Toro, "They pounced upon me from all sides. They were hitting me with their fists on the face and on the body. They threw me on the floor and began jumping on my stomach and on my chest." When he passed out they threw a pail of water on his face and as soon as he revived they continued to interrogate him, punching him and beating him on the soles of his feet.

It was almost daybreak when his attackers began to question him about accomplices, the men who presumably had taken part in the shooting incident in southern Chile, hundreds of miles away. When he still tried to assure them that he knew nothing about it, they began to twist his arms and legs until the pain became insufferable. At that point, he told Toro, "I broke down; I began to name friends, even my brother—people who had nothing to do with politics. With that, the tormentors released me and took off, probably to torture the innocent friends I had named."

It is against this background of contradictions—greater political assertiveness, on the one hand, and continuing repression, though not on as great a scale as before, on the other—that Chile is moving toward the election showdown at the end of 1989.

Because of the slow pace with which the seventeen-party Opposition has been getting its act together, in terms of either naming a presidential candidate or outlining programs dealing with a host of problems affecting most of the citizenry, much of the popular fervor and enthusiasm that followed the plebiscite has dissipated. And yet there appears to be a widespread, stubborn, visceral confidence that neither Pinochet, should he suddenly demand to run, nor any candidate backed by the Junta will win.

Most disturbing to many in the Opposition camp is that the wrangling by their top party officials has left little time for consideration of some of the country's most urgent priorities—hunger, sickness, unemployment, and repression.

In the past few years Chile's revenues from abroad have risen substantially and are reflected in a prosperity that is confined almost entirely to Chile's power elite. There is little if anything of this economic revival that trickles down to the have-not sector of the population. As a matter of fact, the living standards of about half the nation's population have plumetted dramatically.

An estimated 50 percent of the shantytown dwellers in Santiago, about one million people, consume less than 1,600 calories a day. The minimum caloric intake necessary to maintain adequate health is put at 2,310 calories a day by the World Health Organization. Since Pinochet's seizure of power in 1973, the per capita calorie consumption has dropped by 9.4 percent, according to the Academy of Christian Humanism, a Chilean-based institution. The Academy also reports that in these fifteen years the supply of goods and services were 16.3 percent lower than in the Allende days. Coupled with widespread malnutrition, there has been a serious rise in the incidence of hepatitis, typhoid, tuberculosis, and skin diseases among the poor. And because of severe overcrowding and poor washing facilities there are recurrent measles epidemics.

A great number of families subsist on a few slices of bread and tea as their daily diet. They lack the most basic necessities. Children have discovered glue smelling as an opiate to lessen hunger pain. To provide food for their children many women have been driven to prostitution to supplement the family's incidental earnings. And among these prostitutes are thousands of children, some as young as ten years of age. Outraged Santiago residents say that this is a totally new phenomenon, never seen before in Chile.

Pinochet boasts that the unemployment rate has dropped from about 32 percent to approximately 8 percent. But labor economists reject this figure charging that the government figures have been "cooked." They say that among those considered employed were people able to find work for only one hour in the week that the census was taken. Actually, these economists insist, the jobless constitute about 20 percent of the workforce.

Chile presents a stark paradox. Since wriggling out of near bankruptcy in 1983, Chile's gross national product has grown steadily, reaching the rate of 6.8 percent in 1988. Once again Chile is being hailed as an "economic miracle," especially when compared to its neighboring countries. Chile's first "miracle," discussed in the previous chapter, began in the mid-'70s, when the Junta's young technocrats, the "free market" exponents, took over Chile's economic reins. In a matter of three years "los Chicago boys," as they were called, stripped the country of what industries it had and ran it into the ground.

As Gonzalo Martner, a renowned Chilean economist, sees it, Chile's present boom is tied to a steadily rising world demand for Chilean copper, the nation's principal revenue producer, as well as the development of other exports such as fruit, wood products, and fish. But above all, Martner believes, "the so-called boom is related to the government's obsessive drive to privatize all publicly-held enterprises and to the low wages paid to Chile's labor force." Chile now holds the edge in its competitive standing,

Martner says, "because its wage scales have reached even lower levels than those of Southeast Asian countries, long considered among the lowest in the semi-industrialized Third World.

"The ideological push to privatization," Martner declares, "has nothing to do with national reality. What we see is the surrender of our national resources and nationally-owned industrial entities to foreign conglomerates." The government, he says, "is now putting Chile up for sale on the world market to the highest bidder."

Martner cites the recent sale of Chile's entire telephone system to an Australian conglomerate. He then points to the sale of major timberland areas to New Zealand and Japanese companies through which some of Chile's choicest forestry is being cut down. The Japanese have also taken over the major fishing grounds, where their round-the-clock operations are depleting the country's fish stocks, thus posing the possibility of an ecological disaster. There appear to be no Chilean government controls to regulate these practices. U.S. banks and insurance organizations dominate pension and insurance programs as well as the major financial transactions.

Currently there is a heated, agonizing debate about Pinochet's plan to divest Chile of its prime resource—copper. The same fate awaits Chilean oil facilities, the highly-profitable fruit and wine-producing areas, the Santiago subway system, the government-owned TV stations, and even the State Bank.

Much of this trend is in compliance with the Baker Plan, originally launched in 1985 by James A. Baker III when he was Ronald Reagan's Secretary of the Treasury. The plan was designed to extend new loans to Third World debtor nations to service their enormous foreign debts, providing they would be willing to privatize their state-owned enterprises and develop wide-ranging free market policies.

Justification for privatization is based on the Baker view that publicly-held industries are operated less efficiently, and therefore more expensively, than those run by private concerns. (Gonzalo Martner points out that in the early '80s, when privatization was already under way as the economy neared collapse, "the only entities that did not go into bankruptcy were the State Bank and the government-owned copper mining corporation.")

Globally, the Baker Plan never took off. As a matter of fact, when Baker was being confirmed for his new post as Secretary of State under President George Bush in January 1989, he admitted that the plan was a flop. In Chile, however, Baker's "pot of gold," as it were, shining at the end of the proverbial tunnel, was something Pinochet could not resist. The dictator grasped at the opportunity.

As the money began flowing in and more of Chile's resources were put on the auction block, the Baker Plan began to take on the characteristics of a blueprint for Chile's economic dismemberment. According to Wisconsin's Republican Congressman Toby Roth, who lavished praise on Pinochet's anti-Communist stand and his economic policies when he visited Chile after the plebiscite, "no other country has adhered to the Baker Plan as closely as Chile." Many of Chile's resources are bought cheaply by foreign investors via the debt-for-equity transactions.

Considering the negative notices on his plan worldwide, Baker might find solace in the fact that the proceeds from the continuing "sale" of Chile have enabled the Chilean government to repay $3.5 billion of its $22 billion debt and at the same time maintain its interest payments on schedule. Baker may even derive a bit of personal satisfaction because, until his appointment as Secretary of State, he held a substantial number of shares in Chemical Bank, one of the most important lenders of capital to Third World countries.

Most of Chile's income is earmarked to pay off the foreign debt and to support Pinochet's huge armed forces establishment. However, there are also substantial profits from export activities in the hands of a rather small group of landowners and bank executives. The government neither participates in nor encourages investment to develop Chilean industries. Nor are any efforts made to have the millions of Chile's poor share in these recent bonanzas, thus enabling them to break out of their vise of misery.

The contrast between the "haves" and "have nots" in Chile stands out in sharp relief. Santiago, a handsome city for the most part, especially in the lush residential areas, with spotless, well-tended parks, is like a world apart from the grubby, barren *poblaciones*, where 40 percent of the inhabitants of the Chilean capital attempt to survive. Once again, as in the mid-1970's, during its short-lived "free market" boom, the shopping centers on the wide, tree-lined streets of La Providencia district are filled with glittering window displays in well-stocked stores. And the outdoor cafes and tea shops, filled with attractively dressed women, remind one of cosmopolitan European cities.

But only a twenty-minute car ride will take you to the Santiago of slums and squalor. It is here, where shacks made out of scraps of wood and flattened tin cans, so like the "Hoovervilles" of America's Great Depression, are the homes for nearly two million people. In the summer heat, when the temperature soars to the 90's, these shacks become "airless, burning sweat boxes," as one *poblador* described it. And in the winter these shacks go into a deep freeze as icy blasts come sweeping down from the Andes mountains that surround Santiago.

Columbia University Professor Ximena de la Barra McDonald, a Chilean architect and town planner, says that the "current housing scenario is one of degrading living conditions, of overcrowded neighborhoods, of the inability of new families to live independently, of doubling, tripling, and quadrupling in small shacks within the same site." The public services, she says, are practically non-existent. Garbage collection is on a "when and if schedule." There are few clinics; schools are inadequately staffed; and the public transport system is a disaster.

The streets are unpaved, and in the summer pools of dirty water become splashing playgrounds for malnourished children who make do by sailing their little boats made out of newspapers. Every five blocks or so a lonely spigot on a street corner provides the only source of fresh water for the immediate community.

The mood of the inhabitants varies from one *poblacion* to another. In one such settlement that I visited, people were recently transferred by the government from their homes on the fringes of middle-class areas, in keeping with a program aimed at better police surveillance of the poor. Families were forced to move what belongings they had by whatever means available.

There was no assistance from the regime. In another *poblacion*, the people were recent arrivals from the countryside, where they were forced off their lands by powerful fruit-grower organizations. Here there is gloom and concern as they try to adjust to poverty in a big city.

In other shantytowns, particularly those of much older vintage, some going back to the period before Allende, the dwellings are more firmly built and the overall atmosphere is more vital and even revolutionary. One such *poblacion*, La Victoria, is noted for its resistance to the Junta (see Chapter 9). It is probably among the best organized in pressuring the municipal authorities for better subsidies. At La Victoria every bit of wall space on the houses is decorated either with some kind of slogan or with a roughly-hewn mural commemorating anti-Pinochet demonstrations. There are also portraits of Allende and the Nobel Prize-winning poet Pablo Neruda, with some of his verses inscribed alongside. On one wall there is a salute to internationally celebrated May Day, marking the Chicago Haymarket incident of 1886, when police attacked thousands of workers who were demanding an eight-hour work day.

La Victoria and several other *poblaciones* have seized the initiative in pooling whatever resources they have to help themselves—some 300,000 inhabitants. For the most part this effort has been led by women. They have created a variety of cooperative ventures, such as soup kitchens, first aid stations, and even workshops to teach women how to sew. And all of this without the assistance of either the government or private charities.

As stated earlier, keeping people in poverty, many sociologists contend, is part of the government's strategy to maintain a cheap labor force, especially useful in providing Chile with a competitive advantage in its thriving export trade. This strategy has been made possible through repression and the destruction of trade unions, whose function it is to protect worker rights. Wage and labor-protection laws promulgated during the Allende Administration, which so endeared Allende to Chilean workers, were abrogated immediately after Pinochet took over. Most of the labor leaders of that period have either been executed or forced into exile. And even at this time, when there are occasional symptoms of tolerance, labor remains muzzled. Two of the most prominent labor leaders, Manuel Bustos and Arturo Martinez, have recently been banished to internal exile hundreds of miles away from the capital.

Currently only 15 percent of labor is unionized. But there is little the unions can do to improve worker conditions. Strike attempts are limited in scope, and the workers cannot negotiate from strength. The employers are fully empowered to fire workers at will, and they do just that. There is absolutely no job security. Also, in hazardous occupations worker protection is generally up to the employer exclusively. The government has deregulated all industry; the open shop is at the center of its labor policy.

Yet, because of a long-standing Chilean tradition in labor history, workers try to retain what semblance of trade unionism they can. Sometimes they succeed in causing tie-ups, as for instance in the fishing fleets, where working conditions are reportedly insufferable. And in April 1989, there was a partially successful general strike demanding an end to the exile of Bustos and Martinez.

The minimum wage is set at about U.S. $50 a month, and usually there are no fringe benefits whatsoever. When I chatted with members of a road-repair gang during their half-hour lunch period on a hot summer day, a few were quite outspoken about their plight. "We strike these bricks or asphalt with pickaxes and shovels from eight in the morning to six in the evening, six days a week," a man with sunken cheeks and a lean body volunteered. "We do this all year around," he continued, "and we get one week's vacation a year, but it's without pay." Another of the group added, "and we get only 17,000 pesos a month (US $60), which is not nearly enough to feed a family." A pound of bread costs about 20 cents in U.S. currency and a bus ride to work is about the same. The wage scale is even lower for workers on the government's Poverty Alleviation Program for the unemployed. They earn as little as US $25 a month for cleaning streets and trimming park hedges.

What does the future hold for labor in Chile? Will the country return to a democratic form of government? Will repression cease? Will privatization of Chilean industry and resources come to a halt? These and other burning issues are hanging in the balance as Chile enters the last phase of its pre-election campaigns.

All indications are that the seventeen-party Opposition will back Patricio Aylwin as its candidate for the presidential contest. Not a charismatic figure, Aylwin also has an unsavory political background. The sixty-seven-year-old politician, a member of the Rightist wing of the Christian Democratic Party, is still remembered as Allende's adversary, a man who actually applauded the bloody putsch that overthrew the Allende regime.

Over the years Aylwin has distanced himself from the Junta and as a lawyer has defended some of the victims of the regime's repression. In the planning of the plebiscite he was among the chief organizers of the "no" campaign. Basically of a very conservative cast, Aylwin is in concert with the Junta's free market policies. But he has been sounding off very strongly on the urgency for the country to return to democracy and to provide a pluralistic arena of expression for all parties, including the Communists. And he is definitely among those demanding changes in the constitution.

Though it is difficult for many Chileans to forgive Aylwin for his past, anti-Pinochet opponents will nevertheless swallow the "bitter pill" and back him for the country's chief magistrate. At the very least, they feel, if he is elected, there is hope that repression will recede, thus providing a greater opening to pressure the regime for the enactment of reforms.

Even the Communists, though frequently attacked by Aylwin, are ready to vote for him should the Opposition alliance agree to his being their candidate. Jorge Insunza Becker, a top Communist Party leader, declared in an interview that "be it Aylwin or any other choice of the Opposition, they [the Communists] will support him. The main objective at this time," he said, "is to break the stranglehold of the Pinochet dictatorship."

Another plus for Aylwin is that he is very closely tied to the middle class, which at one time was considered an important sector in Chilean society and is still regarded as pivotal in the coming election. Actually many in this group have been battered so badly economically that they no longer, in fact, belong to that class. But because of their tendency to hang on to past traditions in terms of respectability, and because of their disdain for what they regard as the lower class, they might be inclined to vote for a Rightist ticket. And Pinochet's warnings at the time of the plebiscite that a "no" vote would led to chaos and anarchy might still have a residual influence even though nothing of the kind materialized.

However frustrating this development is for many in the Opposition camp, they might find consolation in the fact that the Right, too, is fragmented. For instance, the most important of the Rightist parties, the National Renovation party, has been quite critical of Pinochet, and it also has been calling for changes in the constitution. Its leader, Sergio Onofre Jarpa, Pinochet's former Minister of Interior, indicated his reservations about the dictator even at the time of the plebiscite. He himself may be one of the Rightist candidates for the presidential elections, although officially he has denied that aspiration.

There 'is also the shadow of yet another possible candidate, albeit an unlawful one, since his pursuit of the presidency would violate the provisions of his own constitution that forbid him to run in the elections. He is, of course, Augusto Pinochet. For months after his plebiscite defeat, he remained in sulky silence— wounded, angry, and withdrawn. And, as time passed, it became increasingly evident that he was not being missed. Many of the Rightists appeared to be relieved. They believed they could retain the Pinochet regime without Pinochet. They felt they could mask the regime with modest cosmetic changes, and have it adopt a mild liberal stance. They would be especially secure, they indicated, if they could be spared the embarrassment of a Pinochet at the helm.

Soon after, however, there were hints that Pinochet might be changing his mind, that he could not control his obsessive need to continue as Chile's "man on the white horse." And if he cannot swing it constitutionally, some observers fear, he might mount an "auto-golpe," a putsch against his own Junta, and take over the reins of government personally. Since the army, which he heads, is the most powerful force within the defense establishment, there would be nothing to stop him.

"No" rally, September 4, 1988. (Deborah Shaffer)

Members of the Sebastian Acevedo Movement in the Plaza de Aremas,
September 14, 1988. (Deborah Shaffer)

Women of the Association of Relatives of Disappeared and Detained Persons protest in front of the Moneda Palace, September 15, 1988. (Deborah Shaffer)

"No" rally, October 1, 1988. (Deborah Shaffer)

Voting at a womens' polling station, early morning, October 5, 1988. (Deborah Shaffer)

"Dia De Alegria" (Day of Happiness), October 6, 1988. (Deborah Shaffer)

In an interview with the French newspaper *Le Monde*, Pinochet compared himself to the Roman dictator Cincinnatus. Though at one stage of his career Cincinnatus decided to retire from public life and become a gentleman farmer on his huge estates, he was called back from retirement to save Rome from hostile forces, thus becoming the savior of Rome. This analogy, however ridiculous, is indicative of Pinochet's aspirations to become the savior of Chile.

Some political observers point out that there may be yet another reason why Pinochet would want to hang on to power and obstruct a transition to a democratic government. This has to do with his personal security and that of many of his henchmen. Among the variety of urgent problems that a democratic regime would have to confront, if voted into power, is bringing to justice a considerable number of Junta civilian and military officials involved in the torture and murder of thousands of Chileans during the Pinochet administration. Many were kidnapped from their homes and then disappeared without a trace. But in the case of many other victims there are existing records that include testimony naming individuals and government agencies who were directly involved in the commission of these crimes.

There are a number of human rights organizations that have been collecting this data clandestinely through the years. Perhaps the most important of these is the Vicariate of Solidarity, the human rights agency of the Catholic Church. It began its work a few years after the overthrow of Allende by providing legal and medical assistance to the victims and has since expanded its operations considerably.

For some years the Junta not only maintained a wary eye over the Vicariate but also accused it of providing a safe harbor to terrorists. And in some instances government operatives assaulted Vicariate staff members; several were murdered. In January and February 1989, the pressure on the Vicariate intensified with the demand from the federal prosecutor that the medical records of all those it assisted should be turned over to the government. The Vicariate refused. Its director, Bishop Sergio Vallech, though a conservative, declared that he was ready to go to jail rather than submit to the order. He denounced the order, stating that it was in violation of patient-doctor privacy, an internationally accepted principle. Support for the Vicariate came from liberal bishops as well as from very conservative ones, including the Papal Nuncio. Support also poured in from professional societies, from political leaders, and even from some of the traditionally pro-Pinochet newspapers.

Uppermost in the minds of many was the question: Why, at this time, would Pinochet want to alienate himself from the Chilean people by attacking the Catholic Church, since Chile is a Catholic country? Indignation against the regime reached an all time high when the police began clubbing demonstrators outside the Cathedral who came to show their sympathy for the Vicariate of Solidarity.

It is becoming apparent to many Chileans that Pinochet is getting nervous. The notion of a democratic government taking over, as a result of the December 1989 elections, is giving chills to many in the Junta establishment. For there is a great likelihood that a hue and cry would then develop to have Pinochet and others of the Junta High Command go to trial.

On the eve of the election, and regardless of the worries that may confound him, Pinochet is still at the summit of power. It is still up to him whether changes will be made in his constitution so that a new government would be able to govern without his having the last word. In the five months following the plebiscite, Pinochet would not yield to the demands of the Opposition to proceed with negotiations on this matter. As pressure grew, from the Right as well, Pinochet's Interior Minister Carlos Caceres agreed to have a joint working commission deal with some of the provisions that the Opposition finds most objectionable.

Should the Opposition succeed in getting the constitution revised and its candidate into the presidency, this, indeed, would make history. But almost immediately after taking over La Moneda, the presidential palace, the new government will be confronted with a variety of urgent issues, "all of which are of the first priority," as one politician described them. A number of these will be viewed from different angles, perhaps as many as seventeen, since in many instances the parties that make up the coalition are marching to their respective drummers.

Perhaps among the first issues to face the new lawmakers will be the decision to lift the various edicts regulating repression and to outlaw the secret police. While these steps will probably get quick approval from most of the Coalition, this is not likely to be the case with the constabulary and the armed forces in general. After all, the basic preoccupation of the police and much of the army during the dictatorship was not with plans to defend Chile's territory from attacks by its neighbors—Bolivia, Peru, and Argentina. Their main targets were their fellow Chileans who were fighting for democracy. In effect, Chile's military became Chile's army of occupation.

Therefore these questions. How can the military establishment be integrated within a new civilian government? What employment can Chile provide its armed forces, if they no longer have to do what they were assigned to do by Pinochet? Even if they were to remove themselves from politics, pick up their weaponry and move back to the barracks, the threat of their return to government would hang over the heads of the Chilean people like the sword of Damocles. This has been one of the principal reasons for the political instability in Argentina and Uruguay since the withdrawal of their military from government following the demise of the Fascistic regimes in both countries several years ago.

There is expectation that Chile's military will not yield that easily. They are likely to demand a very special role for themselves within the government. They have come to believe in their superiority as administrators and as custodians of law and order. And that again raises the serious issue of the culpability of the armed forces during the reign of terror that has marked the fifteen years of Pinochet's dictatorship.

Already some of the Opposition parties disagree as to how to mete out punishment for these crimes. Although the general consensus is that those guilty of torture and murder must be brought to justice, there are those in the Opposition who favor a case-by-case indictment of the accused. Others, on the other hand, lean toward the Nuremberg approach. Still others, in the interest of national "reconciliation," would advocate amnesty, as has been adopted in Argentina and Uruguay, much to the dismay of thousands of families and friends whose relatives were disappeared, that is, murdered.

The other "first priority" is the economy—as it will affect the well-being of that half of the population that has been reduced to a marginal existence, and the direction it will take to retrieve Chile's national integrity from foreign domination. In terms of planning for the long run, the seventeen-party Coalition is likely to be in agreement that Chile's immense foreign debt is the main obstacle to any significant development of the country. Chilean people bear the highest per capita repayment obligation in Latin America. The country is squeezed dry to continue repaying the debt.

Once the Opposition is the government, pressure will mount for programs to meet the immediate and acute needs of the poor. Because of the massive budget cutbacks dictated by the foreign debt and the privatization fixation, there has been a virtual elimination of public health and social services, as well as government-supported higher education. The slum dwellers have no place to turn for assistance. Dental care is scarcely available for this sector of society. And in the few, understaffed, city-run hospitals, the patients must bring their own bedsheets and pillows. They even must buy blood and syringes if transfusions are indicated.

Considering the urgency of these compelling needs, will the Opposition government join with other debtor nations to demand a drastic reduction of its debts? And how will it deal with the growing unease concerning Pinochet's policy of repaying the debt with the revenues from the sale of Chile's resources to foreign conglomerates? Some of the Opposition parties have already declared that they would press to annul these transfer agreements once the Pinochet dictatorship is voted out of power.

In that connection Washington would find itself in a dilemma, because such a development would contradict its basic commitment to having debtor countries repay their debts regardless of how much pain it may cause. At the same time, since 1984 or so, the State Department has become increasingly aware that Pinochet's murderous tactics against the Chilean people no longer spell security in the region. And so it has swung around to support the Opposition in the hope of having it replace Pinochet with minimum damage to the basic principles of "Pinochetist" economic policy. As one Chilean journalist put it, "It has become increasingly obvious that the United States is playing both ends against the middle." Certainly during the plebiscite Ambassador Harry Barnes went out of his way to indicate his pro-Opposition bias in a number of instances. He aroused Pinochet's ire so much that when departing from his post following the plebiscite, no one from the government was at the Santiago airport to see him off. But only three weeks after the plebiscite, the United States voted in favor of yet another loan to Pinochet by the Inter-American Development Bank. This time for $35 million. Was it a pat on the back for Pinochet because he permitted the plebiscite to take place? These ambivalent moves by the United States have created uncertainty in both the Opposition as well as in pro-Pinochet circles.

A major challenge confronting an Opposition government is that of restructuring Chile's economy so that the country avoids becoming a "banana republic," dependent almost entirely on the export of raw materials. The recent scare concerning a shipment of grapes to the United States, in which a few of the grapes were found to have been poisoned, had a sobering effect even on the pro-export enthusiasts. In a matter of days many countries shut down all imports of fruit from Chile. This resulted in a $100 million loss for the Chilean economy and in thousands of job layoffs. The answer to this dilemma, many Opposition economists maintain, is in the development of industries designed to fill the needs of Chile's domestic consumption.

The list of urgencies facing Chile is enormous. Notwithstanding these difficulties there is a strong optimism that if the Opposition prevails in the elections of December 14, 1989, Chile will find its road to recovery. But even in the worst case scenario, that is, if Pinochet retains power by means of his unchanged constitution, the dictatorship is seen as doomed, in the process of disintegration. What little political relaxation followed the plebiscite will be difficult for Pinochet to undo. The country is determined to move ahead.

INDEX

Rightists *(cont'd.)*
production, 202; and consumerism,
203-4; and economy, 268; *see also*
Patria y Libertad *and* Junta
Rimbaud, Arthur, Junta and, 214
Rio Chico, 114-16
Rivera, Diego, 127, 215
Rodriguez, Ancieto, *105*
Rogers, William, 57
Romania, 155
Ropa Usada Americana (Used Amer-
ican Garments), 242
Ross, Jorge, and CRAV, 267-8

Sanchez, Roberto, 21-3
Santiago, curfew in, 10, 32, 34, 76,
132, 134, 185, 228, 233, 245;
blackout, explosions, and bombing
in, 73, 237, 271-2; Pinochet and
Junta members at Cathedral of, 79;
prisoners return to, 117; children of
slum areas of, 198-201; morgue of,
234; impression of prosperity in, 245;
shantytown people and, 246, 256-7;
see also shantytowns
Santiago National Stadium, *see*
Estadium Nacional
Schneider, General René, 13, 50,
52-4, 77
Schweiker, Richard, 40n
Science, and education, 260-1
secret police, 10, 115, 247, 248n, 274;
see also Junta
Senora K., *see* Joanna K.
Sepulveda, General José Maria, Junta
and, 23
shantytowns, attack on, 39-40, 94;
media and, 49-50; and Allende, 56,
80, 201-2; military and, 71, 207;
reaction of, to putsch, 158-60, 170-3;
life in, 158, 164-8, *165*, 183-4, 198,
201-2; youths of, and soldiers, 172;
students and illiterate of, 183; housing, malnutrition, and unemployment in, 190, 255-7, see *also*

housing, malnutrition, *and*
unemployment; women of, 197n,
199-202; aid for and opposition to
aid, 198-202, 201n; JAP in, 203; and
free vacations, 205; poverty, begging,
and prostitution in, 207, 245-6; Jara
and, 212, 220-1; demands of workers
and families in, 237, 252; Father
DeMott and, 239; priests and, 251;
pauperized woman of, 255
Sieveking, Alejandro, 222
Silva, Cardinal Raul, 252, 254
Socialist Party, 11-12, 65
Solidaridad, 257
Soto, Dr. Oscar, 24, 37, 67
Souper, Colonel Roberto, 73-4
Spain, Chileans in, 273
Spanish Conquistadores, 196
Southern Cone, unrest in, 43
spare parts, U.S. embargo on, 59, 60,
66, 78
steel, expropriation of, 56
Steinbeck, John, 218
strikes, 55, 66-8; controversy about, 68;
women and, 197-8, 251, 254-5; in
textiles, 237, 258; in copper, 238,
258; hunger, in Swedish Embassy,
257; increase in, 257-8; hunger, of
students, 262
students, as Allende supporters, 178,
262; activities of, 178, 180-4, 237,
252, 259, 262; meals for, 183, 183n;
women as, 197n; expelling of, 260,
262; sacrifices of, 261-2
sugar refining enterprise, collapse of,
267
Suharto, General, 138
Sule, Anselmo, 82
Sumar, nationalization of and results,
169-70; workers of, and putsch,
169-77; improvements at, 170
Sweden (Embassy) and Chilean refugees, 136-8, 140-4, 152, 155, 273;
and Edelstam, 137-8, 155; and Allende program, 139; and milk,
139-40; people of, and "house of